FLY FISHING

The Way of a Trout With a Fly

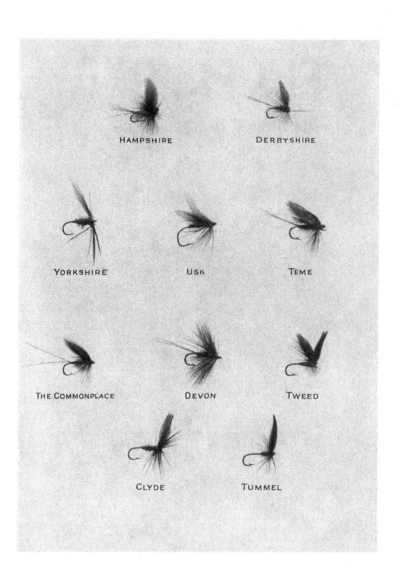

HAMPSHIRE

DERBYSHIRE

YORKSHIRE

USK

TEME

THE COMMONPLACE

DEVON

TWEED

CLYDE

TUMMEL

PLATE I.   THE BLUE DUN.
As rendered in ten different schools.

FLY FISHING

The Way of a Trout With a Fly

G. E. M. SKUES

DOVER PUBLICATIONS, INC.
Mineola, New York

Bibliographical Note

This Dover edition, first published in 2017, is an unabridged republication of the work originally published by A. & C. Black, Ltd., London, in 1921 under the title *The Way of a Trout with a Fly.* Two color plates from the original publication appear in black and white in this Dover edition.

Library of Congress Cataloging-in-Publication Data

Names: Skues, G. E. M. (George Edward Mackenzie)
Title: Fly fishing : the way of a trout with a fly / G. E. M. Skues.
Other titles: Way of a trout with a fly
Description: Dover edition. | Mineola, New York : Dover Publications, Inc., 2017. | Originally published under the title: The Way of a Trout with a Fly (London : A. & C. Black, Ltd., 1921).
Identifiers: LCCN 2016044705| ISBN 9780486814629 | ISBN 0486814629
Subjects: LCSH: Trout fishing. | Flies, Artificial.
Classification: LCC SH687 .S45 2017 | DDC 799.12—dc23 LC record available at https://lccn.loc.gov/2016044705

Manufactured in the United States by LSC Communications
81462901   2022
www.doverpublications.com

DEDICATED

TO

THE FLY-FISHERS' CLUB

IN GRATITUDE FOR MANY HAPPY HOURS
AND SOME PRICELESS FRIENDS

Myself when young did eagerly frequent
Doctor and Saint and heard great Argument
   About it and about, but evermore
Came out by the same door wherein I went.

RUBAIYAT OF OMAR KHAYYÁM.

THE WAY OF A TROUT WITH A FLY

WHEN the Wise Man laid it down that there were three things which were too wonderful for him—yea, four which he knew not—he came to the climax with " the way of a man with a maid." Some future Solomon will end with a fifth—the way of a trout with a fly—for it combines the poise of the eagle in the air, the swift certainty of a serpent upon a rock, and the mystery of the way of a ship in the midst of the sea, with the incalculableness of the way of a man with a maid. Our aviators seem to be on their way towards a solution of the way of the eagle in the air. The mystery of the way of a ship in the midst of the sea has yielded all its secrets to the persistence of modern man, but the way of a man with a maid and the way of a trout with a fly remain with us to be a delight and a torment to thousands of generations yet unborn.

FOREWORD

AUTHORITIES darken counsel. An authority is a person engaged in the invidious business of stereotyping and disseminating information, frequently incorrect. Angling literature teems with examples. I imagine that few anglers have devoted more time than I have to the study of authorities. From Dame Juliana to the latest issue of the press there is scarcely a book on trout-fly dressing and trout fishing which I have not studied and analyzed, and this conclusion seems to me inevitable. It was not until I realized this that my reading became any use to me. Up to that point I had been swallowing wholesale, with my facts, all sorts of fallacies and inaccuracies, alike in the matter of dressings and their use, and what they were intended to represent. From that point on an author became merely a suggester of experiment —a means of testing and checking my own observations by the water side, and no longer a small god to be believed in and trusted as infallible. And that is all an author, writing on any progressive art or science, ought to be. It is good now and again to have the ideas and discoveries of an epoch analyzed in the crucible of some acute intellect, and the problem restated, but this age has put an end to all belief in finality, and the business of that analysis should be to clear away the lumber of the past, while preserving all that is of value, and not to add more than can be helped to the lumber that some later writer will strive—probably in vain—to clear away. An authority who lays down a law and dogmatizes is a narcotic, a soporific, a stupefier, an opiate. The true function of an authority is to stimulate, not to paralyze, original thinking. But then, I suppose, he wouldn't be an authority.

Since the very beginning of things men have talked fish and fishing, just as they have talked religion and metaphysics, without progress commensurate with the amount of labour and energy expended, and with as many divergencies to right and left and as much slipping back and floundering in morasses of error. That the subject is so eternally interesting is my only excuse for the collection of the speculations contained in the ensuing pages. That they advance the sum of human knowledge on the subjects with which they deal is too much to hope.

For more years than I care to look back upon it has been my ambition to write a work upon trout-fly dressing, and it was my desire that it should exceed in scope all previous books on the art, and should examine and elucidate the methods of all the schools of dressing which this country has produced. But I was determined not to rush hastily into print before experience had sufficiently ripened my knowledge to give me assurance that my deductions were sound. I read omnivorously all that had been written on the subject, and the more I read the more I became impressed with the conviction that to make any advance upon the past it would be necessary to discard much of the learning of the past, to go back to the beginning, and to think out and rediscover the principles upon which the practice of the art should be based.

It is a singular fact that among the many works which have dealt with the subject of trout-fly dressing, it is impossible to find one which deals at once practically and comprehensively with the theory of the art. Cutcliffe's " Trout-fly Fishing on Rapid Streams," one of the most intelligent works on fly fishing ever written, explores a corner of the subject, but his patterns are mainly lures, and when he comes to deal with patterns which are, or purport to be, imitations, representations or suggestions of the natural fly, he is manifestly out of his depth.

It therefore became my plan to attempt a work on the theory of the art of trout-fly dressing, with enough of the practice to illustrate the various points made and the methods of the various schools. I would give much to be able to leave behind me, when I pass over the ferry, a work which would extricate the subject from the confusion in which generations of inaccurate observation and loose thinking and writing have involved it.

It was an ambitious project, but that would not have deterred me from the attempt; and I only gave up the project when I reached the conclusion that there is one governing factor in the treatment of the subject upon which I know nothing, and upon which—so far as I can learn—the scientific knowledge of my age is unable to help me. I refer to the vision of the trout. As those who penetrate beyond the opening pages of this volume will discover, there are, in my opinion, reasons for suspecting that the eyesight of the trout differs from that of man in its appreciation both of form and of colour. In what these differences consist, if they exist—and I do not pretend that the evidence of their existence is conclusive—I am entirely ignorant, and I see no means of lightening my darkness any more than, as a being of three dimensions, I see any prospect of appreciating the secrets of the fourth dimension. If I could understand these differences, and if, understanding them, I could put them into simple, lucid English, comprehensible to fly dressers of every class, then I could have given this generation a work on a subject never yet comprehensively treated in any language, which would at any rate have registered an advance in the art, and would have done something to elevate it out of the rut of convention, aggravated by empiricism, in which the practitioners of the ages down to this have toiled. It was not, however, to be, and I have arrived at a time of life when I have little hope that the advance of science will have solved the questions I would pose to it, while I still have the energy to undertake such a work as I have indicated. In these circumstances I have no wish to add yet one more to those primers on trout-fly dressing, accepted by a too credulous public as authoritative and for the time being final, of which the literature of angling with the fly is full. To do so would be but to add to confusion already more than sufficiently confounded.

I have, however, thought it might be of service to collect in book form my reflections on a number of considerations leading up to an understanding of the true theory of trout-fly dressing in the hope that at some not too distant date some scientific angler and fly dresser of a younger generation may be induced to take up and solve the at present unsolved problem, and to give his solution to the world, not in the difficult language of science, but in such clear and simple words as may be understanded of the people, and thus provide a sound basis for the ascertainment of the principles and considerations constituting the true theory of dressing the artificial trout-fly.

For some time after the publication of "Minor Tactics of the Chalk Stream," I not infrequently had occasion to regret that I had not delayed publication for a year or two so that I might have incorporated in that volume matter on which further experience and further observation had given me more light. I take this opportunity of collecting and giving to the fly-fishing public in the second division of this book such of the supplemental matter to which I refer as I have embodied in articles in the press.

Much of my matter has already appeared in *The Field*, *The Fishing Gazette*, and *The Journal of the Fly-Fishers' Club*, to the editors of which I record my acknowledgments.

Plates II. and III. are reproduced from exquisite coloured drawings made from my handiwork by Captain S. Barbe Goldsmith.

To my friend H. T. Sheringham I tender grateful thanks for his encouragement and for his help in seeing this work through the press.

G. E. M. SKUES.

CONTENTS

DIVISION I

PART I

PART II

PART III

THE VISION OF TROUT

PART IV

How

PART V
WHAT

PART VI

DIVISION II

SOME FURTHER MINOR TACTICAL STUDIES

ILLUSTRATIONS

xvi

THE WAY OF A TROUT WITH A FLY

DIVISION I

PART I

I

CONSIDERATIONS OF MOTIVE

ONE frequently sees it maintained in books and in articles
in the press that it is impossible to say why trout come
on to the rise. With all possible respect for the distinguished authors of those books and articles, I venture to
disagree. Trout come on to the rise for two reasons in
combination—(1) because they are hungry, and (2) because
there is food. It is no answer to say that frequently fly is in
quantity on the water and is neglected. That is quite true,
and yet it is consistent with the trout not being hungry—
being perhaps gorged—or being busy with some preferable
diet under water. It is clear that the trout do not rise
without something to rise at, that when they come on
to the rise they do so with remarkable unanimity, that
they leave off with a unanimity almost as remarkable, that
when fly food is scarce they do not rise as freely as when it is
plentiful. And when it is plentiful and they are not rising
it is not too great an assumption to suggest that it is because
they are not hungry. It is probably within the experience
of most chalk-stream anglers that fleets of upwinged duns
sail down neglected, with only a trout rising fitfully here
and there among them, and that that trout here and there
is singularly amenable to the attraction of an iron-blue dun.

That only means that trout have a preference for one food over another and are at times so gorged as to be dainty. After a long course of one insect they are apt to prefer another. In liking a change of diet they do not differ greatly from ourselves. That diet may be sought on the surface, in mid-water, in the weeds, or on the bottom. It is an entire mistake to assume that the trout is only feeding during the rise. It is indeed probable that there are few hours of the day when he is not feeding on something—mainly down below. And if his subaqueous supplies be plentiful and filling it would easily account for his not being excited by a plentiful exhibition of surface food. Indeed, the examples of dour rivers like the lower and middle Kennet and the Middlesex Colne prove that there are cases where the supply of bottom food is so large as to keep the trout down below in the absence of the rare attraction of the May fly or the large red sedge, and at times the grannom. The Kennet at any rate breeds large quantities of duns. The fact that the upper Kennet is less dour only proves that the supply of bottom food is less satisfying. But it is still more satisfying than that of such rivers as the Itchen and the Test and free-rising streams of that class. And there are all degrees of stream in between these two ends of the scale. There is, therefore, no real mystery about the question why trout rise to the fly. The only real problem is why at times, when everything appears in favour of their doing so, they do not. It may, however, be assumed that there is a common-sense reason for it. In nature nothing happens without a reason. The difficulty for the angler is merely that the reason is hidden some way beneath the surface. There may be occasions when trout take the fly for sport or high spirits, jealousy, or curiosity, or some by-motive; but on these occasions it may be taken for granted that the temptation is scarce and that hunger is in abeyance.

II

THE WHY

The question why the trout takes the artificial fly is another question altogether and deserves a separate examination. Speaking generally, it takes the fly as food. But it may be induced to take it from hunger (deceived by its resemblance to the natural insect), as in the case of the floating fly or the sunken nymph; from hunger (attracted by the motion of a tripped or dragging sunk fly rather than by any close resemblance to a natural insect); from curiosity (attracted by some fancy pattern, such as Wickham's Fancy, or Red Tag); from rapacity (excited by the spectacle of some big dragging fly); from tyranny (induced by the spectacle of something seemingly alive and in distress)—or there may be a combination of some or all of these motives. The angler will, therefore, be wise who considers, in relation to the water it is his privilege to fish, on which of these motives he can most profitably place reliance, and adjusts his methods accordingly. In some waters the fish are generally risers. In others, where the appeal of the fly is more commonly to motives other than hunger, they are strikers. The American angler seldom uses the term "rise." He has "a strike." And it may be believed that the term is just. A book of American trout flies shows a large majority of them to be fancy flies, appealing to curiosity, rapacity, tyranny, or jealousy, rather than to hunger. There are British waters and parts of waters where strikers are more common than risers. For instance, in a slow, almost still, mill-head the trout, moving about on the bottom or at the surface in search of food, will (unless smutting) with difficulty be tempted to take a floating fly, however good an imitation it be of a natural insect, but will without difficulty be lured to slash at a dragging fly, the resemblance of which to a natural insect is not marked. In such a place the angler has often the choice between not catching the fish and applying the appropriate method of the dragging fly. I do not approve of the dragging fly on the open chalk stream, but in the case of such a mill-head I should not hesitate to use it, though confessedly it is, as a method, far less interesting than is the taking of the trout with the genuine imitation or representation or suggestion of the natural fly.

Why does the trout take the natural fly ? Undoubtedly, as the contents of his stomach prove, as food. Why does he take the artificial fly ? In my opinion, in the vast majority of cases, because he supposes it to be his food. On occasion the motive may be curiosity, jealousy, pugnacity, or sheer excess of high spirits. But if I did not believe that the trout took the artificial fly not only as food but as food of the kind on which he is feeding, the real interest of trout fishing would be gone, so far as I am concerned. That is the reason why, for me, trout fishing on chalk streams transcends in interest any other kind of trout fishing. For on streams where the fly is comparatively scarce trout are more apt to take any kind of insect that may be on the menu, and are to be taken freely on patterns which do not represent the fly on the water. But chalk streams are rich in insect food. The duns come out in droves, and the fish show a discriminating determination to take only one pattern at a time, which convinces me that they mean to have nothing which does not satisfy them as being that on which they are feeding. Even on chalk streams there are occasions when there are exceptions to this rule, but in my experience, stretching over thirty-five years, these occasions are few.

III

FREEWILL AND PREDESTINATION

A year or two before the war a learned German Professor, Herr Ludwig Edinger, contributed to the *Field* an article entitled, " Fish and Freewill," in which he sought to prove that it was by an involuntary reflex action that the trout took the fly. " The trout," said he in effect, " is a creature of very little brain." In the higher vertebrates a special portion of the brain—the cortex of the cerebral hemisphere —has alone the function of combining different sensations and of drawing conclusions from them. If deprived of their cortex they exercise no choice, and have no power of deliberation, but react in a definite way to each definite change in their surroundings. " A study of the anatomical and microscopical structure "—I quote his exact words— " of the brain of fish shows that there is no structure corresponding to the cortex in the more highly developed forms." Hence he declared that fish have no power of combining their sensations, and that they cannot exercise choice. So that the action of the trout in taking the fly is purely reflex, depending on two factors—viz., upon the stimulus being adequate and upon the degree of excitability of the nerve centres—and the Professor went on to develop his argument in some detail.

The fly so cunningly cast by the Professor evoked several rises. More than one angler rushed into print with facts confirmatory of the Professor's theory.

I suspect Professor Ludwig Edinger of being a humorist of the most cynical and heartless type. Who that was not could so wrap up a platitude in learned language and spring it upon innocent anglers in such a way as to lead them to think that they were trembling on the verge

of a portentous discovery which should knock their dearly
loved art into the proverbial cocked-hat? "Has a fish no
option when it takes a fly?" "None," says he, "when
the temptation is irresistible." Only he does not put
it in that nice plain way. He envelops his proposition
in a cloud of cortices and reflexes and other fearful wild-
fowl; and scared readers rush into print with their evidence,
confirmatory or negative. The Professor neatly brought
down his game, and must have chuckled in his sleeve.
I suggest to him that his next quarry be a theological
Congress to whom he might propound similar riddles on
the fall of man—and was Eve compelled to eat the apple,
and what was the nature of the reflex of which Delilah
was the victim which compelled her to keep Samson's
hair cut? And were Eve and Delilah respectively *sans
cortex*, or were there only rudimentary cortices in their
skulls?

But be reassured. Professor Ludwig Edinger is quite
right. The trout has no option when he takes the fly,
and it doesn't matter in the least to the art of angling.
The art is to present the lure so that it shall be an
irresistible temptation. If it isn't so, in the circumstances
the trout won't take it. Why is the artificial fly irresistible when he takes it? Because he thinks it is a natural
fly and good to eat, or else because it excites his curiosity
or bullying propensities. Then the reflex acts. If it
doesn't look to him like a natural fly and good to eat, or
if it doesn't excite his curiosity or bullying propensities,
the reflex does not act, because the stimulus is not there.
"That's all there is to it," as they say in the States. So
the angler is still faced with the eternal problem, how to
provide the stimulus which excites the reflex action, and how
to place it so as to excite that action. It is just as difficult
to do these things since Professor Edinger flung his epoch-

making discovery before an astonished world, and it will probably go on being difficult just so long as trout are trout. The trout, being a slow-witted person and so fashioned by a merciful Providence, is apt to look twice at a solitary specimen of any kind of insect before attacking it. But, given a sufficient supply, he awakes in time to the notion that there is game afoot, and it is probably just the same if the artificial fly be tendered him again and again without a mistake. He may begin to suspect a hatch, and may irresistibly be led to respond to the stimulus. Fortunately there are other stimuli to which he responds with equal inevitability—funk, for instance. So that the fearful may take heart of grace; and may even suspect that, when the learned Professor had had his laugh out at the readiness with which the anglers' reflexes responded to his stimuli, and had settled whether there were any or only rudimentary cortices to their brains, things went on just as they were before, and that they will so continue.

It doesn't matter a bit in the world whether the trout reasons that the artificial fly is unsatisfactory or whether his sensations suggest to him that it is not a fly. In either case the angler won't get him that chuck. It does not matter whether his perceptions or his reason suggests to him that that is a fly and good to eat. Perceptions which lead to logical conclusions are as near a form of reason as is good for the angler, even if the premises or one of them—the fly, to wit—be a wrong 'un.

PART II

I

THE SENSE OF TASTE

THAT trout have some sense of taste can, I think, hardly be doubted. The excitement with which they come on to a rise of iron-blues must indicate that the fly or nymph gives them some special satisfaction. Their greedy devotion to the black gnat, too, and, on occasion, the eagerness with which they take willow fly and alder are evidence of the same kind. They take the artificial fly as food, but are extremely quick to reject it from their mouths, and that is why quick striking is necessary. Probably they have more sense of taste than have chub. I recall casting an artificial Alder to a chub which lay in a still little pool among lily pads. As the fly lit the fish turned and lay at right angles to its former position. I did not strike, as I thought the fish had missed the fly, but I waited some couple of minutes to let the fly and gut sink well below the fish before I attempted to retrieve my cast. But when I did so I found to my astonishment that the fish was hooked. It must have sucked in the fly as it turned, and the fly must have been in its mouth a couple of minutes before my attempt to retrieve it pulled in the barb. If the fish had any appreciable sense of taste it would have ejected the bunch of feather and herl immediately. A trout would certainly have done so.

II

THE SENSE OF SMELL

It is equally certain that trout have some sense of smell. They can find their way by it to a place baited with worms even in the thickest water; and in thick water they would probably starve but for the sense of smell. But it may well be doubted whether they place any reliance on it when taking the fly, natural or artificial. Here, one must infer, they are guided entirely by sight. If they relied on smell the paraffin anointment of the artificial dry fly would hardly fail to put them off; and the absence of an insect smell in the case of a wet fly might be expected to warn them to be careful. Insects have, many of them, quite a strong scent. A box of stone-fly creeper is very distinctly odorous.

It is, moreover, well known that a gentle or a caddis worm on the hook of a fly often proves irresistible to a trout, and the fact is made use of by unscrupulous anglers. But here the fish is taking the savoury gentle or caddis worm and not the fly, and it is still true that in taking the fly he depends so much more on vision than on any other sense that for the purposes of fly fishing smell and taste may be disregarded. But the vision of the trout, in its nature and peculiarities, deserves a closer study than it has ever, so far as I know, received.

PART III

THE VISION OF TROUT

I

IN a well-known Greek myth, Semele, one of Jove's many mistresses, is presented as having persuaded her lover to reveal himself to her in his Olympian majesty, and as having been burned to a cinder in the conflagration;—the moral of this being that man is not intended to see things as they are, but only in such form and to such extent as is good for him. This is, I believe, in full accord with the views of modern science, which holds that man sees nothing absolutely as it is, but only relatively and as is necessary for the purposes of his being. Even so his perception of things seen is not the sole result of the image on the retina, but is a subjective effect produced upon the mind by the combination of the image and the results of experience gained through the sense of touch and possibly other senses connecting and co-ordinating the image thrown upon the retina. A baby, it is supposed, sees everything flat at first. He has to feel his way through his sense of touch to a sense of distance and per-spective. Man's eye therefore is not in the absolute sense a perfect organ, but only relatively perfect for the purposes of the needs and nature of man.

I do not think that, if this proposition be true of man, it can be any less true of fish, and, in considering the way of a trout with a fly, whether natural or artificial, it may be worth while to spend a little time in an endeavour to see what can be deduced from known facts about the nature and characteristics of the eyesight of the trout.

The nature and the needs of trout differ greatly from those of man, and it need not therefore surprise us if examination should lead us eventually to the conclusion that his perception by eyesight differs materially from that of man. Indeed, I think it would be remarkable if, living in a different medium that is subject to certain optical laws from which the air is free, and having different needs and modes of being from man, the trout were to see things in all respects as man sees them—even after making all allowance for the correcting and co-ordinating effects of tactile experience.

To begin with, while man's eyes are placed in front of his head and operate together so that his vision is stereoscopic, the trout's eyes are on the sides of his head, slanting slightly forward and operating separately, so that it may be inferred that in most cases his vision of an object is monocular. It may be that in the act of taking a fly, whether on the surface or below it, both eyes may be trained forward upon the object, or, alternatively, that one eye only may be on the object and the other attending to business in another direction.

Then, though the vision of a trout is astonishingly quick, enabling him as it does to pick out and capture minute living objects, often in rapid and turbulent streams, it does not seem to be greatly concerned with a sense of form or detail. Otherwise it is extremely difficult to conceive how he can take a hackled fly, such, for instance, as the Straddlebug May fly, with its long straggling fibres of summer duck, in circumstances which can leave no doubt in any unprejudiced mind that he takes it for May fly or a hatching nymph. In the case of smaller soft-hackled patterns the case is only a shade less wonderful, and even in the cases where the imitation or representation of the natural fly is most lifelike, it cannot be suggested that the likeness is so precise that it could for a moment deceive the eyesight of man.

In the matter of the trout's colour perception there has been much divergence of opinion among anglers. Some have gone so far as to suggest that the trout is colour-blind. Some say he perceives tone only and not colour. Others would have you believe that he sees colour precisely as does man. I am not of the school which would class the trout as colour-blind. I am assured by a man of science who has studied the subject that in the retina of the trout, the seat of colour vision, no differences in quality from that of man are to be found. The same elements are to be found in human beings and in the trout. These are, of course, structural differences. The medium, water, in which the trout lives renders a spherical lens behind a flat cornea necessary. The method of adjustment of focus differs from that of man, the eye of the fish being accommodated for near vision, and the entire retina of the trout's eye appears to be sensitive, instead of merely one spot. But, allowing for these differences of mechanism, there is no obvious or apparent essential difference. And I am asked to infer from this that trout see colour precisely as do men. It may be so. I do not know. But I would ask whether an examination of the retina of a man who is wholly or partially colour-blind shows any differences from the retina of a man of entirely normal vision. If no differences are shown, why may not the trout, notwithstanding his similar retina, be partially colour-blind without the fact being betrayed by his retina? The lines of the spectrum are numerous, and I would ask, is it not conceivable that the trout may have a faculty of perceiving some to which man is insensitive and even some beyond the range of colour visible to man at either or both ends of the spectrum ? I do not know, but Nature is so marvellously various and so fertile in expedient that I should hesitate to call it impossible that it should be so. The subject is one which will bear a good deal more thinking over and investigation than it has hitherto received, and I propose to examine it at more length at a later stage.

II

THE SENSE OF FORM AND DEFINITION

The trout is credited on authority with being the keenest-eyed of animals, and doubtless most of us have too frequently found him keener of sight than we have cared about. Yet the nature and limitations of that keenness are well worth examining if we are to get a working grip of the principle which should underlie the art of trout-fly dressing. In examining the question of the possibility of successfully using imitations of larvæ or nymphs for trout fishing, Mr. F. M. Halford, after supposing that the angler has turned out a fairly good imitation of the nymph, and tries it at a time when the fish are bulging incessantly at natural larvæ, says:

" Alas ! how woefully is he *désillusioné*. The fish will not look at this, although it is an admirable representation, both in colour and shape, of the natural insect. . . . How is it to be expected that a timid, shy fish like a trout, who from painful daily, and even hourly, experience is warned to use the keenest of all the senses with which he has been endowed by nature—viz., his sight for his protection, should mistake that motionless, supine compound of dubbing, silk, quill, and hackle, drifting helplessly and lifelessly like a log down the stream, for the active, ever-moving larva sparkling in the sunshine, and varying in colour at every motion as rays of light strike it at different angles ?"

Now, accepting for the sake of argument this presentation of the action and appearance of the larva as correct, we have to reconcile it with the fact that this shy, keen-sighted fish does not infrequently take the artificial fly of the angler, floating, sunken, or semi-submerged, at times and under conditions which can leave no doubt in any reasonable mind that he takes it for the natural fly which it feebly pretends to represent. What is the inevitable conclusion ? Undoubtedly that the eyesight of the trout, though perfectly adapted for all his purposes except defence against the wiles of man, is defective in some direction or directions, since it permits him to make such fatal mistakes. But how can we know the nature and extent of these defects in his eyesight ? There are two ways of getting at it. One is by microscopic examination of the trout's eye by a skilled oculist or optician—a method beyond me; the other is by reasoning from the innumerable data which a prolonged experience of trout-fly fishing gives to every observant angler.

The first point to which I invite attention is that a trout is a predaceous animal, and his eye may be expected to evince the peculiarities of the eyes of other predaceous animals whose business it is to catch their prey in motion. One naturally turns to the cat for a familiar example. If anyone has watched a cat at play, he may guess to what I am leading up. For a moving object her sight is of amazing quickness, but she is far more stupid than the dog at finding a stationary object, unless guided by the sense of smell. Is this true of the trout ? Let us follow the inquiry further. The cat not only sees things in motion, it sees them moving in the dark. The trout also has a faculty for seeing —at any rate in his own element—in the dark, and even distinguishes colour well—quite well enough to enable him to take one artificial fly rather than another. Most anglers who have fished wet-fly streams in the late dusk with a team of flies could quote occasions when one fly has been taken by every fish to the exclusion of a choice of other patterns, and that fly not necessarily either the lightest or the darkest.

Let us grant, then, that the trout's sight is quick; let us concede him a strong sense of colour or texture or both; but is that sight clear ? Has the trout even a rudimentary sense of form ? There are grounds for doubting it. I am going to get into hot water with the apostles of the " precise imitation " school, but I am not going to dogmatize, but to call attention to facts.

If we take the most exquisitely dressed Olive Quill or Iron-blue dun and compare them with their prototypes in nature, can we honestly say that the resemblance of form or attitude is marked ? We know it is not. We are satisfied if in colour and size the imitation is approximate. If the fly be tied with rolled wings reversed, it is frequently as good a killer as, or even better than, the ordinary pattern. Yet the fly with dense, stiff wings thrown forward is really not, in shape at any rate, a striking likeness of the natural insect, with its wings sloping just the other way. A good instance of this is the Mole Fly—a sedge; instead of having its wings laid back over the body, it presents them flung forward in the opposite direction. Yet it is indubitably a successful pattern. Then, does the trout pay much attention to the fact that the floating fly of commerce is generally able to give the centipede fifty legs and a beating ? There are times when he does not. Does he even mind where the legs occur in the anatomy (if one may be pardoned the term) of the artificial fly ? They may, as in the Wickham or any of the sedges, be in spirals all down the body, but what does he care? Take the Dotterel dun. This is a hackled imitation of a light yellow-legged dun. The dotterel hackle is a brownish dun feather with yellow tips to the points of the fibres. The dun colour represents the wings, the yellow tips the legs. But does the trout resent being offered a fly with yellow legs at the tips of his wings, and these wings spread mopwise all round his body? If he does resent it, the popularity—the well-deserved popularity—of the Dotterel dun is hard to account for. Making every allowance for some disarrangement of toilet in a natural fly which has become submerged or caught by the current, can we say that it ever has its wings starred all round its head or shoulders in a palpitating mop? Then the honey-dun hen hackle. This is the same thing again. And we know that the honey-dun hen feathers are among the trout-fly dresser's most cherished treasures.

Let us turn to the Iron-blue dun. The natural insect has lead-coloured wings and red feet, and the artificial may be dressed either winged or hackled. If hackled, a dark blue dun feather with copper-red points is an admirable feather to use. But the trout does not mind a bit that your Iron-blue dun has a mop of blue wing all round its head, with a little red foot at the end of each fibre. It is a commonplace of fly dressing that, in translating a winged pattern into its hackled correlative, you select a hackle combining as far as possible the colour of wings and legs, and, so long as you keep the colours, their relative position is of little consequence. As an instance, let me quote the case of the Lead-winged (i.e., starling-winged) Coachman and the Little Chap. Each has a peacock herl body. The dun of the starling wings in the Coachman is reproduced by the dun centre of the hackle of the Little Chap, and the red hackle of the Coachman by the red points of the hackle of the Little Chap. But if they be dressed on the same size of hook, when one will kill, as a general proposition the other will kill. If the artificial fly lay on quite still water it may be doubted whether it would often be taken; but in general the movement of the stream imparts an appearance of motion to the fly, and the trout, catching a general impression of correct size and colouring, absorbs it, hook and all, without too nearly considering the things that belong to his peace. Taking it by and large, the fact is indisputable that the shabbiest, roughest, most dilapidated, most broken-winged fly is as likely to kill as the newest and freshest of the fly-tier's confections—provided size and colour be right. What is " right " must be the subject of further discussion. Meanwhile, I think I have established this, that in appreciation of form and proportion and detail the sight sense of the trout is defective.

III

THE INVISIBILITY OF HOOKS

But there is another matter in which his eyesight sometimes serves him ill. Dr. Watts—I think it was that great and good man—represented a wise old mother trout assuring her too ardent offspring that "that horrid fly is meant to hide the sharpness of the hook." It may be so, but performance, alas! often falls far short of intention, and the instances are few in which the horrid fly does anything of the sort. Indeed, a very competent school of Scottish fly dressers is all for minimum of wing and body, and the rankest exposure of the hook which is possible, so that the fly is the merest sketch, and the hook is the prominent thing. Therefore, in speculating on the vision of the trout, we have to make our account with the fact that, whether the hook be blued or brown, it does not deter trout from frequently seeking to make a meal of the artificial fly. The trout, therefore, must either fail to see the hook, or, seeing it, must ignore it. If he sees it and realizes that it is an unnatural appendage to the artificial fly, he could hardly ignore it. He must therefore either take it for a natural appendage, or for some casual, but quite irrelevant, attachment, or be so obsessed by his intentness on his food as to see only what he wants to see—namely, that combination of colour which seems to him to correspond with the natural insect in favour for the moment. It is impossible to say that he does not take the hook for some casual attachment, for all sorts of odd things float down the water with the natural fly. Yet he will not as a rule take a fly to which a weed attaches. The trout are familiar with those nasty little thin leeches which attack their own heads and bodies. Whether these ever attack floating flies I could not say, but I never saw or heard of their doing so. The balance of probability, I think, leans to the theory that the trout is so obsessed by the pressure of appetite that he only sees what he wants to see—his supposed insect prey—and ignores the hook as an irrelevant detail,* all of which goes to prove that the wily trout of the poets and journalists is—may Providence be devoutly thanked for it—really rather a stupid person.

IV

THE SENSE OF POSITION

If it be true, as has been suggested, that the trout is so obsessed by the pressure of appetite that he is when feeding lost to the sense of all things connected with his food except

* This is in keeping with his being satisfied if his colour sense be satisfied and with his lack of a clear sense of form.

colour and size, that would tend to account for a phenomenon which anglers at large accept with a philosophy
born for the most part of ignorance, but which is a distressing problem to anglers of a more entomologically
learned and conscientious type. The phenomenon is his
willingness to take the winged fly under water, where
winged flies are comparatively seldom found. An ultra-
conscientious angler might go further and be pained by his
willingness to take nymphs floating high and dry above
the surface, a position in which nymphs are not to be found
at all in nature. But at this point the ultra-conscientious
angler usually stops, and, obsessed by the appetite for
catching his trout, sees only what he wishes to see, and
persuades himself that the bright cock's hackles on which
the artificial nymph body is held high and dry above the
water really represent the much denser and duller-hued
wings of the natural dun, it being generally known that
the dun not infrequently stands on the points of its wings
on the water.

It is a fact which no arguing can get over that the trout,
whether of chalk stream or rough river, will, so frequently
as to take the case out of the exceptional, take a winged
fly wet and a hackle fly dry, as well as a winged fly dry
and a hackle fly wet. In particular, when bulging, a
trout will be so set on his subaqueous meal that he becomes
almost unconscious of what is going on on the surface
(and is, therefore, much less readily put down than a trout
which is taking in the hatched fly), and accepts with almost
equal readiness the natural nymphs and the angler's
winged Greenwell's Glory, provided the colours appeal to
him as right. He seems able to obliterate from the field
of vision all irrelevancies such as hooks and wings, and to
concentrate on the olive of the body.

There is less difficulty in accounting for his taking a

hackle fly on the surface. If it represents a spinner, the
effect may be right enough, but if it represents a dun,
either hatched or in the nymphal stage, then it is possible
that the bright cock's hackles surrounding it are the
" trailing clouds of glory " with which it comes, and they
may lead to an early closing about it of the shades of
the prison-house which every trout carries with him, and
then all is well with the angler.

If I were really spiteful, I might suggest that many of
the winged floating patterns are only taken because of their
resemblance to nymphs, the wings being ignored. And,
truly, I could elaborate quite a pretty argument on the
subject, with instances in point.

But be all that as it may, it would seem that the vision
of the trout is defective in not keeping him alive to the
incongruity of the winged fly under water and the hackled
nymph on the surface. The only alternative explanation
is that his observation, his memory, and his power of
reasoning from the known to the unknown are much to
seek.

V

A PROBLEM FOR THE OPTICIAN

I was casting a fly one sunny July day upon a shallow
Berkshire brook, which, cutting its way through a boggy
surface soil, babbled gaily, seldom more than eighteen inches
deep, over a hard-core bed of chalk and gravel. The brook
swarmed with trout, few apparently under the half-pound,
and very few over the pound; and when first I arrived
at the water-side the only fish taking were a few casual
feeders, which picked up a miscellaneous *hors d'œuvres*
under the bushes which lined a part of one bank where
the stream, being deeper, was also slower. But as I moved

upstream, at every bend I came upon a new group of trout, which darted up stream and down in a great state of agitation, long before I could come within casting distance of them. After I had walked up three or four of these groups, and could see that the character of the stream for some distance ahead differed in no material wise from that part under my elbow, I returned to my starting-point and sat down on a stile to give the trout time to settle. In less than half an hour dimples here and there in the runs between the cress-beds a little way up encouraged me to try again. What a change! Fish, that half an hour before had scuttled desperately while I was yet a long way off, took no notice of me now, went on feeding gaily, and did not disdain my Olive Quill on those occasions when it was put to them right. To cut a long story short, I landed during the daytime twelve brace, retaining two over the pound limit; and going out again in the evening I landed other five brace, of which one was over the pound, and was retained.

Next day was similar in conditions, and I fished for a couple of hours in the morning, catching five brace, of which one was one and a quarter pounds, one a safe pound, and the rest went back. All the while that the fish were feeding they took no notice of me—comparatively speaking, of course—until they were hooked, when they made a fierce resistance. When they were not feeding they were wild as hawks, and scuttled over the shallows in droves while I was yet a great way off. Nothing remarkable in all this, of course—nothing that is not within the experience of all anglers for trout. The experience, I admit, is quite commonplace. It is only because of a train of thought to which it gave rise that I mention it, and mention it in detail. Were the trout so infatuated with their food that they did not care about me during the rise, or was it that, with their eyes concentrated on the nymphs and duns coming down to them, they could not see me without a special effort, or without some special cause attracting attention ? If one supposed that for reasons of self-protection, or for some other sound natural cause, the eye of the trout had a wide range of focus, so that he could see—even behind him—to quite a distance out of water when not intent on his food, and that when food was toward that focus shortened to a few—perhaps a very few—inches to deal with the business in hand, would not that explain his comparative unconsciousness of the angler's presence far better than the supposition that appetite was so strong upon him as, without diminishing the acuteness of his vision, to cast out fear ? It is worth thinking about.

The human eye focuses itself upon an object, and it sees that object clearly—its immediate surroundings clearly enough; but those which are not the object of attention are often blurred and impressionist in outline and effect. If the object of attention be near, the effect of distant objects is blurred and lost. Imagine a like result in the eye of a trout, and allow for a denser medium than air. While the attention is focused on the food, feet or inches off, it may well be that the mechanical effect on the lens of the eye is to blur or even to shut out altogether comparatively long-range objects, such as an angler in the rear extending forty feet or forty-five feet of line in his direction. It might even be that, with the focus of his eye shortened, a trout becomes incapable of seeing through water on one side when the light is in a particular direction, while remaining quite capable of seeing distinctly what is behind him on the other side. In earlier pages I have endeavoured to show that the vision of the trout is defective, at any rate as regards the form of the fly, while attentive to colour and size. The mouth of the trout is large, and when he takes in the fly he does not, as so many artists depict him as doing, snap it. He expands his gills so as to induce an entering current through his open mouth, which carries fly or nymph in with it. Therefore he has no need to see the detail of his food very clearly in order to take it in. May it not be that this defective near vision when concentrating on the fly is the correlative of the distortion of the eye from its more general business of keeping a watch for possible enemies?

Whether it is so or not I am not prepared to say. I am no optician; but if some angler who is an optician would make a study of this subject, and could deduce from his anatomy of the eye of the trout the truth of this matter, he might be conferring upon anglers some knowledge worth having.

VI

THE SENSE OF NUMBER

If the conclusion from my argument be accepted that trout have a defective sense of form, and will often take for a fly something that is either so tumbled or so differently arranged from the natural insect it is supposed to represent as to be very unlike it to the eye of man, the reader will have no difficulty in accepting the corollary conclusion that with the sense of form (and probably from the same cause) the sense of number is also at fault. Countless writers have poured scorn on the imitation theory, because the hackle of a winged fly suggests many more legs than the natural insect possesses. I suggest that the fish gets only a general effect, and that, provided the excess of hackle be not so pronounced as to spoil the general effect by producing an appearance of clotting, it will not be fatal to the fish taking the artificial fly for a natural fly.

VII

THE SENSE OF COLOUR

1. *A Query.*

So many who have argued in print on the subject of the
colour-sense of trout have argued as if there were only two
possible alternatives—namely, that trout must see colour
as mankind see it, or else must be wholly colour-blind.
I venture to suggest that that attitude of mind takes too
little account of the wonderful variety of nature. It might
well prove to be the case that, without being colour-blind,
trout are more sensitive to some colours than to others,
or they might be wholly colour-blind to one primary colour
and keenly sensitive to others.

A person completely colour-blind sees all objects in a
neutral grey, the form and reflected light alone distinguishing
one from another.

A simple way of illustrating what I mean is to take
things in their simplest form. There are three primary
colours—violet, red, and green. All other colours are a
combination in varying proportions of two or more of
them. The simple combination of any two of them makes
the complementary colours. Sensations of different colour
are produced by rays of light of differing wave-lengths.
Now assume, for the sake of argument, that trout are
sensitive to red only, and colour-blind to violet and green.
Then a combined colour made up equally of violet and red
would look to him precisely like a combined colour made
up of red and green in equal proportions, for his eye would
only accept the wave-lengths to which it was sensitive
and reject the rest, thus selecting that part of the combined
colour to which it was sensitive, and rejecting that part

to which it was blind. And any shades made up of a combination of green and violet, in whatever proportions, without any red, provided the tone were the same, would look much the same to him.

Let us go a step further and imagine him confronted with a combination of orange and green, making a sort of dirty brown: his eye would pick out the red from the combination, and would reject the violet and green; and, the less red there was, the fainter the object would appear. Again, if he were confronted with a combination of green and pink, making another combination of a sort of brown, his eye would select the red and reject the green and violet. And the two quite different shades of brown would look practically identical to him, provided there were the same intensity of red in each. Again, if the combination were violet and orange with the same amount of red in the orange as in the other two combinations, his eye would again select the red and reject that part in those parts of the combination to which he was blind. So that this combination would again look the same to him. In fact, his only test of colour would be the extremely simple test, the degree of red in it. If that were constant all colours would look alike.

Yet one step further and imagine your trout sensitive to red and green, but entirely blind to violet. Then any combination of red and violet entirely free of green, or of green and violet entirely free of red, would be judged by the amount of red or green in it, as the case might be. But if red and green were together in any combined colour, then the fish would begin to be able to perceive distinctions.

It is unnecessary to drag the reader through the further combinations to make this point clear.

Now all this is extremely crude, and it is not put forward

as suggesting an opinion that trout are blind to any one or two of the primary colours. That is not the suggestion at all. Nature is not so simple as that. But it is quite another matter to say that, because man has a highly-developed sense of colour, therefore trout, if capable of colour-sense at all, must see colour as man sees it. There are degrees of colour-consciousness in man, and it would surely not be a great stretch of imagination to conceive that trout's sensitiveness to different colours may well be different from that of man. He may be more or less sensitive to some colours, and relatively less or more sensitive to others—possibly extremely insensitive to some; and he may be sensitive to some beyond man's colour scale.

If this be conceded, merely as a basis for argument, it would certainly be found to result in trout seeing likenesses of colour where man sees differences, and perhaps differences of colour where man sees likenesses.

In a previous chapter I have, I think, made it fairly clear that trout do see likenesses where man sees differences, and differences where man sees likenesses. Is it too big a jump in reasoning to infer that there may be some variation in degree of sensitiveness to different colours between the eye of the trout and the eye of man?

But can it be doubted that if the fly dresser knew exactly the degree of the trout's sensitiveness and insensitiveness to different colours, and also knew the combinations of colour producing any particular shade for the trout, he would have gone a very long way towards solving the secrets of fatally successful trout-fly dressing?

It is, I think, beyond dispute that trout are extremely sensitive to red and are greatly attracted by it. Witness the value of a Red Tag to a fly. Living as so many do among surroundings of green weed with a diet of insects in so many shades of green, it seems unlikely that they are insensitive to green, but there are practically no blues in the trout's habitat unless you count the blue of the sky seen through the circle of vision above him. And it would not surprise me if it were proved that trout are comparatively insensitive to blues.

It may be that Sir Herbert Maxwell's famous red and blue May flies were, in fact, the one the colour of supreme attraction, the other a neutral grey.

On no point is there great divergence of opinion among anglers than on this of the power of the trout to distinguish colour; but it is only possible to reason from one's own experience, and to appeal to that of others. For the moment we are dealing with the colours suggesting current daily food, and setting aside the colours of lures which excite tyranny, rapacity, or curiosity. These latter are usually bright and stimulating, and they are rather beside the point for our argument. The colours of the nymphs, duns, and other insects which form the daily menu are in general sober, and if trout were incapable of making fairly fine distinctions of colour, it is hard to account for those frequent occasions when fly after fly is tried, seemingly like enough to the fly on the water, in vain, and finally a pattern is found which kills fish after fish. Again, on wet-fly waters, where the angler is laying a team of flies across the stream, one fly out of the three or four will be persistently selected by the trout, and if two or more anglers are using the same pattern on diverse casts they all find the same pattern selected. My own belief, for what it is worth, is that where the supply of food is moderate or small and the fish is hungry, his taste is apt to be far more catholic than on those occasions when there is a strong hatch of one or more varieties, one of which appeals most strongly to the trout. There must have been days within the experience of most of us when the water has been covered with yellow duns and small pale olives, with a sprinkling of iron-blue duns among them, and all else has been neglected in favour of the iron blue. Here it is true that the fly is quite distinct in colouring from the others on the water at the same time; but on similar occasions, when the iron blue is not to the fore, the trout will as a rule not be mixing their diet, but confining themselves to fly of one kind, and sticking to that, and that only, and letting all else go by.

So far we have been dealing with surface feeding mainly, but where the trout are bulging it is not so easy to ascertain what they are feeding on. It involves an autopsy—a messy and uncertain business at best—for it is impossible to say when and where the nymphs in the gullet were taken; one can only make an approximate guess. It is true that one generally finds one type of nymph predominating, but one often finds odd specimens of other kinds, and it may be suspected that the trout, accustomed where no rise is on to forage among celery beds and other vegetation in search of nymph and larva, shrimp and snail, is then much more catholic in his tastes than when he is busy gathering in the surface duns. If one puts down a soft muslin net among celery beds just before the rise is expected one will bring it up wriggling with larvæ and nymphs of very varying dimensions and colouring, from darkest olive to something like bright dandelion and primrose. So it may easily be true that the trout when nymphing may more readily be induced to make a mistake than when feeding steadily on the surface. There it is much more important to get the right fly. And the right fly is that which the trout finds to be the right colour. It does not always seem the right colour to the angler, and so it may fairly be questioned whether the trout sees colour just as man sees it. This is a question which deserves to be pursued further, but this is not the place to pursue it.

2. *A Speculation.*

To set about discovering in what the difference (if it exists) of sensitiveness to colour in the eye of the trout and the eye of man consists, is an extremely difficult matter. I do not profess the anatomical or optical knowledge which would enable me to probe it scientifically. I do not know whether the problem is or ever will be soluble, whatever be the scientific advance of man. I hope it may be possible to solve it some day, if it be for the good of fly fishing as an art. In the meanwhile I may perhaps be forgiven some empirical speculations in the direction of a solution, some gropings after the truth.

It may, I think, be taken as a starting-point that, whatever be the nature of the trout's faculties of vision, they are designed to subserve his earning his living and the preservation of his species.

One starts by observing that in weedy rivers trout live in an environment of green; in gravelly or rocky rivers they live in an environment of brown. One knows from the attractiveness of the Red Tag and the Zulu that they are peculiarly sensitive to red.

In their food one finds among the duns a prevalence of greens and yellows; among the sedges reds, orange, and brown; in the Perlidæ, or willow flies, browns; and in the alder brown and plum colour. There is not, however, except very faint in the wings of duns, any great quantity of blue in the food of trout, nor does it prevail in their habitat, except in combination with yellow to make green. I am not forgetting the iron-blue dun. That is easily to be picked out as a very dark fly against the light, and not necessarily because of the blue in it. Indeed, the base colour of the iron blue, as disclosed in its spinners, is a shade of red as exemplified in the claret spinner and the Jenny spinner. The wings of duns, standing up in the air or seen spread out spent on the water, are generally very colourless, and it is known that many anglers fish hackled flies habitually in preference to winged flies.

It would not perhaps be the worst guess that could be made if one were to hazard that blue was the colour to which trout are least sensitive.

It is the colour of sky and cloud, the background against which they see their surface food.

The reference to a neutral grey recalls a greenheart rod of mine made by Farlow and painted heron-blue, and its extra-ordinary invisibility to the trout. Again and again I have held it over a trout lying under my bank, and have waved it to and fro without scaring him until I showed myself, and it certainly seemed as if it were of a colour to which the trout was almost insensible. I remember speculating at the time whether it was by reason of his scheme of colora-tion that the heron was able to get within striking distance of the fish. I afterwards had a split-cane Test rod built by Messrs. Hardy Brothers, and I got them to colour it similarly, but the varnish put a flash upon it which dis-counted its invisibility, and that and the fact that the colouring matter under or in the varnish added not a little to the weight of the rod led to my discontinuing the use of heron-blue colouring for my rods.

VIII

THE SENSE OF SIZE

" The fuller the water the larger the fly " is a good general working rule, and so it follows that where, as in the chalk streams, the flow is steady and constant, there is seldom any occasion to increase the size of the artificial fly above the normal size of the natural. And on these streams one is liable to find that the presentation of a fly above the normal in size is apt to be resented, and many experienced anglers advise a size smaller than the natural fly rather than an imitation of equal size. What, then, is the ground for the use of a fly larger than the natural upon rougher and less constant streams ? The only one which suggests itself is that a full water (once it clears enough for the fly) stimulates the fish to such high spirits and such extremity of hunger, that the added size of the angler's lure, so far from giving rise to suspicion (as it would in more normal circumstances), becomes an added attraction in its promise of satisfaction of an oppressively vigorous appetite. The angler therefore may be sure that he will be wise to pay attention to this matter of size, as it is one of which, for good or for ill, the trout takes notice. It is a curious point that the wet fly may be fished a size larger than the dry representing the same insect. I record this as a matter of experience without being able to give, off my own bat, even a guess at a reason. A very skilful and observant wet-fly angler of my acquaintance says that the nymph and the creeper *are* larger than the winged insect.

The conclusions which I venture to submit as the sum of the foregoing arguments and inferences are that in flies purporting or intended to imitate natural insects, size and colour are the matters of consequence, and that, apart from mechanical considerations as to the structure and wearing power of the fly, shape is of very secondary consequence.

IX

TONE

One theory of some who do not believe in the colour vision of trout is that it is tone only of which they are conscious —meaning by tone, I assume, shade of colour, irrespective of what that colour may be—so that all colours of similar shade look alike to him—say a neutral grey as to a totally colour-blind man. It is an attractive theory in that it might account for cases of trout seeing likenesses between the artificial fly and the natural fly where man sees only differences—such as the case of the Blue or Grey Quill being taken for the pale watery dun at least as well as, if not better than, the Little Marryat, or of the Orange Quill being taken for the blue-winged olive or its spinner—at dusk. It does not, however, seem to account for cases within one's daily experience on chalk streams where a single pattern proves fatal to the trout after a whole series of other patterns of apparently similar shade have been ostentatiously ignored. It is suggested by some that trout looking up at the fly from below always see it more or less black against a background of sky. There may be instances where this is approximately true, but they must be comparatively few, and more frequent at night than by day, and in either case only when the fly is between the fish and the source of light. Where the source of light is behind the fish or at either side he will, I am convinced, see (or at any rate be in a position to see) far more colour than the theory under consideration would permit one to suppose. The position is, of course, quite different where the light is in any way in his eyes or eye. He might therefore be far less critical of a fly passing on the sunny side than on the shady side of him. The theory allows nothing for the fact that so many natural flies have bodies· more or less translucent, nor for the light thrown on to the underside of their bodies by reflection of light from the surface of the water, from the bottom (brown gravel, grey chalk, or red rock), or from the often brilliant-coloured weed-beds below. Looking up from a glass-walled chamber beneath water-level at artificial trout flies floating on the surface, one certainly sees them in much more detail than the theory under consideration would suggest—to say nothing of their being enveloped in iridescent colours, an effect which may be due to their being seen through a prism of water. One sees them thus even where the body of the fly is opaque and gets its effect from reflected light; and it may be that it presents to the trout by reflected light the same effect as the semi-translucent natural fly presents by means of light partly transmitted and partly reflected. There are, of course, many artificial flies in which, by means of dubbing, or celluloid, or stained gut, or horsehair, an effect of translucency of body is obtained similar to that of the natural insect represented, and often a bit more brilliant. In such cases the trout would get the effect of transmitted as well as reflected light—and one may appeal to the experience of anglers as to the efficacy of such patterns to combat the tone theory. That theory, moreover, hardly accounts for the specially attractive effect of scarlet on the trout. It is not one with which the writer holds, and accordingly he sees no special advantage in the silhouette fly patterns advocated by that very interesting writer and skilful angler, Dr. J. C. Mottram.

X

IN DUSK AND DARK

The capacity of the trout for distinguishing flies in the dusk or dark has often been the subject of comment. I first noted it in September, 1888, on the Coquet, when, the August dun being up, its spinners, after looking like red-hot needles dancing in rays of the setting sun, were later on the water. I was fishing the tail of a run under trees with a team of three flies, all representing the spinner, tied on eyed hooks with gut bodies dyed a flame-coloured orange, a reddish furnace hackle, and wings from the ruddy feather of a partridge's tail. One of my three flies was winged from the portion of the partridge-tail feather which is finely freckled with black, the others from the unfreckled part of the same feather. On several evenings I found the trout invariably selected the fly with the freckled wing and entirely ignored the others. On a Norwegian lake, fishing during the short July night when the wind had dropped dead, I have found the same one of a team of flies accepted again and again while the others were ignored. On the chalk streams again, the ability of the fish to draw fine distinctions at night must have struck every observer. I recall one evening when the trout were taking the natural blue-winged olive well. I tried a Red Quill dyed orange on a No. 1 hook, after getting my solitary Orange Quill soaked and slimy through killing a brace; but the trout would have none of it—though they took the Orange Quill again when I had washed and dried it. Yet the only distinction between the two patterns was that the quill of the Orange Quill was plain condor, and in the Red Quill it was the usual ribbed peacock. It was dyed in the same dye in each case. In fact, the Red

Quills had been supplied to me as Orange Quills. That was years ago, and I have the remains of the dozen still, for they have never been any good to me. Again, I recall one evening when I rose eighteen trout, all short, to a Tup's Indispensable dressed to represent a spinner with a ruddy colouring, and then, putting on a fly of identical size with a body of rusty-red seal's fur, I began to get firm rises immediately. This must have been something more than a coincidence.

I have had it suggested to me by a distinguished angling writer, whose opinions deserve respectful consideration, that trout disregard colour during the daytime, but distinguish it at night. While accepting the latter proposition, I do not accept the former, though I do not profess to understand how they see colour under either condition.

It might seem bold to express the opinion that they distinguish textures at night, seeing that they undoubtedly take confections of feathers, silk, and fur for natural flies; but I think it clear that at times they evince at night a preference for artificial flies of one texture of body or wing rather than another, such as herl, rather than quill, or *vice versa*, as indeed they do by day. For instance, the difference between landrail and starling dyed to landrail colour is not very obvious to any but the trained eye of the fly dresser, but I have known trout reject the sedge fly winged with dyed starling and greedily accept an exactly similar pattern winged with landrail. Again, it is well known that an Iron-blue nymph hackled with the blue-black feather from the throat of a jackdaw will be accepted freely when a fly hackled with an apparently identical hackle from the crest or other part of the same bird will be contemptuously ignored. In the same way the Water-hen Bloa must be hackled with a feather from one particular row of feathers from under the waterhen's wing—

the similarly coloured feather from the next row being useless. Other less well-known instances will be familiar to North-Country fly-fishermen. Numerous instances could no doubt be recounted where trout drew no such distinctions, for their fastidiousness is much more marked on some waters than on others. Indeed, I once fished a tributary of the Test where my host told me the only fly I need use, whatever might be on, was the Red Quill. It was an August day, with a nice rise of pale watery duns, but the trout took the Red Quill all day. Thank goodness, the trout of my length of the Itchen know enough to keep one guessing all the time.

And now comes the time to consider the upward vision of the trout.

XI

LOOKING UPWARD

At this stage I should like to consider further the theory put forward by writers well deserving of attention that the colours of flies, natural or artificial, are not distinguishable by the fish because the fly comes between the trout's eye and the light.

In order to do this effectively it will be well to get some idea first of how things look to the human eye from under water, not because the trout necessarily sees exactly in the same way, but because it is the only way in which it is possible for man to realize the lighting conditions of the under-water world. The theory above mentioned is generally supported by reference to the experiment of placing a glass dish containing water in such a position that lying on one's back one can look up through it at a floating fly. In such a position no doubt the fly would be against the light, and it would probably appear indistinct in colouring, for one would be looking perpendicularly upwards into the light. A trout, however, seldom sees a floating fly by looking perpendicularly upwards at it. Indeed, at the moment of taking it it must be at least the distance from his eye of the tip of his neb, and while the fly is approaching the trout more or less rapidly it must be seen at an angle to the perpendicular from the trout's eye to the surface. In these conditions the trout cannot always have the fly between him and the strongest light. If the sun be low and be shining directly down-stream towards the trout, then the conditions would approximate to those of the experiment quoted, and the light would be entirely from behind the fly, and its colour, unless it be transparent, would not perhaps be readily distinguishable.

But if the sun were exactly the opposite way and were shining exactly behind the line in which the fish is swimming, would not one suppose that the approaching fly would receive enough illumination to enable the trout to apply to it such appreciation of colour as he possesses? Between this condition of things and the condition prevailing when the light is coming right down into the trout's eyes, there must be a large range of conditions in which a greater or less degree of visibility of colour would appear to be possible.

This is, of course, all upon the assumption (which may not be correct) that the trout sees as man does. His eye is adapted to the medium in which it works, and it is at least conceivable that it is so constructed as to enable him to overcome the difficulty of appreciating colour with the light behind it. It is certain that it has a faculty of choice of fly, indicating a degree of appreciation of colour, or tone, or texture in the dark or deep dusk, so that it might not want much light on the underside of the fly to enable it to appreciate its colour, tone, or texture in any direction. The light reflected from the bottom, gravel, rock, or weed, might be enough. We do not know.

I was given the privilege, some few years ago, by Dr. Francis Ward, the author of " Marvels of Fish Life," of spending some hours in his underground observation chamber built below water-level on the side of an artificial pond with plate-glass sides cutting off the water from the chamber; and with the assistance of Mr. H. T. Sheringham, the Angling Editor of the *Field*, I made some brief experiments in the direction of trying to divine how trout see the fly, whether floating or sunk.

The pond was a cement construction, lined at bottom with rock and pebble, but showing from the darkened observation chamber in one side a far side of bare cement. The water came flush with the top of the glass window. The first thing that struck me was that the whole cup of the pond seemed reflected upside down except for a little semi-circle of light just above my head, and as one looked up into the semi-circle of light it seemed as if one were gazing into a big ball of water with a little round hole of rainbow light at the top, and except at this hole the sky was cut off by a sort of mirror, like plate-glass. But the tank was full of light, reflected from the bottom and no doubt back again from the mirror made by the underside of the surface. The semi-circle, of course, indicated by its edge the margin beyond which rays from above proceeding in the direction of the observer's eye ceased to penetrate the surface. I believe that rays striking the water at an angle of more than 48 degrees to the perpendicular above the eye of the observer will be reflected back skywards and substantially do not penetrate. In the same way if one looks beyond the edge of the semi-circle—*i.e.*, outside the angle of 48 degrees—one does not see through the surface, but only sees the bottom of the tank reflected on the surface. Thus a fly floating on the surface outside the angle of 48 degrees from the perpendicular to the eye of the observer is unseen, unless it or a part of it penetrates the surface, or makes some impression on it breaking up its mirror-like smoothness. If some impression only is made, it may, and no doubt does, afford the fish some indication that something, which may be fly-food, is approaching. If it, or any part of it, breaks through the surface, then that part only which breaks through the surface becomes visible outside the angle of 48 degrees, and it is reflected against the underside of the surface. This was well illustrated by the effect produced by the gardener's birch broom being thrust into the water to sweep aside some discarded shucks which had fallen from budding trees into the water. Only that part of the broom which was put through the surface was visible, and that was duplicated by reflection. The rest, for all that could be seen of it, might as well not have existed.

But inside the semi-circle, within the angle of 48 degrees, everything floating on the surface was not only visible, it was extremely clearly visible, and was surrounded by a prismatic radiance which was more specially in evidence the nearer the fly was to the outer edge of the semi-circle. There was no difficulty about distinguishing the colours of flies on the underside or on the sides. Indeed, the effects produced were all much what I have suggested above may be the light effects where the light is behind, or at any rate not directly shining into the eye of the trout.

I blame myself for not having ascertained and recorded precisely the position of the pond and the observation chamber in relation to the points of the compass, and the relative position of the sun at the time of observation, so that I might be able to deduce with more certainty the difference in appearance of a fly with the light between it and the fish and a fly between the fish and the light. The day, however, was very overcast.

A May fly was the first subject—one tied with summer duck wings, red hackle and tail, and a brown dappled pseudo-natural body—a most effective pattern, by the way, in Southern Germany. The first thing we noticed was that, when thrown on the surface dry, the gut was not noticeable from underneath, except in the semi-circle of light, and not very noticeable then. Outside that area the fly was like the broom. No part of it could be seen, except what had broken the surface film and passed through it. Thus, one sometimes saw the hook only—more generally part of the body and the lower part of the hackle—and we could conceive that, to a trout, a floating artificial May fly, not too dry, passing outside the transparent circle above his head, would appear at a little distance like a nymph, only taking shape as a winged fly when he got it within the circle of light above his head. Beyond this there was the fact that to us the under-water parts were duplicated by reflection. In the rainbow semi-circle of light above the observer's head in the pond the whole artificial May fly became not only visible, but extraordinarily and brilliantly so. The wings seemed coated with a spun-glass brilliance which was most attractive. It may have been all in the observer's eye, because it is quite conceivable that, looking up through a triangular wedge of water, one may have been looking through a sort of prism, which perhaps gave the rainbow effects above referred to.

With the May fly sunk below the surface, much of the brilliance was lost, and the gut became obvious at once. But whether the fly was outside or within the rainbow hole at the top, it was extremely difficult for the observer to say that it was not on the surface, except by deduction from the fact that it was visible, and would not have been so outside the semi-circle had it been floating. A sunken fly was readily visible at quite a distance through the water, when a floating fly at much less distance was, but for the hook, clean out of sight. The insistence of the dry-fly angler on extreme accuracy of casting and absolute dryness of gut and fly seems, from these observations, so far as they go, to be thoroughly justified. It is also obvious why a trout which will move a long way to intercept a nymph or sunken fly is not to be tempted by a dry fly that does not come accurately over him into the circle of light above his head.

Later we sank a large Pink Wickham, and it looked dead as mutton, and with the light behind it all the golden brilliance of its body was lost. Not even in the magic semi-circle above the observer was the glitter visible, but it is conceivable that, were the fly floated over brilliant green weed in sunshine, the green of the weed might be thrown upwards on to the belly of the fly, so as to reproduce the effect of a green-bodied sedge. In the dull light which we had, the brown stone bottom sent off too little reflection to give any noticeable effect. Even as it was the body did not look black. But some silver-bodied and gold-bodied salmon flies, which were dangled over sheets of metal painted blue, green and red, took up these colours, despite the dull day, very splendidly. So there can be no doubt that the effect of colour reflected from the under-water surroundings on the body and hackle of a trout fly is a question of degree. It may be considerable. The old trout-fly dressers were well aware of the ability of hackles—especially cock's hackles—and furs to take up light and colour from one another, so as to attain unsuspected harmonies. Thus, you might take two dun cock's hackles, apparently exactly alike, and, trying one over a mole's-fur body, get a dusty grey effect, and, tying

the other over a hare's-ear body, get a rusty brown effect!
They also knew the value of an admixture of seal's fur or
mohair in the body, in throwing up and affecting the colouring of the hackle. And I cannot help thinking that the
rage for quills sacrifices a great deal that was of value—
and still would be—in the dubbed body of the trout fly.

A small spent spinner—one of the then new Halford
patterns—dropped on the surface showed nothing whatever,
except an extremely black and obvious hook, duplicated
by reflection, breaking through the surface in a tiny patch
of blurred and broken light, due, no doubt, to the hackles;
and when viewed in the rainbow semi-circle one could not
candidly say that it looked (apart from the hackles) at all
fly-like, or anything but dense and hard against the light.
But my friend told me that when the spinner was floating
less high on its hackles, and was in fact somewhat water-
logged, it looked very fly-like and attractive. A home-
made Tup's Indispensable, tried next, had a distinct
advantage over the spinner when floating. Sunk, it
presented quite a nymph-like appearance, and it was quite
comprehensible that a trout might come some way to
fetch it. The same might be said of some seal's-fur-
bodied nymphs which we also tried. In a dull, shabby
way they had a lot of translucency. We next tried to
fathom why a Greenwell's Glory, fished wet, should be
taken at all below the surface. As my companion said,
it was " a fine representation of a Greenwell's Glory," and
on the surface it might have passed as a rather shabby
olive. Under water it went down always with its narrow
wings upright, and it may be that it is taken because the
trout is too foolish to realize that it is not on the surface.
Much the same might be said of a small dotterel hackle,
tied Stewart-wise, with waxed primrose silk on a No. oo
hook. It might have been taken for a hatching nymph

caught at a disadvantage with its wings half out, or, again, it might not, but I cannot think of anything else.

I was not below in the observation chamber to observe the effect of a floating Coch-y-bondhu made in the old style, or a Kennedy's floating Coch-y-bondhu beetle. Our last experiment with the trout fly was with a good-sized floating Sedge, but I recall nothing new or of interest about it.

I recognize that it is not safe to dogmatize or deduce very much from these very incomplete, very brief, and very imperfect observations, made by one like myself not equipped with the scientific knowledge to draw the inevitably right deductions from them, and the little which I have since observed does not take me much further. I do not know the true meaning of the structure of a trout's eye. I cannot tell what may have been the disturbing or distorting effect of the sheet of plate-glass between me and the water. And there are doubtless many other factors I have not allowed for, and I recognize that the course of experiment ought to be pursued systematically for weeks and months and years in all sorts of lights and all sorts of weather before any safe deductions can be drawn. So my readers (if any have got so far) will understand me that I am putting forward this record of my observations, not as establishing anything, but as containing perhaps some suggestions for investigation which others, more fortunately situated and better equipped than I am, may be able to follow up and verify or disprove.

XII

LOOKING UPWARD IN DUSK AND DARK

Under another heading we have considered the trout's vision looking upward in daylight. Let us now try and put ourselves in his place after the sun has gone down and darkness is supervening. What effect has this upon the trout?

It is a remarkable fact that, until the sun's rim dips, the evening rise does not begin. Often it does not begin then; but, though a stray fish may take a fly here and there, generally in parts when the sun shines down-stream, the evening rise proper never begins before, and it often begins directly after—immediately, that is, that the sun's direct rays are off the water. It is true that this is the time that spinners choose to come down upon the water—sometimes spent and dying, often with wings erect. But at times one sees quite enough new subimagines hatching just before sunset to bring on a rise if it were at any other time of day, and often there are many spinners then on the water. And if there be a hill, or high river bank, or a screen of trees which takes the direct sunlight off the water earlier than the hour of sunset, there one sees the evening rise accelerated. This is a fact of which the angler, desirous of making the most of his evening, may make profitable use while waiting for the general evening rise to begin. It would seem, therefore, that the diffused light reflected from the sky after sunset provides the trout with better conditions for seeing his surface prey than are afforded by the sunlight impinging directly, but at a low angle, upon the surface. The lighting may be scanty—but what there is of it strikes to a large extent straight down from the sky—and it would almost seem as if the trout could thus see better than if vision were confused by the almost horizontal rays of the setting sun. It would be interesting to see whether similar conditions prevail just before sunrise. I have never been up early enough to see. I have often observed that on a dull day, with diffused light only, the trout are much more alive to the presence of the angler on the bank, and much more cautious in their scrutiny of the artificial fly than on a bright day with full sunlight. The dull day of milk-and-watery glare makes the water look much clearer and full of light than does the bright day.

We have seen from previous investigation that trout have a strange power of drawing distinctions of colour, and perhaps of texture, in the dusk and dark, and it may be that the under-water world is then relatively better lighted for the trout than the above-water world is for man. If this were so, it would account for the trout being able to distinguish colours from underneath.

Years ago I picked up from a pedlar on Ludgate Hill a square of plate-glass mirror about five inches by five, in the hope that by means of it I might be able to get some idea of how an artificial fly looked to a trout. I placed it at the bottom of a large papier-mâché basin, and floated flies over it. But though no doubt it gave a fair idea of how a fly looked in point of shape, I soon concluded that its value from the point of view of colour was probably largely discounted by the fact that the mirror reflected on to the underside of the fly light which in quantity greatly exceeded and in quality of colour greatly differed from that which would be reflected by rock or gravel, or sand or green weed. I therefore carried the matter no further, and the mirror went the way of all mirrors.

Recently, however, a friend in the medical profession procured and sent me a laryngeal mirror, one of those little circular mirrors on a long metal bar, like those by the aid of which dentists manage to see the interiors of the hollow teeth on which they are working, while they are working on them; and he suggested that by means of the mirror I might readily see how the artificial fly looked to the trout. Though it seemed to me that this experiment must be subject to much the same objection as the former one, yet, seeing that the mirror could be adjusted to get a variety of points of view, I tried it. First I was unable to find in my house a bowl which was not white inside; so, rather than do nothing, I filled a white slop-basin with water and floated on it a pale watery Tup's Indispensable. There could be no doubt about one being able to see the entire coloration of the fly reflected in the mirror just as clearly as one could see it from above. But this may have been, and probably was, largely due to the white colour of the bowl and possibly in part to the light reflected from the mirror. I tried a Whirling Blue dun under the same conditions and with the same result, and the only good I got from the experiment was to prove the fact that, at a distance which might be measured in fractions of an inch, the mirror, if held only just under the surface, showed no part of the fly except those parts of hook and hackle which had penetrated the surface. At this stage I abandoned the experiment with the white basin, satisfied with having seen again how it might be that the deeper a trout lies the larger is the circle through which he is able to see the floating fly, and the nearer the surface he lies the smaller the circle, and that as he approaches it or it approaches him very closely he may scarcely be able to see anything of it but the impress of its feet or hackle on the surface, and thus may be blind to its incorrectness of detail, and may be satisfied with the general impression which he gained while it was farther off.

The next step was to procure coloured jars for a resumption of the investigation with the laryngeal mirror, and I selected jars of dark green and dark brown as being the colours best approximating to weed and rock, and deep down in them, in a room too far from a window for direct light from the sky to strike the surface of the water, I floated a Red Quill and a Pheasant-tail Red spinner. Putting the mirror deep under them, I saw every detail with all the clear-

ness of detail with which I saw it looking down upon it in
the open.   Later on, in a corner of the Itchen in the shelter
of a boathouse and a bank, I placed the mirror under some
natural red spinners and pale watery duns floating spent
upon the surface, and again every detail was as clear from
below as it was to me looking down upon the flies from
above.   This test may have been vitiated by the fact that
it was carried out under the open sky, so that the little
mirror may have reflected upon the flies the light which
made the detail clear.   At any rate, up to this point I
have seen nothing to prove that the trout looking up at
the floating fly, natural or artificial, sees it in silhouette
without colour (except, perhaps, when the fly is directly
between him and a strong light), and much to lead me to
think that he probably sees it, according to his capacity
for appreciating colour, as clearly from below as man
does from above.   I consulted Dr. Francis Ward, the
author of " Marvels of Fish Life," upon the subject, and
he suggested the use of a trench periscope so boxed in as
to exclude all possibility of the mirror reflecting back
upon the underside of the fly the light of the sky, but up to
the present I have not been able to give the scheme the
necessary attention.

There is, however, the indisputable fact that the trout,
which at dusk, in the absence of moonlight, is unable to
distinguish the angler casting a short line close behind
him, is able to make fine distinctions of pattern in the flies
presented to him, and that fact suggests to me that the
under-water region is better lighted for his vision than
the air above.

PART IV

HOW

I

THE MOUTH OF A TROUT

"And lo, it stuck
Right in his little gill."
DR. WATTS.

AMONG the many hundreds of trout which have been the
victims of my luck or skill, I have never known one which
was hooked in the gill, *pace* the good Dr. Watts. So it is
not unreasonable to conclude that the indraught of water
which takes the angler's fly into the trout's mouth does
not, by some miracle of contrivance, project the fly against
the gills by which the indrawn water is expelled.

The mouth of a trout is, relatively to his weight and
length, larger than that of any, I think, of our fresh-water
fishes, except perhaps that of the pike. It is serrated all
round the edge with fine teeth, and the roof of the mouth
and the tongue are armed with far more formidable ones.
For the purposes of taking and retaining the fly I cannot
conceive that these teeth are of much service. They seem
better suited to the purpose of the capture of minnows
and other small fry, which but for them might escape by
wriggling, and I have little doubt that the escapes so
often made by a too lightly held trout are often due to his
using the tongue-teeth as a sort of toothpick, to extract the
hook from the roof of his mouth or the side of his jaw.

If the angler in his bath makes the experiment of trying from below water to catch some small floating object on the surface, he will find it evade him again and again, pushed away by the current set up by his approaching hand, and it looks a miracle that the same thing should not occur with the trout, especially when his approach is swift. But if the feeding trout be watched as he rises to the fly, it will be noted that there is, as he opens his mouth, an expansion of the gills which carries a stream of water, and with it the insect, in with a rush. What is the process by which, on the water being ejected through the gill, the fly, natural or artificial, is retained is not known to me. It may be an operation of the tongue, but I think not. In any case, until the water is sufficiently expelled to enable the fish to feel or taste the capture, there is necessarily an interval, which constitutes the angler's opportunity, when that fly is his artificial one, to pull the hook home. When the fish is taking larvæ, or nymphs, or other subaqueous life carried by the current, the process is just the same. It is probable that if, in either case, the fish lipped the hook or the gut, there would be an instantaneous ejection of the dangerous morsel. Taste (which is, after all, a phase or development of the sense of touch) would warn him that at best the object was indigestible and unprofitable; experience might hint that it was dangerous. When trout are well on they take with a big gulp, often accompanied by a distinct " gluck " or smack of the lips; but there are days when the fly seems to be sipped in with a minimum of water through scarcely opened lips, and on such days the angler is apt to miss an abnormal proportion of rises.

This, then, being the method of the trout in feeding, one can readily see that minute accuracy of observation of the relative parts of a fly, as regards arrangement and proportion, is not of consequence to him, except to guard him against the angler. Innumerable natural flies come down to him partially entangled in their shucks (is it possible that the bronzed hook is ever taken for an adhering shuck ?), or in disarray through some misfortune or another, and all that is essential for feeding purposes is that he should take that which in size and in combination of colours is like that on which he has been feeding. Any closer noting of detail would be as much thrown away as would minute observation of the detail of each fish be thrown away in the case of a diner eating whitebait at the Carlton. Each fly is too tiny a morsel, and passes too quickly, for much leisure to be spent on inspection.

II

A SPECULATION IN BUBBLES

In the oft-repeated description of the imagined introduction of the novice to the dry-fly art, the typical classic touch in the drama is the disappearance of the dun and the single bubble floating where a moment before the dun had been. But never in all the papers and articles in which I have read this description have I seen the faintest speculation as to how the bubble comes about. Yet it may be worth while to consider the way in which it is produced.

It is true that, if one lies supine in a deep bath full of water with one's arm submerged and brings one's finger-tips to the surface, like the neb of a trout taking down a fly, and then turns them sharply down under water, one may produce a bubble or bubbles—generally the latter. It will, however, be found that some degree of violence is needed to produce the effect. But when a big trout is taking flies under a bank, and sending down single bubbles at each rise, he usually seems to be taking so softly, with such a minimum of effort and such an almost imperceptible dimple, as to exclude the idea of the degree of violence necessary to produce the tell-tale bubble. Clearly the air which fills the bubble is not in the mouth of the trout as he rises. There is, however, another possible explanation. When the trout sucks in the floating fly, is it not likely that he at the same time sucks in some air with it, and that he has to expel it: that in the act of expelling the water which he draws in with the fly he also expels the air with the water in the form of the bubble which gives away the position? It is in favour of this solution, that when trout are bulging, or in softer fashion taking nymphs under water, or even spent spinners flush with the surface, one does not note the bubble. It is only when floating flies, standing up on the surface, are being absorbed that one sees it, the reason probably being that it is more likely to require a gulp of air to take down a creature standing on the water and in the air than to take anything under or even flush with and adhering to the surface. The value of this, if it could be established, is that the presence of the bubble would be a fair indication that the trout producing it was engaged in the taking of floating duns.

III

THE RISE

When the angler sees a tell-tale ring upon the surface of river or lake, he is apt to say, "There is a rise." But if, when fishing, he should have his fly taken by a trout, whether under the water or at the surface, he would in recounting the incident say, if he were a Briton, "I had a rise." If an American, he would say, " I had a strike." The term " rise " is, therefore, used rather loosely—so loosely that for the purpose of considering the subject thoroughly it is desirable to start with a comprehensive definition of what it is intended to cover by the term in the course of this discussion. I propose, therefore, to use the term here, not in the sense of indicating the break in the surface caused by the movement of a trout in the act of feeding on insect life, but as covering every movement of the fish in the act of so feeding.

Now trout inhabit waters of all degrees of pace and stillness, and of all degrees of depth and shallowness. In all of them they feed on insect life; and it must be manifest to the merest tyro that differing conditions produce differing evolutions in the act of feeding. The items of insect nourishment absorbed by a trout are, in general, individually small, and, as a mere matter of instinctive natural economy, it could not pay a trout to expend in securing his prey more effort than the nourishment produced by the food would replace, or even so much, if he is to live and thrive.

From this reasoning one can see why big trout tend to feed on the natural fly less and less, and are often only to be tempted by the May fly or a big sedge. They prefer to spend their efforts in securing prey of a size which will more than repay the effort expended in securing it. From this cause the older trout are apt to become cannibals. For the same reason the trout of comparatively gentle and not too deep streams, where the fly is secured with the minimum expenditure of effort, will continue to be fly-feeders till they have reached a greater size than the trout of faster streams or of deeper, slow streams or lakes, where the coarse fish and the life of the river or lake bottom present larger individual items of diet in sufficient profusion.

The trout, therefore, though a powerful and vigorous fish, may be accounted a lazy one in the sense that he persistently maintains the utmost economy of effort consistent with living and thriving, and with the satisfaction of a healthy appetite as a means to that end. He will never face a strong stream for the mere pleasure of doing so. At times he may seem to be doing so, but careful observation will generally show either that he is in dead or comparatively slow water, or that he is getting such a supply of food brought to him by the current as to compensate him for the effort. He need not be seen to break the water, for a stream of subaqueous food is being brought to him, so that the faintest turn to right or left, or upwards or downwards, enables him to field it with the minimum of exertion. Again, except to intercept another fish or to prevent the imminent escape of his prey, he will seldom swim against a strong or even moderately strong current to get food which the current would bring to him. An apparent exception, which may at times be noted at the beginning of a rise, of a trout, generally a big one, cruising upstream and feeding as he goes, is not a real exception; for that trout, if he be watched, will be found to have been proceeding from his hole or shelter to a corner where he may expect a concentrated stream of fly-food to be brought to him by the current.

Thus, in still or slow waters which do not bring a sufficient supply of food quickly enough, trout either feed upon the bottom, or in mid-water, or near the surface, but in either case must cruise to find the food which is not brought to them.

Again, in eddies of swift or comparatively swift streams, where during the rise little fleets of becalmed duns or other insects lie almost motionless, trout will be observed cruising slowly along, picking one here and another there, and luring the angler ever upward till suddenly the rising ceases, and the trout is seen ready to resume his beat at the bottom of the eddy, which he will do unless scared by the angler or his rod.

Thus it appears that in different conditions trout rise in a variety of ways, and the observation one hears made that one has to strike more rapidly to hook the trout of this river than the trout of such and such another river only means that the conditions of the former river exact a quicker rise than those of the latter. This may in part be due to the fact that the trout of the former river run smaller than those of the latter, as, the larger the trout, the slower, other things being equal, is his rise.

With these preliminary considerations before us, let us proceed to examine the action of trout rising under varying conditions. A good start may be made in the High Street of Winchester, where below the Town Hall a fast but narrow stream runs from a culvert between brick walls alongside the Public Gardens. There one may generally see several brace of vigorous trout, but it will be rare to see one break the surface in feeding. Yet that they are well fed is evident. The stream is shallow, but they lie as deep as they can, and the swifter part of the water passes overhead. To test how they feed, however, make a few little rolls of new bread and throw them in. In a moment the fish is in the current. He does not rush to meet the bread. He merely adjust his fins, and the current swings the roll to his mouth, where it is sucked in by the expansion of his gills. In just the same way the trout of a glassy glide, just below and flush with a carrier which prevents them from seeing many natural insects on the surface, may at the time of a strong rise be seen busily stemming the strong current and moving slightly to left or right to meet and take in the ascending nymph, or whatever it may be, brought down by the stream. If, however, the food supply brought down be scanty the fish may be seen lying in holes and behind or in front of rocks and weed patches, and either inert or picking food off the weeds, or lifting for a moment into the current to annex something, and dropping back again to a position of shelter which deflects the main weight of the current from them.

Looking over a stone bridge one will often see a good trout just above a pier or pillar which divides the current, where he is in a sort of cushion of slow water which makes the least demand on his energies, but leaves him free to move rapidly into the stream to either side to intercept subaqueous food. In such a position he but rarely comes up to the surface, whether for a natural or an artificial fly.

Another position of great advantage for a trout is the tail of a pool. There he can lie low in comparatively shallow water with the weight of the current passing over him, and the whole of the food coming down from the pool concentrated into the neck, as it were, of the bottle, so that with a minimum of exertion he can take toll.

Similar positions of vantage are to be found in rough streams where the current pours between two rocks, and the trout can swing out from shelter into the current to snatch his fly and be back again.

In all these instances the trout will take far more food below than at the surface. Let us suppose, however, that lying deep he sees a fly coming down the stream on the surface. He is lying horizontally in the water. He shifts the plane of his fins, the current sends him upward, and thereupon his body, instead of meeting the current end-on as hitherto, receives some of the force of the current on its underside, and, exposing thus a larger surface to the force of the current, he tends to drop back down-stream, as his mouth comes up to meet the fly, with the body at times almost perpendicular to the surface. Then, opening his mouth, our fish by means of an expansion of his gills induces a small current of water, carrying the fly in with it. It is at this stage that he makes the only real effort, beyond the initial alteration of the plane of his fins, in the whole process. He has to turn down to regain his station, and this requires a vigorous turn of the whole body in order to overcome the upward thrust of the current, and to convert what was an upward movement into a downward one. It is this turn downwards, with its brisk curving of the body and sharp thrust of the tail, that produces that surface effect which, in the case of a fish feeding under these conditions, is commonly known as "the rise." And it follows that the faster the water the more vigorous that turn must be, though a swirling water will disguise and carry away its effect much more than will a smooth stream.

The structure of the vertebral column of the trout does not permit of much movement in any direction, except the lateral. Therefore the downward turn, where it cannot by reason of the force of the stream be effected by means of the fin planes alone, has to be effected by a sideways twist, the flash of which (as "the little brown wink under water") has so often afforded to the wet-fly angler the one hint that it is time for him to tighten on his fish. Chalk and limestone streams generally present numerous points of vantage where the stream, with or without the aid of the wind, concentrates a steady sequence of surface food, and it is at such points that trout will be poised, either in shelter, ready to ascend, if the stream be strong, or near the surface, if the stream be gentle. These points are generally under banks or at the tails of weeds from which the ascending nymphs are shed, and these are accordingly the places watched by anglers. And it will often be found that, even when there is no rise of fly, a small Sedge fly floated over such a place will bring up a trout which, perhaps for fear of being displaced by a rival, is hanging on to his place of vantage.

But, alike in chalk streams and in other streams, there are slow lengths where the surface food does not come rapidly enough to permit of a fish waiting for it. In these, therefore, he will be cruising, either at the surface or in mid-water or deep, with an upward eye on the surface and the intervening water. If he be cruising at the surface he will sip the fly gently with a minimum of effort. If, however, he be lying at mid-water or deep and comes up to the fly, he will do so with a slash or a "strike," as if he feared to be intercepted by a rival; but he will gather most of his food in mid-water or at bottom. In these conditions it may well be understood that a big fly of a beetle type, well sunk and drawn slowly or in short darts, may often prove far more attractive than a floater. The Ramsbury water on the upper Kennet, rented for a term by Mr. F. M. Halford and his friends, is in its lower lengths, at any rate above the Mill (locally called "pounds"), nearly all of the mill-head character, and that no doubt accounts for the failure of the most able management, in spite of lavish expenditure on stocking and on destruction of enemies, to convert it into a free-rising water. It may therefore be judged that such waters present a legitimate case, not only for the wet fly, but for a dragging wet fly.

It is the stream of moderate pace and comparatively even flow, therefore, that is suitable for the dry fly. The upstream wet fly fished without drag is suitable to that type and to faster and rougher streams, and the dragging wet fly may be used at both ends of the scale.

My lake-fishing experience has been so slight as to

disentitle me to say much about it. But it seems to me
that the same principles which apply to the rise of trout
in slow or still waters in rivers must be found in action
in the case of trout in lakes. In my limited experience all
the big fish have seemed to be found as a general rule on
shelving ledges where the water ran from six to ten feet
deep, and they lie or cruise at the bottom and come up
with a slash at the fly. Often the only rises seen are
those which are evoked by the angler's flies; and it would
seem that the main food was at the bottom, but that
surface food, if sufficiently attractive, was not despised.
That would seem to account for the fact that lake flies
are dressed larger than corresponding river flies, for I
suppose experience has proved that the trout is unwilling
to come up far for a small fly.

Occasionally, however, when the wind has dropped, trout
may be seen making small dimples on the surface of a lake;
and I recall one such occasion when I picked up in a
morning six brace of fish approaching a pound average,
fishing a long line ending with a Greenwell's Glory, double-
dressed on gut with No. oo hooks, and cast behind the
eye of the fish, which again and again turned and took it
with the greatest innocence.

So far in my observations I have dealt with the fish
taking the fly as food, and not from any other motive,
such as curiosity, tyranny, jealousy, rapacity, or pugnacity
(when the action is generally, even in fast water, more in the
nature of a strike than a rise); and I have not dealt with the
nature of the indications of the rise afforded to the fisherman
under differing circumstances—for to do that it is essential
to consider not only the position and convenience of the
trout and the nature of the water, but also the character
and condition or life stage of the food which the trout is
taking. For it will be found that different classes and

conditions of food are taken by trout in different ways. And all the movements described are, moreover, further conditioned by the season of the year, the health and vigour of the fish, and his ability to contend with fast waters, and his hunger or sportiveness, and his appetite or preference for special varieties of food; also by the state, temperature, and colour of the water, and the character of the light in relation to the fish's position. Sometimes in streams trout are so full of vigour that they throw themselves right out of the water, taking in the fly in the upward rush, and come down head first into the water to resume position. The effect of the character and condition of the food of the trout upon the action of the rise and its indications, and the clues which rises of different character accordingly afford the angler as to the food which is being taken, must be the subject of a separate chapter.

IV

ASSORTED RISES

A close study of the form of the rise may often give the observant angler a clue, otherwise lacking, to the type of fly which the trout is taking, and to the stage and condition in which he is taking it.

So far the present writer has found in angling literature, whether permanent or ephemeral, no systematic attempt to differentiate the varying forms of the rise of trout. There has been little evidence of any general consciousness of distinctions more precise than that between bulging, or under-water taking, and surface feeding, and in this respect this deponent makes no pretence of having been more acute than his fellows. It has, however, for some time past been growing upon him that, as no phenomenon in nature but has its cause, so the varying forms of rise, which every angler with the fly must have observed, are all dictated by the nature of things. It is conceived that there are several things which naturally influence the character of the rise, these being the position of the trout in the water, his degree of confidence or appetite, the smoothness or roughness of the surface, the pace of the current, and the nature and stage of the fly-food being taken.

In the examination into these matters which follows, the writer makes no claim to be authoritative or exhaustive, but he hopes to awake among the keener minds an interest in the questions discussed which may lead to some pronouncement which shall be at once exhaustive and sound in all its conclusions.

The chalk streams and rivers of quiet and even flow obviously afford greater facilities for observing the phenomena of rises than do streams less clear or of more turbulent habit, and it is from the chalk streams that one can most easily acquire the bulk of the data which may be applied, with the necessary qualifications, to the solution of similar questions on other streams. The illustrations here given will, therefore, in general be found to be taken, unless otherwise stated, from chalk streams and chalk-stream fishing, and it is not proposed to deal here with the effect of rapid current on the various types of taking.

Every chalk-stream fisherman, however much or little he may have thought about the subject, will recognize that there are a great many forms of rise. It is now proposed to consider some of these, and to try and ascertain what clue they severally give to the food the fish is taking.

Analyzing broadly, the insect taken will be either— (1) poised on the surface; (2) flush with the surface, as being either spent or entangled by wetting of the wings, or in the earlier stage of the process of hatching; or (3) subaqueous.

The best known and the most obvious rise is that in which the trout takes the floating dun or upwinged spinner. It is the foundation rise of dry-fly theory and practice, and it is to this, with the spent spinner rise thrown in, that the dry-fly purist would, in theory at any rate, confine the angler. But, as a matter of fact, this super-surface taking forms only a small part of the evidence of a trout's feeding known as the rise, and it is often supremely difficult to determine whether a given rise or series of rises be at food superaqueous, flush, or subaqueous. Much of the floating fly-food of the trout is very small and hard to detect on the surface, and it requires some close watching to say whether it be sipped from above, or at, or just under, the surface. Thus it must come about that many a would-be dry-fly purist has spent busy hours presenting a floating fly (and at times with a measure of success) to trout which are only taking subaqueous food. From this painful and humiliating position there is little chance of escape unless the purist makes a point of actually seeing the fly on the surface taken by the fish (and preferably identifying the insect) before he ventures a cast. Not a great many purists are always so perfectly pure as all that.

Assuming, however, that the insect be seen coming down to where the fish is seen or known to be lying in wait, the trout comes up from a greater or less depth, with more or less diversion to right or left, and, with more or less confidence or eagerness, and, with a smack, a suck, or a sip, takes down the fly. The smack involves some exposure of the neb and a considerable ring in the water; the suck shows the neb under a small hump of water which never ceases to cover the fish. The sip does not expose the neb at all. A fish coming from a depth and turning

down again naturally makes more of a swirl, from the energy
expended in the movement of turning down again, than
does a fish hovering just below the surface and merely
putting up a nose. The size of the fly also makes a
difference. The tiniest insects are sipped, the larger ones
are taken down with much more of a swirl. The rise to the
blue-winged olive at night (and by day, too) is indicated
by quite a large kidney-shaped whorl; and the large dark
olive of spring and late autumn is taken in a similar way.
The degree of eagerness of the fish also has an effect on the
size of the swirl he makes in taking. The fondness of the
trout for the iron-blue dun, for instance, leads him to take
it with an agitation which betrays him to the observant
angler as feeding on the iron-blue dun or its nymph,
though no iron-blue dun may have been observed on the
surface or in the air. Naturally, too, the trout makes less
of a ring when he can be confident of securing his fly than
when he has to hurry to secure it ere it be whipped off the
water by wind or its natural tendency to take flight.

Where duns are floating in eddies one often sees trout
sailing gently under and sipping them softly. Occasionally in these positions one sees a succession ·of head-and-
tail rises—first the neb appears and descends, then the
back fin, and then the upper portion of the tail fin. It is
my belief that this in general indicates that the trout is
taking duns which through accident or defective hatching
are lying spent or on their sides on the surface. The
same type of rise in the open stream may generally,
especially in the morning, before the dun hatch, and in
the evening, be taken to indicate that the trout are taking
spent spinners. In the eddies and over weed-beds, however, when no fly is visible on the surface, it may mean
that the trout is taking nymphs, just in the film of the
surface, about to hatch, or, it may be, swarming for refuge

in eddies after a weed-cutting; and these may be nymphs of duns or gnats. In these circumstances nymphs seem to be taken with a quiet deliberation very different from the swashing eagerness with which the bulger swirls to meet his under-water prey. Very often, however, in streams the trout will be nymphing for hours together with just the same quiet deliberation and with just as little excitement as when taking floating duns; and, as on these occasions there is no head-and-tail rise, the angler is usually immensely puzzled to make out on what they are feeding. The writer does not profess to have worked out any reason why nymphs should be taken on one occasion with the head-and-tail rise and on another with an action apparently differing in no appreciable respect from the ordinary rise to floating duns. The nearest thing to a clue he has been able to observe is that while spent spinners are taken with the head-and-tail rise, floating upwinged spinners are absorbed, especially if small, with a soft suck which spreads a ring so thin and creating so little disturbance as to be scarcely visible in the dusk or the moonlight, while within its circle the water looks like a little pool of fine creaming lines whorling towards a pinhead hole in its centre. Again, occasionally on a windy day one sees a head-and-tail rise in quite rough water. The inclination therefore is to suspect that the trout is taking an insect blown over or caught by the waves with just the action with which he takes a spent spinner or a drowned dun in the eddies, and to deduce that the head-and-tail rise is to a quarry at the surface with no chance of escape, and to make the further deduction that, when nymphs are being taken thus, they are in some stage or condition where they have no chance of escape, and that where they are taken with what looks like an ordinary rise they are capable of some, but not a great, degree of activity, and may be below the film of the surface. Then there is, of course, bulging properly so called, where the fish move to and fro to intercept the nymphs carried down by the current. Here in general the indication of the rise is the swirl of the fish as it turns after capturing its prey. There is also the rise to hatching caddis, such as the grannom—having an appearance much like bulging; the rise to the running sedge—something of a slash; the rise to tiny midges and curses, which may be an example of the ordinary rise to surface food if the insect be perfect, or of subaqueous taking if the insect be yet unhatched.

Of the rises of cruising trout in still or extremely slow water it is not necessary to add anything, except to say that at times they partake of the character of the slash and at times of the sip.

Of the rise to snails spoken of by Mr. Halford in one of his works, the present writer has had no experience.

Summarizing briefly the types of rise we appear to have at least the following:

Over-Surface Rises.

Ordinary rise to floating dun or upwinged spinner and its variants, namely:

Big rise with kidney-shaped double whorl to large floating dun (such as blue-winged olive or its spinner).
Sucking rise to medium-sized floating flies.
Sipping rise to smallest floating duns, spinners, and midges, and
The slash—most commonly to running sedge, or to flies on slow water.

In addition to which there is the plunge where an eager fish comes almost entirely out of water and takes the fly either as he leaves the water or as his head re-enters.

On the Surface or Flush Rises.

Head-and-tail rises to wet duns or spent spinners or
nymphs of duns or gnats suspended inert in the
surface film.

Subaqueous Rises.

Bulging to nymphs.
Bulging to hatching caddis flies, such as the grannom.
Nymphing in eddies ⎫
Nymphing in streams ⎭ to mobile nymphs.

There are doubtless other types which a more observant
eye would be able to distinguish, and there must be many
among the large body of fishers with the fly who are well
qualified to indicate them.

V

" FAUSSE MONTÉE "

There is one form of rise which I have not dealt with,
to which, indeed, it is difficult to give precise designation.
Speaking generally, when one sees the surface broken one
says, " There is a rise," and one means that the surface
is broken by the emerging or almost emerging neb of a
trout. But the rise I am here speaking of is quite other
than that. True, there is a boil on the surface, but it is
not an indication that the trout is there. On the contrary,
it is an indication that he is gone. And, if he has taken
the fly, any hope of hooking him that is based on striking
when the boil is seen is likely to be vain. It will be too
late, probably much too late. This form of rise is much
commoner in fast, fairly deep water than in water that
is slow or smooth. And when the angler finds that he is

apparently getting, and certainly missing, rise after rise, he may suspect that what he is really getting is this kind of false rise, and he should, if possible, seek a position where the light falls so as to enable him to see through the surface the turn of the fish under water, and strike at that instead of at the following surface indication.

How fallacious that indication can be I saw very clearly one sunny June morning a few years back on the Kennet. I had put my rod together for a day's May-fly fishing on a beautiful length of that river, and I was waiting on a bridge above which a lovely clear shallow deepened and narrowed towards the arch. In the eye of the stream—a nice eighteen or twenty yard cast upstream—a yellow trout of near two pounds, and obviously in prime condition, lay rather deep, yet not in that glued-to-the-bottom way which rendered it hopeless to attempt to get him. There was, in fact, an air of suppressed energy and eagerness about him which tempted me to stretch over him the summer duck straddlebug which was ready attached to my cast. The fly lit beyond him, but a yard or more too much to the left. But he came at it with a flash, took a scare, turned, and was gone—three or more yards to the right of his original position; and as he came into the straight, all that way away, a huge boil on the surface surrounded and took under my fly. It was the effect of the vigorous slash he made in his turn away from the fly that only materialized on the surface when the trout was well away from it. It was obviously no good to strike, but if the light conditions had not enabled me to see the whole process quite clearly, I might have struck under the impression that I had had a fine rise, and have gone in the belief that the fish had risen " short," or that I had mis-timed my stroke—and have found any explanation but the true one.

I think it will often prove that when fish are rising what is called short, whether they take the submerged fly or baulk at it, as did the trout in the incident described above, what is seen is no true rise in which the fly is taken, but the belated after-effect of the trout's turn away under water coming to the surface. This turn may vary enormously in its degree of violence, and the gentler it is the better the angler's hope that the fly has been taken and that he may pull in his iron.

VI

THE MOMENT

As Captain Cuttle is recorded to have remarked, " The point of these observations lies in the application of them."

I propose, therefore, to consider the rise at the artificial fly, and to examine its indications as guides to the angler telling him when to strike.

There is, of course, no mystery about the taking of the floating fly. Provided the angler is certain that it is *his* fly that is taken, and not a natural fly an inch or more away, he has only to strike more or less rapidly according to the size of his fish. Matters are often nearly as simple for the wet-fly fisherman if the trout comes up to his fly with a swirl, but he has to remember that if his fly be well sunk he must be very quick or he may be too late, for the swirl is often (as shown above) an indication not that the trout is there, but that he is gone. That is why in a rough river a wet fly fished upstream should be fished on a short line with most of it out of water, so that the trout turning down may if possible be felt, or at any rate that there may be no loss of time in pulling home when the flash of the turn is observed. But often the trout takes so

far below the surface, or with so little motion, that there
is no swirl or break on the surface to indicate that he has
taken.   Then the opportunity may be missed unless some
other hint be noted by the watchful angler.   On chalk
streams or smooth placid streams such indications may be
found in the draw of the partially floating gut, in the flash
of the turn (but this is comparatively rarely seen), or in
the appearance of a faint hump on the surface, often
accompanied by a tiny central eddy caused by the suction
with which the trout has drawn in the fly.

Sometimes the entire process can be seen, though the
fly be invisible, and then the angler will be wise if he
tightens at the least motion of the fish to left or right, or
at the opening and closing of his mouth, or, if the cast has
fallen wide, then at the moment the fish is seen to turn
back.   It is surprising how often he will be found to have
collected the fly.   I have seen a trout let an artificial fly
of the nymph type go past him, turn and follow it for
several yards, and, striking as he turned upstream again,
have found him fast.

PART V

WHAT

I

FLIES AS FOOD

A GENERAL survey of the circumstances, stages, and conditions in which the insects which serve the trout as food may be preferably simulated or represented may not be amiss.

The larvæ of the Ephemeridæ have been classed as digging larvæ (of which the May fly larva is an example), flat larvæ (of which the larva of the March brown, clinging to the bottom and hiding under stones, is the most obvious), swimming larvæ, and crawling larvæ.

The digging larvæ are hidden from the trout until as nymphs they crawl up into the weeds and let themselves go into the current preparatory to hatching out as winged flies. This, then, is the only subaqueous stage in which they are exposed to the trout and can legitimately be simulated or suggested by the fly-fisherman. In the winged stages they are surface flies either floating with upright wings or flat with wings outspread, damaged, or spent or dipping on the surface if egg-laying.

The flat larvæ, of which the March brown is the most prominent example, can seldom in normal times be seen by the trout, since they hide under stones and seldom venture out till the time comes for their ascent to the surface to hatch out. Probably when there is a spate which tumbles over the stones, these larvæ are exposed and carried down-stream, and the trout get an unwonted good chance at them, so that they are not as unknown to the fish as the digging larvæ. At the time of ascent to the surface for hatching the trout get their real chance at them, and it is in this subaqueous stage, rather than in the stage of subimagines, that the fish feed on them most ravenously. The hatches occur in flushes, and it probably pays the fish better to slash the ascending nymph (which they can see farther than they can see the floating subimago) than to await the subimago passing almost vertically overhead.

The stages, therefore, in which the Ephemeridæ which have flat larvæ are legitimately to be imitated are the ascending nymphal stage and the winged stages, either floating or flush with the surface.

The swimming larvæ are obviously much more familiar to the trout. Living in vegetation or roaming over stones and gravel they are easily routed out by the trout. A familiar example of this is to be seen when the trout are tailing. Then larvæ, nymphs and shrimps are bustled out of the weeds, and are captured in the open by the fish. Then, again, at the period of ascent to hatch, these nymphs are exposed in mid-water and near the surface, and are swung down by the current to the waiting fish. An imitation nymph or larva will at times take a tailing trout, but, generally speaking, the stage in which an imitation has its legitimate chance of success is at the time of ascent, or any other time (such as weed-cutting) when the larvæ or nymphs are in open water exposed to the fish. The wriggling action of its swimming cannot, of course, be reproduced in the artificial fly, but when the swimming larva, like the other larvæ, comes up to hatch it is practically quiescent.

The crawling larvæ have a way of hiding snuggled under a thin layer of sand or weed, so as to be practically invisible. It follows that they must frequent quiet waters. Yet when spates occur they are no doubt washed out of their shelters and become a prey to the trout. They too, again, have an exposed stage when they ascend to hatch out as winged flies; and it is in these exposed stages that the imitation nymph or larva has its proper chance of success. Obviously the nymphs or larvæ cannot be imitated either on the bottom or in the weeds.

The winged insect will be taken hatching or hatched, floating cocked, or caught and disabled, and again in the spinner stage, floating cocked, or disabled, or spent, or, again, dipping to lay her eggs.

There are said to be cases where the female spinner " creeps down into the water (enclosed within a film of air with her wings collapsed so as to overlie the abdomen, and with her setæ closed together) to lay her eggs upon the underside of stones." I have never seen such a happening, but it is quoted from no less an authority than the Rev. A. E. Eaton, and must unquestionably be in accordance with the facts.

The net result, therefore, as regards the Ephemeridæ is that effective representation of them for fly-fishing purposes is as larvæ or nymphs, when in open water, and in the winged stages.

Then there is the willow-fly or stone-fly series (Perlidæ), which in the subaqueous stages live on the bottom among stones; and though in those stages they are no doubt avidly taken by the trout when the trout can get at them, they do not in those stages lend themselves to representation on a fly hook, and they are seldom in mid-water. They can, therefore, only be usefully simulated in the perfect or winged form.

There are also the caddis or case flies (Phryganidæ), which again, with the exception of the grannom, do not lend themselves to imitation, representation, or suggestion otherwise than in the perfect or winged form.

The grub crawling on the bottom in its sheath of stones or sticks or sand is no doubt frequently eaten by the trout, but does not, either in form or habitat, lend itself to representation by the fly dresser. It might be that occasionally the ascending pupa about to hatch into the perfect fly could be approximately reproduced. Indeed, the grannom is more often taken by the trout when ascending to hatch out than as a perfect fly, and a brown partridge hackle with a green silk or wool body is readily accepted as a substitute, but the ascending pupæ of other case flies are not so easy to reproduce.

There is the alder, sometimes confused with a case fly, which spends its larval stage in the mud, crawls ashore and pupates in the earth; and, though it frequents the water-side, it only drops on the water, much in the same way as a land fly, as a casualty. In the larval form, however, it would not be badly represented by a Honey-dun Bumble dressed with a palish Tup's Indispensable body; and I once had a fly, so dressed, torn to pieces by eager May trout in Germany.

There are also the gnats which breed freely in stagnant or slow water, and are taken in the subaqueous as well as the perfect and winged stage, though seldom imitated by anglers in the subaqueous stages. Finally, there are various small midges and beetles.

The land flies which get on to the water are less important. They are all in the nature of casualties, and comprise ants (of which trout are inordinately fond), sundry flies of the house-fly and blow-fly type, the oak fly or downlooker, and sundry crane flies, etc.

I do not purpose to go into the entomology of the subject, since that has been adequately dealt with elsewhere.

It follows, however, that the Ephemeridæ, the gnats and some beetles, and possibly the alder, are the only flies which have subaqueous stages calling for representation by the fly dresser. The perfect stages of all the classes of insects named may be dressed to be fished either dry or semi-submerged, or even, so foolish at times is our quarry, definitely submerged.

I think, however, it should be the ideal of the sportsman angler to take his trout, where he can do so, by means of imitations, representations, or suggestions of its natural food presented in the conditions in which the trout is feeding on it.

It is very usual to find writers declaring that to attempt to represent or suggest the natural fly with sufficient exactness to deceive the fish is absurd, and that one fly will do as well as another, provided the size and something of the modesty of nature be observed. I can only say that thirty-seven years of fishing of chalk streams have convinced me that this is not true of them, and that the trout will, more frequently than not, refuse any but one pattern which for the time being appears to them (though it is not always obvious to the angler why it does so) to be the natural fly on which for the moment they are feeding. For instance, it is not very clear why, when the blue-winged olive is rising at night, and the trout are taking it on the surface, a large Orange Quill on a No. 1 or even a No. 2 hook is accepted readily by them, but a large Red Quill of the same size, dyed or undyed, will either be utterly ignored or will put down the trout. The only difference is the colour of the quill. Other instances of unlike likenesses being taken are the taking of the Blue Quill when the pale watery dun is on, the Gold-ribbed Hare's ear when the large spring medium olive dun is hatching, and the Whirling Blue dun for the big autumn olive.

Often, of course, the insistence of the fish is upon closer likenesses. Yet it is my constant experience that on such waters a minute variation makes the difference between failure and success.

For instance, in July, 1919, the July dun was coming up freely on the Itchen, and I was introducing a guest to the water. He put up a fly which to all appearance was a close imitation. Dark starling wings, yellow silk body ribbed with fine gold wire, and greenish-yellow olive hackle and whisk. He was an excellent fisherman, and he spent a full quarter of an hour over a vigorous trout, never putting him down or scaring him. Out of my experience I had made him tender of a pattern of July dun, which differed from his only in having the body silk clothed with pale blue heron herl, dyed the same colour as the silk, a dirty greenish-yellow olive, but he had refused with the remark that his fly was " near enough." After a while he said to me: " Well, give him a chance at your fly, since you think it better." The first time my fly covered the trout he had it, and my friend netted out a nice two pound six ounce trout. He then accepted another fly similarly tied, and putting it on got the next two fish he tried directly he covered them.

I have had too many similar experiences to have any doubt about the matter.

Of course, the Itchen is a river which breeds and maintains a large quantity of fly-food. In rough rivers where fly food is scarce I can understand that the fish will often rise at any fly or any suggestion of a fly which comes over them. But even there, when there is a rise or fall of an acceptable species of fly, I have known occasions when the trout refused everything but a fairly satisfactory representation of that fly. For instance, on the Coquet one afternoon, seeing that there was a heavy fall of small spinners, I put on a solitary fly which I had dressed the previous day to imitate the same spinner, and I caught no less than eight-and-thirty trout with it, while a much more experienced rough-water fisherman, fishing with me on the other side of the same water and using three or four flies, one of them a wool-bodied Red spinner, but not true to shade, took three trout only. I am therefore convinced that what I call "appropriate representation" rather than exact imitation is seldom thrown away.

Every rule has its exception, and the exception is the occasion when the hatch or fall of natural fly is so copious that unless your fly has the luck to fall so near to the trout as to be the absolute next to be taken it is in competition with too many natural flies to invite selection. On such an occasion there should be something special about your fly to attract the trout's attention from the stream of natural insects.

II

FLY DRESSING AS AN ART

I imagine that no art has ever been learned from books; fly dressing is no exception. As a mere mechanical art it can be learned in the workshop or at the fly-dressing table. There, from teaching and example, the student may acquire with practice a certain knack and deftness. But when he has acquired these it is far too soon to imagine himself a master of the art.

Many writers have attempted to teach it in their books by verbal description and by illustration, but apart from the fact that most of them leave unexplained a whole series of details of each process, which seem to them from habit to be so simple and obvious as not to require explanation, there seem to be none who go to the real root of the matter, and tell the student what he is or should be aiming at when he sets out to dress an artificial fly. In saying this I have not forgotten Cutcliffe and his " Trout Fishing in Rapid Streams." In that work, one of the soundest and cleverest in the whole range of fly-dressing literature, the author does propound, in language which lacks nothing in clearness and sincerity, a system of dressing and fishing the artificial fly as a lure. But that is only one, and far from the most important aspect of fly dressing and fly fishing; and when he deals with fly dressing from the imitative, representative, or suggestive side, he does so in a very perfunctory manner; for, for the streams of Devon to which his fishing was confined, that was not a side of the subject to which he attached much importance.

Most, if not all, of the other writers who have dealt with the subject have dealt with it locally and almost entirely as a mechanical art. While saying this (and I hope I am doing no author an injustice) I should like to make it clear that I have never read one of them and attempted the method he describes without learning something from him, and no method portrayed has proved entirely without merit.

Still, the writer has yet to come who will treat the art of trout-fly dressing as a whole, and will make clear to the learner the aims, objects, and advantages of the varying styles and methods adapted to varying conditions of brook, stream, river, and lake, and the processes by which they can be achieved.

The first stage must, I suggest, be the adoption of a clear terminology as an aid to clear thinking. For instance, most of the writers above referred to tell us that the natural fly must be " imitated "—and then they are quite likely to teach you how to dress a straddlebug or a palmer—and it is more than probable that in most cases by imitation they mean " representation " or " suggestion." Even those distinctions are insufficient. Imitation may mean imitation of life, of activity, of colour, and size. It may be obtained by transmitted or reflected light where the colour of the natural fly is reflected or transmitted. And these things are equally true of the artificial fly that is a representation or a suggestion of the natural fly.

III

IMITATION, REPRESENTATION, SUGGESTION

It is a common and a just observation that the best artificial fly bears but a poor resemblance to the natural fly which it is supposed to stand for. But, for all that, artificial flies dressed to imitate, to represent, or to suggest natural flies do take trout, and take them in such conditions that no unprejudiced angler can doubt that they take them for their natural prototypes. This suggests defective vision on the part of the trout, and this question of vision and the nature and extent of the defect are examined elsewhere. At this stage it is sufficient to indicate the distinction to be drawn between artificial flies which are imitations, representations, and suggestions respectively of the natural insect.

Where, as for instance in the case of the Olive Quill or the Iron-blue dun, a determined effort is made to reproduce the natural insect in colour, shape, and attitude, the artificial fly may be called an imitation. It is of little consequence whether the effect be got by reflected or transmitted light. A less ambitious effort may be called a representation, while a pattern so sketchy as just to give the effect of a tumbled specimen (as, for instance, a dotterel hackle, or light snipe and yellow for a pale watery dun), may be called a suggestion.

Every artificial trout fly is necessarily a compromise. It has to carry a hook; to float or to sink; to be durable; to be attractive:

(*a*) by appealing to hunger or appetite; or

(*b*) by exciting curiosity, rage, rapacity, pugnacity, or jealousy.

It appeals to hunger or appetite by suggesting an insect either living, or newly drowned, or otherwise dead, in one of its aerial or subaqueous stages, or a shrimp, or (as Dr. Mottram will have it) a small fish.

Such insects may be suggested by shape; by colour; by carriage; by shape and colour; by action; by action and shape; by carriage and shape; by action and colour; by action, shape, and colour; or by carriage, shape, and colour.

The shape cannot be precise because of the hook, and because of the action of the water on feathers, and because, in the case of a floating fly, of the refractive operation of light passing from air into water.

The colour may be suggested by translucency (or transmission), by reflection, or by both.

Action may be suggested by motion in or on the water, or by position on the surface, and by such a use of hackle as to suggest a buzzing action.

The imitation may be Impressionist, Cubist, Futurist, Post-Impressionist, Pre-Raphaelite, or caricature. The commonest is caricature. It therefore catches most fish.

IV

STYLES OF FLY DRESSING

The angler who has fished with the fly in different parts of the country cannot fail to have noted the extraordinarily differing ways in which the same natural fly is imitated, represented, or suggested in different parts of the country and for different rivers and streams.

As nothing of any permanence is without reason, it must be inferred that these differences correspond to differences in the conditions under which fly fishing is pursued in streams of different classes.

In Plate I. I have reproduced a series of patterns of the same fly—the large dark spring olive or blue dun—dressed according to methods prevailing in different parts.

Fig. 1 represents an attempt at what is styled, for lack of a better term, "exact imitation." It purports to represent the natural fly sitting up cocked on the water in the attitude in which it may commonly be seen on the clear chalk streams of the South. It has wings (double dressed) and legs, body and tails; and the colours of the different parts purport to correspond with those of the natural fly. It is fished in conditions in which, by reason of the clearness and slow pace of the water, the trout has time for a good look at the fly ere it takes it. Fig. 1a is a Derbyshire dressing from the hands of Mr. C. A. Hassam, of the Fly Fishers' Club—than whom no more exquisite artist in trout flies, whether amateur or professional, has ever come within my ken. The wings are single dressed and the whole fly a model of lightness and delicacy.

Fig. 2 represents the same fly as dressed for the tumbling Yorkshire and North-Country brooks and rivers. It is dressed with a fur body, which, when wet, is remarkably transparent and lets through, while it darkens and accentuates, the olive colouring of the waxed silk with which the fly is tied, and the tumbled hackle from the waterhen (moorhen) suggests the tumbled, dilapidated state in which a fly whose wings have been caught by the current might be whirled down-stream in such waters. If used as a dropper, fished upstream and across, this type of pattern with its mobile wings may well constitute an effective suggestion of a fly struggling with its difficulties upon the surface. All the Yorkshire and North of England patterns seem to be dressed upon this theory. Both these types of fly are meant to be fished upstream, or up and across. Fig. 3 is a dressing from the Usk. The Usk is a broad, solid river, where, I imagine, the bulk of the fishing is to be done by casting across stream. Here the theory appears to be that the artificial fly is a sketch. Note the slight shred of wing, the slim body, the slight but active hackle. Fig. 4 is a dressing of the fly intended to be fished down-stream, or rather across and down, in such solid streams as the Teme. It has, therefore, what is described as a good entry; that is to say, a shape which is calculated to create the least unnatural disturbance through its breasting the current or swinging across it. It is to stand hard wear, so the wings are rolled into a single solid pad.

Fig. 5 is a single-winged pattern—i.e., a pattern dressed with only one thickness of wing fibre to represent each wing of the natural fly—and in a variety of quality it is perhaps the commonest and least rational of all the types of fly dressing. Fig. 6 is a Devonshire pattern, dressed with sharp, bright, dancing hackles, probably intended to suggest a struggling nymph rather than the hatched winged fly.

Fig. 7 is a rolled-winged pattern with upright wings akin to the Greenwell's Glory. It is one of the few winged patterns of the Northern English counties and the South of Scotland, and its upright split wings will either enable it to go down-stream almost afloat like the natural fly, or, if it be drawn under, it will be whirled about in a way to suggest considerable life and activity. It is suitable for upstream fishing—even in chalk streams.

Fig. 8 is a type of fly affected by the fly fishers of the Clyde and its tributaries. It is extremely sketchy, but as I have never fished, or even seen, the waters where it is used I am unable to do more than guess at the theory of its operation. It appears somewhat akin to the Tweed type.

Even sketchier is the type of pattern illustrated in Fig. 9, but I have known Scottish burn fishers fill bumping creels with just such simple patterns busked before setting out with a mere wisp of feather for wing, a tiny hen hackle pulled from a fowl caught for the purpose, a few inches of tying silk, and perhaps at times a tiny pinch of wool from coat or cap for the body.

Then there are Stewart's patterns (illustrated in " The Practical Angler "). Of these the winged flies are much like the Teme flies, No. 4, but, fished upstream and across as droppers, are drawn down by the current ahead of the gut cast head upstream, while the hackled type are just soft hackled palmers which, while of the sober colours of the water insects, must really attract by reason of the mobility of the hackle fibres presenting an appearance of a struggling creature.

All these methods have their merits and all deserve study; for the fly fisherman who is also a fly dresser can be none the worse for being able to adapt his methods to the type of water he is fishing or going to fish in.

The number of ways in which flies can be tied is incredible. There are hardly two books which lay down identical methods unless one is a crib from the other. And of all the methods in which I have experimented, from Walton downwards, I have never come across one which had nothing to recommend it, and I should be glad to be master of them all.

V

KICK

This is a quality which every hackled wet fly, for use in rough water, should invariably have. Without it, it is a dead thing; with it, it is alive and struggling; and the fly which is alive and struggling has a fascination for the trout which no dead thing has. How is this quality to be attained? It is a very simple matter. Finish behind the hackle.

Suppose you are tying an Orange Partridge. You have whipped on the gut, tied in the floss, whipped to the shoulder, wound on the orange floss, whipped down the end, cut away the waste. You then take your brown partridge hackle, and placing it face downwards on top of the hook, with the stump towards the bend, you whip it down with two turns towards the head; then, whipping over the hook and back to the feather, you form the head. Then you take two turns over the butt, and, taking the centre of the hackle in your pliers, you wind at most two turns of the hackle and secure the end with one turn of the silk. Then you pull all the fibres forward over the head, and finish with a whip-finish tight up behind the hackle, and break off the waste. You then soak the whip-finish with celluloid varnish (celluloid dissolved in amyl acetate or acetone), push back the hackle over the bend and varnish the head, and your fly is complete. The turns of silk behind the hackle makes each fibre sit up and stand out, and the fly has kick, and it will improve rather than deteriorate with use. Hackles with good natural resilience are, of course, essential.

VI

EX MORTUÂ MANU

For centuries, more than most anglers suspect, we have in the matter of fly dressing been in bondage to the past. The dead hand has been heavy on us. To the newcomer to fly dressing the taking of a trout with the artificial fly seems such a miracle that he is apt to attribute some special virtue to the confection of fur and feather which has done the feat, and he falls to studying the fathers of fly dressing either directly from their works or second-hand through modern pundits, or the experts who derive their knowledge and experience either from the same sources or from the experts before them similarly instructed. Thus the body of angling lore on the subject of artificial flies is almost entirely empirical and traditional, and as every new blunder is carefully enshrined in work after work, it is tainted with every kind of long-perpetuated error and prejudice, and is distant indeed from the natural sources from which it should have directly sprung.

I have described the trout as " rather a stupid person," and, with an irony more biting than I guessed at the time I wrote, I thanked the powers that had made him so, for otherwise man would be unable to catch him with the fly. I did not at the time mean that angler man was something more than " rather a stupid person," but I say now that if the trout took as long to learn the things that belong to his taking as angler man has done, the word " rather " would be an entirely inadequate qualification for the opprobrious adjective. I speak for myself as for the rest of my craft, from Dame Juliana to the present day. Our faculty for misobserving and for misapprehending the most obvious evidence of our senses would put the most stupid trout to shame. The most caustic phrases of "A Scottish Flyfisher" would be quite too weak to convey any idea of the wrong-headed density of the whole string of writers of fly fishing from A to Z, not excluding the present scribe. From the word "go" fly dressers have built their flies upon the assumption that the winged fly, as seen in the air, is the food of the trout. For generations anglers have fished these winged flies under the surface, because they found the trout would take them there, and it was difficult to make them float. All sorts of ingenious and fanciful theories were conceived to account for the taking of winged flies under water. It took a peasant, whose entire education cost, if his preface may be believed, no more than thirty shillings,* to put first on record—though not without some natural errors of observation—that the trout takes the insect at the bottom, and as it ascends to the surface, as well as on the surface, but even he did not advocate imitating it in the subaqueous stages. It took nearly fifty years more to bring us our "Detached Badger," with his autopsies proving that the vast bulk of the food of the trout was subaqueous; that, as he puts it somewhere (I quote from memory), the under-water feeding is the beef and mutton, the floating fly is caviare to the trout, and he authoritatively squelched in Chapter VII. of "Dry-Fly Fishing" the idea that larvæ or nymphs could be successfully imitated. Hence his demonstration that chalk-stream fish could only be taken with caviare. It took twenty years more to bring me to the definite conclusion that the wet fly had a big future on chalk streams. And it took the droughty summer of 1911 (with scarce a natural dun or spinner on the surface day by day, yet with trout after trout breaking the surface as it fed in all respects as if it were taking floaters, and every

* John Younger, "River Angling," 1840.

trout's gullet containing nymphs and larvæ only) to lead me to experiment systematically with nymphs really imitating the natural insect, and to prove that, notwithstanding the weight of authority to the contrary, the artificial nymph will kill, and kill well, when the trout are taking natural nymphs, or even merely not exclusively occupied with surface food.

Now to those who prefer to catch their trout with caviare only, I have nothing to say except that it restricts their chances, and it seems a dull game compared with that of catching them by simulation of what they are feeding on at the time. It is, however, at least a comprehensible theory, like barring the anchor stroke in billiard matches. But to anglers on wet-fly rivers, and to those chalk-stream anglers not exclusively devoted to caviare, I would ask: Has not the time come when the under-water fly should be habitually presented not only under water like a nymph, but as an effective imitation of a nymph? I am aware that a book called "Fly Fishing: Some New Arts and Mysteries" (Dr. J. C. Mottram) has set out an interesting method of nymph fishing. I do not wish to be understood as disparaging his flies or his methods in any way, as I have never tried them. In theory they seem to me to have the defects of rigidity, density, and dulness of colouring, and a tendency to fall heavily when cast, by reason of absence of hackle. Moreover, they are used dragging. In practice these matters may be of no consequence. My own very encouraging experiments have in the main been made with dubbed bodies containing more or less bright seal's fur ribbed with gold wire or silver wire (thus being full of light), and with just enough short soft hackle to help to break the fall of the hook on the water. But whatever method of dressing is adopted, I, at least, urge the systematic and general working out of a logical system of imitating the natural insect in its natural surroundings. This does not eliminate the winged fly altogether. It can be fished dry or when the trout are taking the natural fly on the surface, though even then I incline to think that the nymph will frequently be preferred. A new Ronalds is called for to classify and illustrate the successive series of nymphs and larvæ for the benefit of anglers. Let him stand forth !

But even without our nymphal Ronalds let us try and see what can be done by the application of the sheer light of common sense. Let us suppose that all the lore of centuries is cancelled out, and the angler sitting down to construct, without reference to the past, a system of trout-fly dressing. What would he evolve ?

He would first, I conceive, ascertain what appetites or emotions lead a trout to take the artificial fly, and he would conclude that they were (1) hunger, (2) caprice or wantonness, (3) curiosity, and (4) tyranny or rapacity. For the purpose of exciting caprice, curiosity, or rapacity, he would evolve the fancy fly, and that might not be unlike some of the more conspicuous artificial flies of the present day, either brightly coloured or active in motion of its parts, or both. For the representations of insects appealing to hunger, and occasionally to caprice or wantonness, he would have to make a first-hand study of the food of the trout when freshly taken. He would net a series of trout at the middle or end of a rise, and analyze the insect contents of their stomachs. If, then, he found—as he would find—that 95 per cent. of the Ephemeridæ there to be found had been intercepted before their wings had emerged, it is safe to assume that he would not give the numerous varieties of nymph the go-by without seeing whether it were not in fact possible to reproduce them on a hook with sufficient exactitude to induce the trout to take hold. It is not suggested that he might not also evolve the floating fly for use on special occasions, but I venture to think it would take a place quite secondary to the nymph, if once the initial difficulty of imitating the nymph were surmounted. He would ascertain that during the period of preparation for the rise these nymphs were floating at large in considerable numbers, and were legitimate subjects for imitation. Not so the larval or pupal stages of the Phryganidæ and the Perlidæ, which, hiding in their cases or lurking under stones, do not, at any stage short of the perfect insect, lend themselves to imitation for the purposes of the artificial fly. The larvæ of the diptera on which the trout feed are in general too infrequent in streams or (like the perfect insects) too small to lend themselves to the purposes of the fly fisherman. Assuming, therefore, that the modern angler determined to discard these types of fly, which, either by their dragging motion or by the brilliancy or challenge of their appearance, excited the curiosity or tyranny or pugnacity of the trout, he would find himself practically confined to the floating fly and the larvæ or nymphs of the Ephemeridæ.

He could not, of course, deny that artificial flies, dressed by the lights hitherto vouchsafed to us, have caught trout in the past, or that they will continue to do so in the future. He would probably recognize that on some, perhaps on many, waters the appeal to curiosity, tyranny, or rapacity which they present affords a better chance than the appeal to appetite which the floating fly and the larval or nymphal imitation presents, and that some waters are unsuited to the floating fly. But I think he would have to admit that for an appeal resting upon appetite alone the floating dry fly, the flush with the surface tumbled floating fly, the dipping egg-layer, and the larval or nymphal imitations are the only strictly legitimate lures, and that the floating ephemera must be imitated either in the dun stage, dry with cocked wings, or spent and semi-submerged with soft dun hackles, or in the spinner stage floating, or semi-submerged with bright cock's hackles to represent the wings. He would recognize that on the surface, whether floating or semi-submerged, all fly wings and most fly bodies present to an eye looking up to them a certain degree of translucency. He would infer that to produce that effect of translucency upon the eye of the trout he would have to use materials which are either themselves translucent or which produce by reflected light the effect of translucency, like some quills in certain lights. But as dubbing will transmit light from whatever quarter, whereas quills will only reflect it if looked at from the proper point of view, he will infer that dubbings of suitable colours have advantages over quills. He will realize that the vision of the trout is not identical with that of man, and if he be a skilled optician he may deduce what that difference is, and how it affects the game. With the nymphal or larval imitation, he will see that translucency is even more important than in the case of the winged fly, and that dubbing has the advantage of quickly absorbing water and sinking his fly. This is, I think, as far as common sense, unassisted by experience on the riverside, would take him. But think of the advance. All the unnatural horde of so-called imitations of natural flies which are used under conditions in which no natural insect is ever seen, would be relegated to the true category of lures, and the angler whose business it is to take the feeding trout with the simulacrum of what he is feeding on would know what he was about, and if he chose to use any of the abominations of the past, he, at least, would do so with open eyes. At last he would be a free man, escaped from the bondage of the past. *Ex mortuâ manu, libera nos Domine.*

PART VI
BAFFLEMENT

No comfort comes of all our strife,
And from our grasp the meaning slips.
The Sphinx sits at the gates of Life
With the old question on her lips.

*   *   *   *   *

We have successes, and build upon them profound and far-reaching
theories—to have them shattered into smithereens on the very next
experience.

*   *   *   *   *

Hold we fall to rise, are baffled to fight better,
Sleep to wake.

*   *   *   *   *

And as we dwell, we living things, on our isle of terror and under the
imminent hand of death, God forbid it should be man the created, the
reasoner, the wise in his own eyes—God forbid it should be man that
wearies in well-doing, that despairs of unrewarded effort, or utters the
language of complaint. Let it be enough for faith that the whole
creation groans in mortal frailty, strives with unconquerable constancy:
surely not all in vain.

I CONCLUDE this section of my book with a sense of
bafflement, fully aware that my speculations are mere
speculations and inconclusive in result. It may be that,
just as man is a creature of three dimensions, and not
constructed to comprehend the matters of the fourth
dimension, to say nothing of the n dimensions, plus and
minus, extending beyond or comprehending the three in
which he dwells, so man is intended never to solve the
mystery of the difference between the eyesight of man
and that of the trout. Be that as it may, it is beyond me,
and I have come to a time of life when I cannot hope to
add much to what little I have so far learned. Such as
that is, however, I dedicate it to my brother fishers with
the fly, in the hope that it may lead to further advances
in the not too distant future, and that in the meantime
it may be of some help to those who seek improvement
in the theory and practice of the art of trout-fly dressing and
of fishing with the fly.

89

DIVISION II

SOME FURTHER MINOR TACTICAL STUDIES

I

SOME PROBLEMS

I. THE HARE'S-EAR PUZZLE.

THE latter days of April, with their outstanding hatch of large medium olive duns, bring back this recurring problem for the colourist. In a sense I am a colourist. That is, I recognize—I am forced by the logic of facts to realize—that the trout take certain artificial patterns for certain natural flies. I admit the likeness is often not obvious, and I infer from that—to the great indignation of " Jim-Jam " and others—that the trout do not, in all probability, see colour as we see it.

For it is the fact that whenever I see the greenish olive body of this spring dun I know that the season of the Hare's ear—the Gold-ribbed Hare's ear—has come; and I put up the Gold-ribbed Hare's ear with the utmost confidence, and I find it more certainly and infallibly right than any other dressing I know, unless I except the large Orange Quill when the blue-winged olive is on. But that is in the evenings, in the dusk, while the Gold-ribbed Hare's ear kills in the full light of day.

Why, then, should a pattern dressed with a body of a dusty grey-brown, ribbed with flat gold and extremely rough, be taken by the trout for a smooth-bodied fly with an olive-green body ?

It is true that fur, when wet, is extraordinarily translucent. It is probable that the gold catches some of the
green of the under-water weeds reflected upward from below.
But still the facts as known to us suggest some problem
of the eyesight of the trout which requires solution if we
are to arrive at a true theory of the art of fly dressing.

It has been suggested that the artificial is taken in
this case for the natural fly, either just hatching out of its
shuck and not entirely extricated, or else standing on its
shuck. But if that is so, why should not all the upwinged
duns be represented upon similar principles ?

At one time the late Mr. F. M. Halford was a great
advocate of the Gold-ribbed Hare's ear, but I believe that
latterly his enthusiasm for precise imitation induced him
to give it up, successful pattern though he knew it to be,
because he could not explain its success to his satisfaction.

I confess I do not take it to be a lure. The trout do
not take it like a lure. I believe they take it for a natural
insect—the medium olive dun—which is on at the time.
But why ? It is, by the side of this problem, easy to see
why the Blue Quill is regarded by the fish as the pale
watery dun.

Still, the Hare's ear kills. And I should like to know
who was the genius who first conceived its possibilities,
and how he got at his theory.

If we had that information progress might be possible.

2. UPSTREAM WIND.

It is true that it had snowed and hailed and sleeted, and
wintry-blasted and rained every day of April up to and including the Saturday of Easter; but my friend " Fleur-de-
Lys" need not have been so demned superior on the telephone
when he cried off our engagement to go down that afternoon
to open our Hampshire season together. It is some satis-

faction to think that he is sorry for it now. I had a sort of notion there was more of a chance than appeared obvious on the surface of things, and the very fact that " Dab-chick," in the *Field* of that week, had issued his most impressive warning that it would be hopeless to expect any sport at Easter, only made me more set in my determination to go down and offer the trout some samples of my fly dressing.

Years ago I was walking by the Beverly Brook in Richmond Park, when I came across a dark secondary wing-feather of a heron, and conveyed it home. I dyed it a rich brown olive, of the hue that goes dirty orange where the pith of the split stalk of the feather is exposed, and ever since I have dressed myself annually a small stock of Rough Spring Olive with a body of that feather, and have generally killed fish on them before the big dark spring olive took his departure about mid-April. Here is the recipe:

Hook.—No. 1.
Silk.—Bright yellow, well waxed.
Wings.—Darkest old cock starling.
Body.—Three or four strands of dyed heron's herl, as above described.
Rib.—Fine gold wire.
Hackle.—Dark brownish olive.
Whisks.—Ginger.

For the wet pattern the hook may be a size larger.

Well, the week-end was bleak enough to satisfy the malicious soul of " Fleur-de-Lys." But the beginning of the new week broke very pleasantly bright and sunny, and so, though I knew from old experience that it was not the slightest use to be on the water before twelve o'clock (Greenwich time, not summer time), yet 10.30 summer time found me in waders and with my rod put together making across the water meadows for a deep length of the river

which I had found in other years the most lucrative length
at the beginning of the season.

The length which I selected to begin upon ran nearly
north-west to south-east, down to a short bend, when the
stream turned due east. The bend is always a satisfactory
place at which to observe fly coming down, as the stream
flows sharply and deeply along the western bank, and seems
to concentrate the hatch of duns into a yard-wide causeway
under the bank. And so, when I reached the spot, quite
naturally I ignored the absurdly early hour, and gave up
watching the snipe and the strings of wild duck and the
two pairs of swans preparing to nest, and the hundred and
one charming things with which the water meadows teem,
and concentrated on the current in the corner. It was
by now ten minutes to eleven summer time (9.50 a.m. by
Greenwich), and consequently at least two hours before
there was any reasonable hope of the fly beginning to show.
But I had my cast soaked and a Rough Olive floater tied
on and oiled, and I didn't feel a bit unreasonable. Presently eleven o'clock (summer time) chimed, and almost
before the echoes of the last stroke had died there appeared a
little dark form on the surface at the lower end of the bend.
It drifted, fluttering, for a little space, and then there was
a cheerful smack and a widening ring, and it was not.
It did not take long to get my distance; the wind, blowing
from south-east by south, though strong, was not un-
friendly, and promptly I was covering the trout. Twice
he rose at natural flies, and three other fish began above
him in the same bend. The next one looked like a bigger
trout. However, I stuck to my fish, and at length brought
him up to my Dark Olive—short. I then cast across to
a fish I had seen rise just by a tussock at the point of the
inner corner of the bend. Up he came boldly—and missed.
I pondered. I knew my pattern was as good imitation of

the dark spring olive as was made, if not better; but something was wrong. I caught a fly and had a look at it. It was not the dark spring olive at all, but the large medium olive which usually comes on about mid-April, a fly which experience has taught me indicates Gold-ribbed Hare's ear. I had only one in my box, but I knotted it on and was presently covering my first riser again. Up he came promptly and fastened firmly, and presently was guided to the net, a nice plump fish of one pound three ounces, in excellent condition. In the course of his struggles he had, however, run up into the province where the bigger trout had been rising above, and therefore, though I had not followed him, I thought it wise to give the corner rest, and I rambled down-stream for a hundred yards or so in search of another riser to keep me occupied. None appearing, I returned in a quarter of an hour, to find all three fish in the bend again busy sucking down the duns every two or three minutes. I offered my Hare's ear to the lowest, and half a dozen times it was ignored. So I cast across to my riser under the far bank. He came up and missed the fly. Something was evidently wrong. I caught another fly, and found that the big dark spring olives were now coming down, and that the few medium olives among them were being rejected in favour of the larger fly. Back went my Rough Olive, and the first time it covered the trout right it was taken. So was the trout—a fish of one and three-quarter pounds. I put down the next fish, and got the third before twelve o'clock.

I had now fished out the bend and had the wind behind me straight upstream, with, if anything, a shade of a push against my own bank. There was a strong ripple in mid-river, with deep oily water under my bank, and it was there I found most of the few rising fish concentrated.

The duns were coming down in quite fair quantity for the time of year; but, in the strong breeze, they were skidding and skating about on the surface, and even being blown upstream, so that the trout could not depend on their coming down to them quietly and evenly; and presently I noticed that these flies were not being taken, but only the disabled flies which were blown on to the water, and had one or both wings caught. I found, too, that my next fish would have nothing to do with my fly floating cocked and well dried; but he had it immediately it was offered semi-submerged. Acting on this tip, I laid siege to some three other trout in the next couple of hundred yards. I cannot claim any merit. It was a duffer's day. I had the right fly, and the wind took it into the mouths of the trout. Anyhow I got the lot, and by one o'clock the strap across my chest began to feel uncomfortably tight.

I was still some way from the luncheon hut, and I occupied the next hour in fishing up to it. But after one o'clock there was a change in the humour of the fish, for though they came up readily enough to the same fly, and were apparently taking the natural fly as well as ever, not one would take soundly, and I lost five, each after a brief run. Then they stopped for the day. I waited in the meadows till four o'clock on the chance of an afternoon rise, but none came on. So well content I conveyed my three and a half brace, of which the first was the smallest, back to my inn, and indited a postcard to "Fleur-de-Lys," because I thought it would gratify him to know what he had missed.

It is perhaps only fair to say that the following day spring set in again with all its arctic severity. There was an icy wind from the west, about a dozen flies seen on the water all day, one fish observed to rise three times— once at me, short—and a toom creel for the writer.

3. A CURIOUS CONTRAST.

It is one of the charms of fly fishing that no two days are exactly alike, however closely the weather conditions may seem to correspond. This is an account of two consecutive spring days on the Itchen which presented a remarkable contrast.

I have long had an affection for the large dark olive, and as it is seldom seen on the Itchen after mid-April I determined, in spite of a keeper's warning that the trout had not yet begun to get under the banks, to snap a couple of days by the water-side, and I chose Wednesday and Thursday, April 9 and 10. Tuesday, the 8th, did not give me much encouragement, for it was a bitter day of north-east wind, and, indeed, that wind had been prevailing for nigh a week. It was therefore more for the pleasure of stretching a line against the wind with my ten-foot Leonard than with any expectation of sport that I strolled into the meadows at about 10.30, fortified by waders and a mackintosh against the icy wind which blew dead down-stream. But by the time I had assembled my rod and had passed the line through the rings I saw, to my astonishment, a large dark olive skating along the surface, propelled by the wind at more than the natural pace of the stream, and before eleven o'clock the first rise was in evidence; and very soon I was ware of no less than three trout on the feed in the short stretch which was in sight. I watched them carefully to see if they were taking the surface duns, and soon made up my mind that they were not. So I knotted on a wet pattern of the large dark olive, and began with No. 1. He, however, was " not taking any," and the same was true of No. 2. The light, indeed, was a bad light—a sort of dull leaden colour in sky and on the water, but everything looking preternaturally clear. The third fish was an inexperienced person, an inch under regulation length, and he was returned to the water to gain his inch and wisdom. Then there came a break in the clouds and a brief gleam of sun; but the large dark olives, which had been growing more numerous, began to slacken, and I could find no more rising trout. On a little bare patch, however, under the far bank, just where a small meadow runnel discharged into the stream, I made sure I spied a sizable trout, and after an ineffectual shot or two I got my fly over him. He looked at it and turned away. The next shot got it in the mouth of the runnel. An under-water turn towards the bank brought the fly into his, as I rightly judged, and I shortly had the pleasure of netting out my first keepable trout of 1913—a well-conditioned fish of fifteen inches. Before I had consigned him to my bag the cathedral clock struck noon. From that time on I did not see another large dark olive.

I had opened on the side-stream, but now I migrated to the main. For a while there was a lull. Then I became aware of a scattering rise of small palish olives. I cast over a number of rising fish with but little success, for though I rose several of them they all came short except four, and I was convinced that they were all grayling, like the two brace I caught. Since grayling were, as the chemists put it, "in excess" in the water, and as the standing rule is to kill all you take, I knocked my two brace on the head. Presently I turned down-stream again, and seeing another grayling put up I cast down to him and let the fly swing over him. In a second he took firmly and was fast. Another followed, and another, almost as fast as I could cast. Fish which came short at a fly floating loose struck firmly and hooked themselves on a taut down-stream line. By degrees ere five o'clock I raised my two brace of grayling to nine and a half brace, and thought I had done good service to the water in doing so. All this time I had not seen another trout put up. Returning to the side-stream I found nothing moving, a fact which did not surprise me at the time of day at that time of the year; but presently I spied a hovering fish of good size over a pale gravel patch. I despatched my dark Greenwell's Glory to him, and at the fourth offer he took it gaily. He proved to be the duplicate of my first trout of the day, both in length and condition. Finding no other fish showing, and feeling disinclined to return to my inn, I strolled back to the main, and between 5.30 and 6.15 I killed another brace of grayling. The startling thing, however, was that the trout were beginning to line up along each bank, as if preparing for an evening rise. I even brought up (and missed) two. I did not, however, wait for the evening rise to materialize, showing thus most commendable self-restraint.

The following day opened rather milder than its predecessor, with the wind from the north veering to the northwest. I was by the water-side punctually at a quarter to eleven, but in spite of the milder weather I saw no fly and no movement of a fish till 11.30. Soon after that hour chimed I saw, about a hundred yards up, a trout of two pounds if he was an ounce show half out of water as he swirled half across the stream to take a nymph. I crawled up into position, but he never showed again, and after waiting a quarter of an hour and making a couple of chancy casts I moved on. Two more fish broke the water, but I failed in much the same way to place them. I now came to a little spinney, just above which there is a sure find for a good fish. There is a little nook in the bank at the far side which is seldom untenanted when any rise is toward. To-day was no exception, for hardly had my wet

Rough Olive reached the holt ere my rod was a hoop and I was battling with a big fish. Alas! he elected to go down, and the spinney and its barbed-wire fence forbade any following. I had to hold and chance losing him, and in a few moments he had kicked off. Two or three minutes later the same fly tempted a very bright fish, just over one pound, and he went into the basket. A few yards farther on, over a bright-green weed patch, a big fish was cruising, and alternating bulging rushes with soft, tiny little rises. I suspected him of an occasional dry fly, and watching him I found him guilty. Accordingly I put up a small Pope's Nondescript, tied with hare's-ear legs, and was about to approach him, when another trout broke the surface a little nearer. He had the first offer, and must have followed the fly down, for I was lifting the fly for the next case when he slashed it and missed. I lost no time in covering the larger fish beyond. He came up promptly and was hooked, but got off after a flounder or two on the surface.

I had now reached a broad shallow in which there were several fish in position, and, selecting a good one, I put the same fly over him several times. Presently, just as I was about to lift it for another cast, the fly was taken by a smaller fish lying below him and to the far side. He was, however, a nice pounder, who looked as if he had not spawned, he was so fat and bright. His struggles, however, put off all the other fish on the shallow and I moved on.

I now came to a place where a long belt of trees protected the water from the north-west wind and left it absolutely unruffled. Under the far bank there were one or two fish rising at intervals to a very small pale dun, which began to hatch out in nice quantity. I missed the first fish, which I covered with a No. 1 Whitchurch, tied with honey-dun cock's hackle on a No. 00 hook; but the second fish, making an almost invisible ring, and putting up a single bubble as he sucked in the fly, proved to be a sixteen-inch fish in beautiful fettle. He scaled two pounds one ounce when weighed in the evening.

The next fish was taking in a similar place and in similar style. After being covered several times he came up and fastened, and after an extraordinarily brilliant fight came to net—one pound four ounces. The next fish I rose and missed—entirely my own fault. Then, almost in the spot where I had taken my second trout the previous day, I saw what looked to me like an exceptionally fine trout move across an open patch. I changed my fly and put on an Ogden's Hare's ear. While I was doing so he rose. He put up a second time within a couple of inches of my fly, and a third time a couple of casts later to take it. He weighed one and a half pounds that evening when I got in. Here the river bent so as to receive the full force of the north-wester up the next stretch, and I turned down again to get to the main. On my way I found one trout only rising, but he was willing, and made up my three brace as the clock struck two. I walked some way up the main, but did not see another fish rise, whether trout or grayling.

A curious contrast these two days! The first, the colder of the two, the rise began earlier and went on till after six, and the grayling were on all the time. The second, the milder day, was entirely a trout day, and the rise beginning at 11.30 was all over by two o'clock. The same flies were on both days. Why this contrast?

4. THE RED QUILL.

" The Red Quill is the sheet anchor of the dry-fly fisherman on a strange river." Thus authority—and it is true enough. Yet in all the years of my fishing I have never been able to persuade myself exactly what the Red Quill means to the trout. According to my experience, it is of no service on a chalk stream in April. But from early May to the end of the season there are few days when it is not worth a trial. But why? Some suggest that it is taken for a spinner. It may be. Others say whirling blue dun. This seems far fetched. On my own water its most deadly time is, according to my observation, when the trout, though feeding freely and to all appearance rising, are in fact taking nymphs just below the surface— but without bulging. The absence of the head-and-tail action proves that they are not taking spent spinner, and they are letting the subimago go by. Why, then, do they take the Red Quill? There is one other fly and one only I know which they take in the same way, and that is Pope's Nondescript. But that they will take at times when they are feeding on nymph in any fashion, either bulging, nymphing without bulging, or tailing.

In the case of Pope's Nondescript, I imagine the broad gold tinsel of the body (a feature shared with Gold-ribbed Hare's ear) is advertisement enough to call attention to an attraction existing in a plane in which, for the moment, the trout is not engaged. The Pink Wickham no doubt attracts the tailing trout in the same way.

But except for the hackle, which, if sharp and bright, may have a certain brilliance, the Red Quill is a modest little fly enough. Yet it does attract many a trout which is normally feeding below to take it on the surface. I have been driven to wonder whether it is taken for a hatching nymph, being generally darker than the fly on the surface. Yet this can hardly be a satisfactory solution. I am left with the facts and no theory to account for them. For this reason I seldom use the Red Quill.

5. THE ENTRANCE OUT.

An Interlude.

It was three o'clock on a hot August afternoon, and such show of fly as was to have preceded the evening rise was definitely over for the day. It was too soon to make for the hut for tea, and there were no carriers in the water meadows handy enough to encourage a tired and, if the truth be told, very sticky angler to seek them in search of a possible willing trout. The weakness of the flesh would have suggested lying down, if there had been any suitable place to lie. The same weakness forbade the attempt on the rough and cow-trodden marshy embankment which contained the river hereabouts. There was no seat and nothing to read, so obviously the line of least resistance led to looking for a fish in the main stream. The morning's operations had yielded a couple of brace from under the hither bank, and the other customers at that counter were probably in retreat. Remained the opposite bank, where, exposed on bare patches of gravel, there might be a fish or two amenable to the temptation of a small Sedge. That, too, was unlikely, for fish in such positions had not escaped attention during the morning rise. Stay! there *was* " the entrance out." The meadows on the far side had some years back been flooded and had never been redeemed, so that beyond the eastern bank there lay some ten acres or so of overgrown swamp, the haunt of coot, moorhen, and dabchick, vilely overgrown moreover with flannel weed, and the mother, o' nights, of innumerable swarms of venomous mosquitoes. Where the water made its entrance into this area had not made itself plain to the angler, but he did know of a recent break in the embankment a little farther down-stream, through which some at least of the overflow found its way back to the river by a shallow and narrow channel. That the overflow carried food of some sort into the river was evident from the fact that the neck of the channel had been occupied during the morning by a biggish black fish which was not breasting the rapid flow for nothing, while a little below in the main stream another fair fish had stood expectant of what his superior might allow to pass. If these fish were still there, they would still be feeding. If feeding, they would be takable. One might as well see. Yes, they were there all right. Seeing, one might as well try. It was better than doing nothing. Such light air as there was helped to carry the little Red Sedge across, and drop it in the little channel neatly enough. No offer— no notice even. Probably a dry fly is a mistake. Try a little wet beetle—say a Coch-y-bondhu. The first time the trout looked at it and half turned. The second time he let it by without a quiver. Yet he must be quite busy feeding. On what ? Why not mosquito nymphs ? But what colour ? A muddy-coloured little beast, probably hanging head downward with his tail at the surface. Here in the fly box is a reversed nymph, with a blob of dirty-coloured dubbing representing head and thorax at the bend of the hook, which might represent him at a pinch if the hackle be cut down. Let us try it first on the fish below in the river. The first chuck is not quite far enough over. The next is a little too far, and drops the nymph in the eddy. What's that ? It looked like a turn of a fish under water. The hand has instinctively responded and the hook has gone home. Down-stream he tumbles, battling bravely, and presently the net receives his fourteen inches.

Is the biggish black fish still in the break in the embankment ? Yes, there he is, stemming the smart little current as busily as ever. It is quite imperative to get the fly

and gut to him wet, so as to have no surface drag (subaqueous drag it is impossible to help). So the nymph
must be switched over to him. The first switch is a bit
short. The next lands the insect on the bank, where for
a moment or two it is hung up in the herbage, but, thank
goodness ! the hook comes away without damage. Two
or three times in a dozen casts the same thing occurs, but
still the fish is unscared and as busy as ever. At last the
fly pitches about a foot above him and a few inches to his
left. There is a quick turn of his head, a simultaneous
turn of our wrist, a violent lash of a broad tail, and the
black trout shoots indignant into the main, tears headlong
down-stream, hooping the little rod, which is at once too
weak and too strong for him. Alas, brave fish ! if for
the nymph of the mosquito that little channel was the
entrance in, for you it has been what an Irish friend of
mine termed " the entrance out."

6. THE ALDER AND CANON K.

For many years after I had become a fly-fisherman I
never did any good with the Alder. I first owned a fly
rod (of a sort) in 1874, but although I had read and loved
Charles Kingsley's " Chalk-Stream Studies," it was not till
1904 that I had any success with his favourite fly. It is
true that my May and June-time fishing had been almost
exclusively on the Itchen (which seldom yields any results
to the Alder) and on the lower Kennet, when the May fly
alone brought up the trout. But in 1904 I took a holiday
in Bavaria which covered the first eighteen days of June,
and for some reason which I do not quite recall I took
with me a small stock of Black Alders purchased of Messrs.
Peek and Son, of 40, Gray's Inn Road, which appealed to me
as being of the genuine Kingsley tie. Kingsley, it will be
remembered, fished his Alder (and his Caperer or Sedge)

well sunk. These Alders, therefore, were tied with long wings of a soppy game hen's wing, tied slanting well back from the shoulders over a peacock's herl body, and there was a soft black hen's hackle tied in front of the wings. The hooks were Nos. 3 and 4 eyed Snecky Limericks.

The May fly was not well on when I arrived, though it had begun to hatch; but at a little distance the water-side bushes looked as if they wore plummy-dun haloes, which on approach disclosed themselves as clouds of humming alder flies. I began fishing on the afternoon of my arrival, and tied on an Alder. I caught a big grayling with it at first cast, and soon after, with the sodden fly, I hooked a trout under the far bank which, judging from the distance between the tip of his tail and the place where my line was cutting the water, I put down at five pounds. I fought him down a couple of hundred yards, he boring all the time under his own bank. Then he turned and forced his way irresistibly, still under his own bank, right back to the cut-weed pile close to which I had hooked him, and of which I had steered him clear, and there he came unstuck.

As I subsequently killed another trout of four pounds six ounces on the same stream, on the same rod with 3x gut on an Alder, and that between two trees which would *not* let me move up or down, I do not think my estimate of five pounds for that last fish was excessive. At any rate, the incident encouraged me to persevere with the Alder, and next day I took eighteen brace nearly all with the same pattern of Alder. I was fishing not many yards behind my companion, who had therefore put down everything on our side of the water, and I got nearly all my trout under the opposite bank with a sunk Alder. Two only were under one pound weight. Next day, on another length, I had sixteen and a half brace, nearly all with the wet Alder fished up or across. Next day the May fly came on nicely, but before it did so I had three brace of pounders in fifty yards with the wet Alder. Towards the end of our stay the heat became very oppressive and the water ran low and stale, but in sixteen days' fishing, some days only partially occupied, I had two hundred and forty-nine trout, of which fully half were taken with the wet Alder.

In the following season (May 22 to June 4), on the same river, I had two hundred and sixty-five in fourteen days, and again the wet Alder scored heavily. From that time on I have given the Alder a trial in its season on various waters, including the upper Kennet (twenty brace in two days), the Nadder (forty-four brace out of fifty-four brace taken in three days), and have always found that it fished better sunk than dry. Of the dry patterns I did best with Dr. Charles Walker's pattern (described in " Old Flies in New Dresses "), but at best it was not in the same street with the wet pattern.

The wet pattern sinks readily and sinks deep. It is not in the least like the nymph of the alder. The trout undoubtedly never sees the natural alder as a perfect insect at a depth below the surface. Yet the successful period of the wet Alder is when the natural fly is out. It will take at other periods, but nothing like so well. I know of no beetle out at that time for which the wet Alder would be taken. I have heard it suggested that it may be taken for a tadpole, but I cannot say I have ever seen trout feeding on tadpoles.

The thing is an insoluble puzzle to me. The pattern is too successful to be readily surrendered. It is obviously accepted gleefully as food, but what *does* it represent ?

7. THE WILLOW FLY.

Another pattern which for some unexplained reason kills best when fished sunk or flush with the surface is the spent Willow Fly. I have killed scores of fish with it sunk for one which I have killed with it floating. Yet I first made the observation of the natural fly, which induced me to imitate it with its fine wings spread out flat to right and left of the hook, on a mill-cauld on the Coquet where the flies were coming down spent on the surface.

It is true that the various Yorkshire patterns dressed to simulate Perlidæ, such as Brown Owl and Dark and Light Woodcock and Orange, are all tied to sink, and are fished wet. But these are for rough tumbling streams, while the successes with the wet spent pattern of which I write have been nearly all attained upon smooth, even, limestone and chalk streams.

II

SOME FLY DRESSING

EXAMPLES

I. IRON BLUE.

IF I had postponed the publication of "Minor Tactics of the Chalk Stream" for a year or two there is one dressing, that of the iron blue dun, given as a winged fly on p. 28 of that work and so illustrated as the frontispiece, for which I could have substituted a far better dressing of the nymph type. Here it is:

Hook.—No. oo round bend.

Body.—Mole's fur on crimson tying silk, well waxed, the silk exposed for two or three turns at the tail end.

Whisks.—Two or three strands of soft, mobile, white hackle, quite short.

Legs.—The very short, nearly black, hackle from the throat of a cock jackdaw, not exceeding two turns.

There is nothing very new in this dressing. The use of the jackdaw's throat hackle for the Iron-blue has long been known as Yorkshire. The only novelty in my pattern is the use of a hackle so small as to suggest legs only. In Yorkshire it appears to be used for wings.

I dressed a couple on gut one May afternoon going down in the train, and next morning, seeing the iron blue on but neglected, and being convinced by the character of the rises that the trout were taking it under water, I soaked my pattern, and as soon as it was soft enough I tied one on and offered it to a trout under my own bank. The cast was a bad one, and the fly went under a full yard outside the trout, but without hesitation he sailed over and gulped it. I wound up with four and a half brace averaging one and a half pounds all on the Iron-blue nymph, and went off without waiting for the evening rise.

After that I always made it my business to have some Iron-blue nymphs so dressed, and they have been worth many a good trout to me.

In and after May, when the iron blue comes on, it will very often be found that the floating subimago is neglected, but that there are splashy, agitated, rather violent rises occurring at some not at all obvious attractions. If the angler is wise, he will have had his Iron-blue nymph in soak and will lose no time in attaching it, and he need not be surprised if his fish comes some way off his beat to collect it.

2. A GOOD SMALL OLIVE.

The July Dun nymph described on p. 32 of " Minor Tactics of the Chalk Stream " has proved a consistent killer, dressed with and without gold wire as therein described.

The floating subimago I tried to imitate with a darkish variety of a stock pattern of olive, which in a range of shades from light to dark I have found fish well from the middle of April to the end of the season. This is the stock pattern:

Hook.—No. o or oo (Shape No. B. 7362 Bartleet).
Hackle.—Greenish-olive cock.
Body.—Primrose or yellow tying silk.
Rib.—Fine gold wire, several turns like a Greenwell's Glory.
Whisk.—Greenish-olive cock.
Wings.—Starling primary, palest to darkest.

The entire fly should be tied so as to be in keeping—all dark, all medium, or all light.

But in July I found it ignored, as were all other patterns, till I put on one which I had casually tied with exactly the same materials with the addition of three strands of light heron herl dyed greenish-yellow olive. This pattern proved very attractive, and each year since I have proved its efficiency when the July dun is on. This is how I came to discover it.

3. JULY DUN.

One July morning some few years back I was occupying a few minutes while waiting for breakfast at my Hampshire inn, by adding to my already excessive stock of trout flies, when the sight of a thin wing covert feather of a heron, dyed a medium greenish-yellow, tempted me to tie in a oo size a sort of pale rendering of a heron herl bodied fly which, as the Rough Olive, had long served me well at the opening and close of successive trout seasons. So I varied a pattern which had served me well in a variety of shades all through the season by giving it a body dubbed with three strands of the herl. Here is the dressing:

Hook.—No. oo down-eyed Bartleet's shape, B. 7362.
Tying Silk.—Yellow.
Hackle and Whisk.—Greenish-yellow dyed cock.
Body.—Three strands of thin heron herl from outer wing covert dyed greenish-yellow.
Rib.—Fine gold wire.
Wing.—Starling, darkish.

I liked the look of the result enough to dress a second to match the first.

It was a sunny morning with a faint air from the south-east stirring when I got down to the water-side, and I ~e to open operations on a stretch of the east bank of ᵸen which runs for a couple of hundred yards from ᵗrth of west to slightly south of east. It is seldom that one gets the wind to serve that length perfectly, but if one does it is well to seize the opportunity, for the trout that haunt that bank run big for that part of the Itchen, and I knew that near the bottom of the length there was one particularly desirable trout.

He did not keep me long before disclosing his position, close up to the flags some thirty yards up. A little darkish dun came over him and was intercepted, and then another and another. I dropped down to the eddy at the bend and netted out one of these little duns, and it seemed to me that the fly which I picked from stock (dressed without the herl, but otherwise precisely like the pattern last above described) matched the natural fly with unusual precision. It was about 9.30 when I delivered my first cast. It was after eleven when, in despair after having tried at intervals a whole series of patterns without having put my fish down, I put on my herl-bodied dun of the morning. It was accepted with the utmost confidence, and in a moment I was battling with a two-pounder, which in due course came to net. The only other fish which I found rising in the length, a trout of about one and three-quarter pounds, followed suit, and I thought I was in for a good thing. Alas! the rise, which was never more than scanty during that morning, did not last me to the next bend.

But the pattern had made an impression on me, and each year since, as March has come round, I have tied for myself and my friends a small supply, which indeed I find difficult to keep, so well has the pattern justified itself. Here is an instance.

My friend B. was a guest on the same water in July of 1919, and we sat down to wait for the beginning of the rise a couple of hundred yards below the length above described. Presently a trout began feeding with great vigour in an eddy just off the centre of the current with occasional incursions into the current. He was taking a little dark dun, and taking it on the surface. I caught one of the flies, and my friend matched it, as he thought, perfectly from his box. "You had better try one of my July duns," I said, offering him one. He wouldn't have it, and I knotted it on to my own cast. For the next twenty minutes B. besieged that trout, casting to him with great skill, trotting his fly down the edge of the eddy, and never letting it get into the drag of it. The trout went on rising busily, taking flies quite close to B.'s, but never taking B.'s fly. At last B. said: "I can do nothing with this fish. You see what you can do with him, while I change my fly." I put my July dun to him, and the first time it covered him it was joyfully accepted, and B. presently netted out for me a beautiful fish in first-rate condition, two pounds six ounces in weight.

Then he said: "If you don't mind, I'll reconsider my refusal of your pattern." So I gave him the only other one I had, and we moved up to the next fish. Sure enough, the first time the fly went over him he had it, and B.'s conversion was complete.

Many angling books give dressings of the July dun, usually with bodies dubbed with a mixture of blue fur and yellow wool, or fur of sorts; Ronalds among others. Curiously enough, I find no mention of the July dun in any of Mr. F. M. Halford's works. It would be strange, however, if all those who have given the July dun in the past were wrong, and I should hesitate to believe it, even if my own observation of the occurrence of a little darkish dun in July were not confirmed by the success which, from 1908 onwards, I have had in July with a little dark nymph tied, as described on p. 32 of "Minor Tactics of the Chalk Stream," to imitate a little dark olive nymph which I took from the mouth of a trout in that month in 1908.

It has proved " great medicine " when the trout are nymphing in July, when the little darkish dun is simultaneously
coming down on the surface.

4. LITTLE RED SEDGE.

It is a good many years since I first dressed the pattern
of trout fly which I know by this name, and I should be
sorry to say how many trout have succumbed to it in the
interval. Although in dressing it I was not consciously
copying any other man's pattern, I cannot pretend to any
originality in its composition; but, such as it is, I have
found it without exception the most killing fly I have used
on chalk streams at all times when the upwinged dun was
not hatching and in all sorts of places. This is its make-up
as evolved experimentally:

Hook.—No. 1 down-eyed, square bend.
Tying Silk.—Hot orange waxed with brown wax.
Body Hackle.—Long, deep red cock, with short fibres,
    tied in at shoulder and carried down to tail.
Rib.—Fine gold wire, binding down body hackle.
Body.—Darkest hare's ear.
Wings.—Landrail wing, bunched and rolled, and tied
    on sloping well back over the tail.
Front Hackle.—Like body hackle, but larger, and long
    enough to tie five or six turns in front of wing.

The *modus operandi* is as follows:—Having waxed a good
length of the silk, one begins winding almost at the eye of
the hook and whips closely to the shoulder, leaving ample
space on which to tie down the wings and wind the hackle.
One then ties in a short-fibred, long, brilliant red hackle,
almost blood red, by the root, and, after breaking or cutting
off the root, whips to the tail of the fly, securing with the last
two or three turns a couple of inches of fine gold wire.
Then it is well to drench the silk, where it is on the hook,
with celluloid varnish. Next one spins on the dubbing

thinly, whips to the shoulder, and takes a half-hitch beyond the hackle. Then, taking the hackle point between the pliers, one takes one turn on the bare hook, and winds in open turns (say three or four) to the tail. Leaving the pliers hanging, one winds the gold wire over the turns of hackle in an equal number of turns, thus securing the stalk again and again. A half-hitch secures the gold wire, which is then *broken* off by a little gentle working to and fro. It should not be cut. The turn of the broken end helps to keep it secure, and the break generally comes closer to the half-hitch than one could cut the wire. The hackle tip can be broken off with a smart twitch.

The next step is to revarnish the head with celluloid varnish. Then, taking a good long slip of landrail wing-feather (nearly the whole fibre of one feather), one straightens it, and, taking it by one edge in a pair of pliers and taking care not to split the feather, one rolls it in a series of turns until the feather is exhausted. It should then be a bunchy roll, readily flattened by being pinched. Laying the roll, well pinched and flattened, on its edge over the hook with the cut end over the eye, one ties it down by taking three firm turns over the fibre, then one turn tight behind and one *under* the roots. If this is neatly done the entire waste end can in general be cut clean away with a single cut of the curved scissors.

This having been done, one drenches the roots in celluloid varnish. This goes almost as hard as metal when set, and holds the wing very perfectly on edge.

The next step is to take a long, short-fibred hackle of the same neck as the body hackle, and, whipping it down near the eye with the root towards the tail, wind the silk tightly back to the base of the wing. Then with the hackle pliers turn the hackle five or six turns over the roots of the wing right up to the wing fibre; whip the tying silk through the hackle to the head, and finish with the whip finish. A touch of celluloid varnish on the whip finish makes all secure. Then the root of the hackle is cut off with a sharp knife, and the fly is complete.

Thus tied it has an astonishing amount of wear in it, and cocks most beautifully. I remember a day on the Chess when I took fifteen trout with one fly of this pattern, and then gave it to my host, who used it for several days afterwards with success.

It is a pattern which I have found successful from May to the end of the season under a variety of conditions, but only when the up-winged dun was not present in quantity.

For instance, it is a nailer for the trout of cross-ditches and drains, however narrow. It is also very attractive to the banker that remains in position after the morning rise is over. And often one may go on securing trout with it all the afternoon and up to the edge of the evening rise, especially in places where the sedges weep over the water.

But there is one set of conditions in which I have found this pattern specially deadly. Sometimes in places where the weeds grow near the surface one may see a movement where the nose of the trout does not seem to break the water, but the back fin and the tail successively show. Just precisely what the fish is doing must be a matter of surmise. I am inclined to think he has dislodged some rather inert nymph from the weed and takes him just below the surface. If you get your Red Sedge to a trout feeding thus, and do not scare him, the odds are long that you get him, and that he will be a good one.

5. PHEASANT TAIL.

I have more than once seen propounded an inquiry to which I have seen no reply—viz., what fly the Pheasant tail is supposed to represent. Well, I can answer that question on my experience. In March, 1910, a friend was visiting Cornwall, and he hoped to get some fishing, and just by way of getting my hand in I sent him some flies of my own tying, with some priceless hackles. Among these flies were three or four Pheasant tails tied on No. 2 hooks. " Ridiculously small for the water," my friend declared; the theory being the smaller the fish the bigger the fly. The Cornish streams were in flood, and he got no chance of using my flies. But he announced his intention of using the Pheasant tails in the Itchen a little later, when the sherry spinner of the blue-winged olive was on. So to prevent him from making an example of himself, I tied him one or two more on something nearer life-size— namely, No. 1—and the result pleased me so much that I tied two or three more for my own use. This is the tie:

Silk.—Hot orange.

Whisks.—Honey-dun cock's shoulder hackle, three strands.

Rib.—Fine bright gold wire, several turns, to secure the flies from being broken by the teeth of the trout.

Body.—Three or four strands of the ruddy part of the centre feather of a cock-pheasant's tail.

Wings.—A sharp sparkling golden-dun cock's hackle of high quality.

The size of hook may, of course, be varied to suit the spinner which is on at the time.

On May 11 I found my friend on the water, not exactly displeased with himself over a basket of two and a half brace, all of them victims of the Pheasant tail. That night I dressed some more of them for my friend and for a guest I had brought down with me, and one for myself. I spent the following morning without using the pattern for some time. Then it occurred to me to try it, and I got a trout of two pounds two ounces. A bit later my guest got a perfect picture of a trout of two pounds with his example, and before I left at 4.30 I got another trout of one pound nine ounces with the same pattern, while my friend owed to it his brace of trout.

I left him attempting to negotiate a trout of two and a half pounds or so. It was two pounds nine ounces, as a matter of fact, for I got him next week-end. There was an admirable procession of red spinners coming down the water, and, though there were few fish moving, this was one of them. He was taking with that head and back fin and tail sort of rise which, to the initiated, indicates spinner-taking; and in an interval between the puffs of down-stream north-wester my Pheasant tail reached him aright, and next moment was pulled home.

Several other trout were hooked and landed, and hooked and lost, to that pattern during that week-end with red spinner on the water, and I came to the conclusion that I had long neglected a very useful pattern, in particular, in the long hot evenings of July, August, and September, when the blue-winged olive is on, and the deep ruddy brown sherry spinner is plentiful.

It is, however, not of an evening only that the spinner is a taking fly. It is often a tender memory to the morning trout, and a fish found feeding before the general rise begins is usually taking spinners, and is very accessible to the temptation of a good imitation.

6. RUSTY SPINNER.

From the time when the pale watery dun first puts in an appearance to the end of the season, one of the most useful of chalk-stream patterns for evening use is the Little Rusty Spinner. Tied on Bartleet's B. No. 7362 (a square-bent, slightly snecked, down-eyed hook) of No. 14 size (about equivalent in this make to No. 00), with hot orange silk dubbed with fine pig's wool or seal's fur of red-ant colour—a deep rich mahogany red—ribbed with fine gold wire and hackled with a rusty dun cock's hackle, sharp and bright, and with whisks of three fibres of a honey-dun cock's shoulder hackle, it proves extraordinarily attractive at the time when small spinners come on the water, and according to my experience it fishes as well slightly submerged as floating. Dressed on No. 1 or even No. 2 hook it is an excellent representation of the male spinner of the blue-winged olive. No angler should be without it at the appropriate season of the year.

7. THE POPE AND THE TAILERS.

Through the bogland of a marshy little Berkshire valley, one of the most delightfully trouty of brooks known to me cuts its way in such wise that though to reach it one has to wade painfully through mud or to stagger from insecure tussock to tussock equally insecure, yet when one gets to the channel one finds underfoot clean hard pan, except where the current has so silted up fine, sharp silver sand as to give the river-weed foothold to grow luxuriantly. The stock of trout is enormous, and but for the fact that they maintain fine condition one would say excessive; for they are so numerous that to scare one means to disturb quite a stretch of water, and to set the trout bolting in all directions. And they are easily scared, for the water is seldom knee-deep, often only ankle-deep, and averages, perhaps, a foot. One would think the business of catching these wary fish with a fly a hopeless one if you did not happen to be by the water-side at the time of the take. Then these trout, having once settled down to feeding, though they still require adroit and careful fishing, are at length approachable, and take a fly, dry or wet, presented *secundum artem* with gratifying freedom. There are innumerable three-quarter pounders in this little river, a good many pounders, and one day this year a friend brought in three brace (the limit that may be kept), totalling nine pounds.

It was my ill-fortune on the two occasions when I last visited the river to light on days which were characterized by bitter north-easterly winds blowing straight upstream, and by an almost total absence of fly. Thus, after getting a nice brace in the one sheltered spot in the whole length, I found the entire morning of the first day blank, for the reason that each movement forward seemed to start some queasy trout, who bolted upstream, and disturbed the next fifty or sixty yards of shallow. The morning thus resolved itself into a series of waits for things to settle.

Just before lunch-time I arrived at a sheep-bridge which crosses the river and the entire marsh from side to side. Here I resolved to eat my sandwiches and await a rise of fly, as it had become evident that without such a rise I was not going to emulate the eight to nineteen brace days of a former visit. But as I approached the bridge I saw two enormous trout (for the stream) rooting like hogs in some weeds just above, and darting rapidly to secure the shrimps or larvæ which they had thus ejected from their fastnesses among the weeds. The weeds were in this part dreadfully full of flannel-weed, so I knew it was no use to put up a wet fly. I put up a Pope's Green Nondescript, size No. 000, and launched it over the sheep-bridge, and over the nearest of the trout. He was on it like a tiger, and on feeling the hook dashed down under the bridge towards me, and smashed me with promptitude and despatch, without neglecting to put down his companion *en route*.

The incident, however, gave me my cue, and after my

lunch I did not waste time in waiting for a rise which never came, but set to work to find tailers. There were quite a few of them, and they were generally good fish. It was often very difficult to get them to see the Green Nondescript. Often one got hung up in flannel-weed; at times one lined them and so scared them, but if they saw the Green Nondescript without having been scared they took it with admirable readiness. I lost many owing to the small size of the hook and to the softness of mouth which seems to characterize the fish of this stream, but the discovery converted an apparently hopeless day into quite an interesting one.

The second day was much like the first; wind in the same quarter, stronger, if anything, than the previous day; there was no fly, and the tailers did not begin till after 12.30, but after that hour I found one at work here and there, wooed him with a Green Nondescript, and ended by topping a nice three-brace basket with a trout of two pounds three ounces. What the trout take Pope's Green Nondescript for, or why they take it when tailing, I have no idea; but it seems equally effective, dry or wet. It must, however, be small. No. o was useless, No. oo would take occasionally, but No. ooo seemed irresistible. This is true not only of the brook in question, but of every other chalk or limestone stream on which I have tried the Pope on tailers.

III

SOME MORE FLY DRESSING

PRINCIPLES AND PRACTICE

THEORIES OF WET-FLY DRESSING OF TROUT FLIES.

THE question why winged patterns of trout flies are used, and used successfully under water, is no new one. It must often have been a cause of bewilderment to the thoughtful angler. But in seeking for an explanation the inquirer only hampers himself if he assumes that the trout takes the winged artificial fly merely as an imitation of the natural fly.

The propensity of a trout to " go for " anything behaving unnaturally is well known. He will lie peacefully among a shoal of minnows, but let one of them be placed on a flight of hooks and spun before him in a series of strange contortions, and he is impelled to attack it. In the same way, let a winged dressing of a fly be dragged across his vision in a way in which no natural fly behaves, and the same impulse is set in motion. This, no doubt, accounts for the taking of the winged fly fished down-stream wet. Somewhat similar considerations apply to the case of the winged fly or team of winged flies dropped under a bank or a bush and tripped across-stream towards the angler.

But winged flies are often presented to the trout much more naturally than in either of these ways, and then, during the rise, they are often, no doubt, taken for what they purport to represent—namely, the subimago hatching, or hatched out. In fishing his team of flies upstream the skilled wet-fly fisherman does not let his flies dwell long enough to be deeply submerged, and he humours his line so that the droppers are kept in the skin of the surface of the water, and are brought down, head upstream, in advance of the gut cast. In this case the flies are taken either, as they alight, as natural flies afloat on the surface, or later in the skin of the surface, perhaps as flies in the act of hatching.

If the artificial winged fly becomes quite submerged it may still be taken, for the water is generally fast; the trout has to make up his mind in a flash to take the fly or to let it go, and the trout is not so clever a person as to measure closely whether the fly be semi-submerged or an inch or so under water.

The hackled North-Country pattern does not necessarily represent a submerged fly, but one in process of hatching or hatched out, and caught by the current and tumbled. Again, the trout, busy in making the most of his meal-time, does not make fine distinctions. Often, too, no doubt, the dibbing dropper attracts by suggesting something alive and in difficulties.

In any case, the winged artificial fly, by its bulk, and the hackled artificial fly, by its kick and action, are apt in rough water to attract more attention to themselves than would a bald imitation or representation of the nymph.

Moreover, for one natural fly that goes down over an individual trout, he is apt to see a number of nymphs. Every fisherman who has fished during a strong hatch of any attractive insect knows how little chance his floating imitation of that insect stands of being taken among the crowd of natural insects. In the same way a bare imitation of a nymph would come into competition with many natural nymphs, and stand a comparatively poor chance of being selected by the fish. A bare imitation would naturally have legs as few and as short as the natural nymph or larva, and, setting aside the difficulty of finding hackles short enough to represent such legs with accuracy, the imitation would look inert.

I have used imitations of nymphs on chalk streams for some fifteen seasons with a measure of success when the trout were not surface feeding, and I use them upstream to feeding fish, and it is my observation that a mere bare nymph without hackle is not so successful as one which is lightly hackled with a short hackle. It is my belief that the artificial nymph lightly hackled with a soft hackle (whether small bird's or hen's) is taken for the natural nymph in the act of hatching, and that in the case of the artificial nymph lightly dressed with a bright cock's hackle of a blue shade, the hackle, being almost water colour, leaves the body of the artificial exposed, tends to arrest speed of sinking, and probably lends the nymph a certain degree of action in the water which suggests life.

Then in practically all my nymph patterns that are not hackled with a soft feather I use a good deal of seal's fur in the dubbing, which gives an effect of brilliance and translucency, to which again a fine gold wire ribbing in some cases lends aid.

All this is very crude, no doubt, and I can cordially concur in the often expressed wish that some wet-fly enthusiast would set to work and make exact reproductions of nymphs and larvæ in the same way as Mr. F. M. Halford treated the floating fly. And these should be submitted to searching tests, not only by one angler, but by a large number of skilled men.

That distinguished angler who writes over the signature " Jim-Jam " has published, both in the *Field* and in his book, a description of a method of imitating nymphs

which he found successful. I hope I may be forgiven
for saying that I do not think his method presents the
right line of approach to the best theory of imitation or
representation of nymphs, for his patterns were intended
to be fished down-stream and dragging, and they therefore
make an appeal to the same propensity in the trout which
attracts him to a spinning minnow or a dragging, winged
wet fly.

In shape of body the nymph may be easily imitated.
Colour is difficult to set down with precision in writing so
that the fly dresser can reproduce it with certainty, and the
best line of attack seems to me to be suggested by one of
the oldest nymph patterns, the Half-stone. Here one has
a bright, almost water-coloured, outer hackle, almost
invisible to a fish looking up, and a nymph-shaped body
well displayed, with the thorax of mole's fur spun on
yellow silk, and the yellow floss lower half of the body
which goes green in the water.

For colour, the angler who desires exact representation
in that respect would have to go to the living nymph.
A dip of a muslin net into a clump of river-weed would
produce a large variety of nymphs in all colours, from
pale yellow to darkest olive, and even to carrot colour.

It was on a variation of the Half-stone dressed with a
lower half of wool instead of floss that the famous Carrot
fly was modelled. In a series of modifications it has killed
for a brother angler many a good fish, fished as a nymph
on crack waters on the Itchen, the Test, and elsewhere.
And dressed large it has served as a May-fly nymph on
some bulging days on the Kennet, and has beaten the
winged fly and the Straddlebug hollow.

Representation or suggestion rather than imitation is
what the dresser of nymphs should aim at. That is one
reason why dubbings outclass quills for bodies of nymphs.

PLATE II.   METHOD OF DRESSING NYMPHS.
From a water-colour drawing by St. Barbe Goldsmith.

THE DRESSING OF NYMPHS.

Various plans have been devised for the making of imitations of nymphs. Years before anyone—so far as the books record—was really aware what a large proportion of the food of trout was taken in the nymph or larval stages the Half-stone was a successful fly. As I have said, I have no doubt it was meant for a nymph. Years ago I had the run of an old Westmorland fly book full of hackle flies, all tied with silk bodies and a bunch of dubbing at the shoulder under the hackle. These, but for the excessive length of the hackle, might have been nymphs. And many patterns described by Theakston in "British Angling Flies" were more like nymphs than the winged fly they are supposed to represent. So it would seem as if some anglers had had their suspicions; but it is only comparatively recently that any deliberate effort to represent nymphs has been made. T. E. P., in the Angling Supplement of the *Field* of April 1, 1911, described a series of flies undoubtedly meant for nymphs, and very effective they looked, though rather long in the hackle. The nymphs of Dr. Mottram ("Jim-Jam"), entirely without dubbing or hackle, I have already referred to. I for some years earlier had been feeling my way, via Tup's Indispensable, to the achievement of a series of nymphs. These have been hackled—mostly with cock's hackle—tied as short, and setting as close, as possible, and the bodies have been dressed with dubbing. The dubbing has always consisted of, or contained, seal's fur, as many of the nymphs are full of lights and glistenings. Partly for the same reason, and partly to prevent the tearing out of the dubbing by the trout's teeth, a fine gold or silver wire ribbing has been generally used.

But the hackle has always been the trouble. It is extremely difficult to get hackles stout enough in the fibre to represent the legs of nymphs, yet short enough for the same purpose, whether one uses cock's or hen's hackles, or the feathers of small birds. Nipped hackles of the latter class will serve, but every self-respecting fly dresser resents nipped or cut hackles, and so I have thought out a method which is, I think, better than using a nipped hackle. Here it is:

Placing your hook—say, a Limerick No. 16—in your vice, begin whipping near the eye, and whip nearly half-way down the shank. Tie in here, with point towards head of hook, a bunch of six or eight fibres of feather of suitable colour, regulating the length so that when the fibre is bent over to the eye of the hook and tied down there will be enough of the points left to be pressed out on either side to represent the legs. Then pass the silk under the ends of the fibres of feather on the side of the bend of the hook, and whip on the bare hook to the tail; tie in two short, stout, soft whisks of suitable colour, tie in gold or silver wire, twirl on dubbing thinly, and wind to the place where the fibre is tied in; wind on the wire in regular spacing to the same point, and secure on the head side of the place where the fibre is tied in; thicken the dubbing, and wind over roots of feather fibre to head. Then divide the points equally, and press backward from the eye; bring over the feather fibre to the head, tie it down with two turns, including a half-hitch, cut off the waste ends, and finish with a whip finish on the eye. Thus the legs are forced to stand out at right angles, or rather more backward, from the eye, and below the level of the hook shank, and the effect of wing cases is produced. (See Plate II.)

A friend with whom I had discussed this method, and with whom I had given the nymphs thus produced a very

encouraging trial on a Hampshire brook, suggests a variation of this method, which has the effect of overcoming
the difficulty present in my conception of judging the
length of fibre to be left out in order to get the legs of the
right length, and the variation has the added merit of
making the legs stand out on each side in the most satisfactory way. Its defect is that it does not lend itself to
nymphs tied with a gold or silver ribbing, as it has to be
finished with an invisible whip finish in the middle of the body,
just behind the wing cases. This is the process (Plate III.):

Placing your hook in the vice, take two turns near the
eye, tie down your bunch of fibres, which are to represent
legs and wing cases, with the points towards the tail, with
one firm turn, then bring the silk under the points close
up against the last turn and pull taut. Now press back
the points firmly. They can be divided a little later.
Spin your seal's-fur dubbing on the silk in just sufficient
quantity to represent the thorax, and wind it on. Then
bring over the waste ends, which were pointing over the
head, so that they point over the tail, dividing the points,
which are to represent the legs, in equal portions to right
and left. Tie down the fibres with two turns, and break
them off, either singly or in groups. Whip to the tail,
tie in the whisks as before, roll on more dubbing, whip
to the wing cases, clear the silk, and finish close up to the
wing cases with a close, hard whip finish, into which a
drop of celluloid varnish has been introduced, by placing
it on the loop of the tying silk as it is being drawn taut.

Both these methods of dressing are carried out with the
same coloured material for leg and wing cases, but there is
no difficulty about using two feathers of differing colours
in much the same way. Begin by taking a couple of turns
of silk near the eye, then lay your leg fibres along the hook,
with the tips towards the tail, take one turn over them,

push the points back towards the eye, divide them equally
and bring over the waste ends, tie down with two turns
of silk, and break or cut off. Next tie down your wing-
case material with two or three turns over the points laid
towards the eye, and cut or break off the points close.
The rest of the operation is carried out as first described.

Any one of these methods, by the way, may be employed for
beetles, more wing-case fibre being used, and the whole being
brought over from the tail instead of the middle of the hook.

For nymphs with freckled legs, brown partridge hackles,
brown or grey partridge hackles dyed, summer duck
hackles dyed in various shades of olives, or even undyed,
make very effective legs. For self-coloured legs the fibre
of the wings of a variety of birds, such as starling, landrail,
fieldfare, etc., are excellent. It must be remembered that
the legs of nymphs are stouter in appearance than the
fibre of the ordinary hackle. Good effects may be produced
with the yellow-pointed fibres of the golden plover. It is
probable that if these patterns are found generally successful there will be a variety of useful suggestions forthcoming.
The grey feather which supports the tail of the peacock,
dyed in a variety of hues, will be found, when wound on
like a quill, to make an admirable representation of the
lower half of the bodies of certain nymphs. It has an edge
which stands up at right angles to the hook, and suggests
the branchiæ of natural insects.

In dressing nymphs one should remember that, though
they should not fall on the water hard enough to scare
the trout, their composition should ensure prompt sinking,
and if the trout be handy I am of opinion that they will
not sink very far. And I shall not be surprised if in a
few years the practice prevails of fishing open rough rivers,
where the wet fly at present holds its own, with a winged
fly at point and two or three nymphs as droppers.

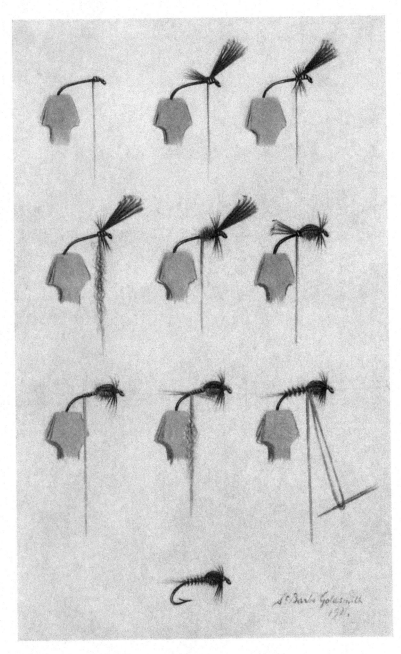

PLATE III.   ANOTHER METHOD OF DRESSING NYMPHS.
From a water-colour drawing by St. Barbe Goldsmith.

THE PURPOSES OF A HACKLE.

The books on trout-fly dressing are to blame for the prevalent opinion that the purpose of a hackle is to represent legs of a fly. It would be wrong to say that that is never a purpose of a hackle, but it is wrong—" the wrongest kind of wrong "—to represent it as the sole purpose or as invariably one purpose of a hackle.

In some of the old books one finds instructions for dressings of winged flies with no hackle, but anyone who tried any such pattern nowadays with moderately shy trout would find them apt to be scared by the violence of the fall of the fly on the water. The first function, then, of a hackle is to break the fly's fall, to let it down lightly on the water. And that is equally true whether it be a cock's hackle, or a hen's, or a soft hackle from any of the small birds.

When the fly reaches the water, another function, or other functions of the hackle, comes or come into play. If the fly be a floater, winged and hackled at the shoulder only, then the functions are, first, flotation, and, secondly (and often in a very secondary degree), imitation of the legs of the fly. Many good fly dressers hold that the body is the really attractive part of a trout fly, and that in a floater a hackle which is sufficient to ensure adequate flotation, and is otherwise colourless and inconspicuous, serves its purpose best. A good cock's hackle, such as is used for floating flies, is extremely sharp and bright when held up to the light, and even in the ruddy shades lets but little colour through. There can, however, be no harm, and it is probably safer, if the hackle, as held to the light, bears a fairly close resemblance in colour to the legs of the fly which its pattern represents.

A winged floater, hackled all down the body with cock's

hackles to represent a sedge—or even a similar pattern without wings—is probably taken for a fluttering sedge by reason of the " buzz " effect.

A floater hackled with a sharp cock's hackle at the shoulder only, and without wings, is probably the best method of suggesting a spinner, spent or still living. The wings of the natural spinner have an iridescent glitter which is well suggested by the extended fibres of a first-rate rusty or honey or blue dun cock's hackle. Such a hackle thus serves (beyond the purpose of breaking the fly's fall) the double purpose of flotation and of imitation of wings.

A floater may, especially in the minute sizes of fly, be dressed with a soft feather, and may be made to float long enough for practical purposes without oiling. Here the hackle serves the purpose of flotation and of imitation of wings and legs. I have often floated a No. oo Dotterel dun, perfectly dry, over a trout when there has been a rise of pale watery duns, and have found it very killing, particularly in eddies under the far bank. The soft tips of the hackle cause it to make a far less alarming drag than does a cock's hackle.

Semi-submerged, the fly tied with bright cock's hackle at the shoulder only, and a seal's fur or Tup's Indispensable body of suitable colour, represents a spent spinner often in the most fatal way. Here the hackle enables the fly, the body of which is waterlogged, to cling to the surface.

Now we reach the sunk flies, and we shall find these present still more complex propositions, according to the way in which the fly is presented to the fish.

Fished directly upstream, a wet fly (whether winged or not), which is hackled with a stiff cock's hackle, has thrown away one of its chief advantages, the mobility of the hackle. In fact, one might be inclined to think that, if a hackle were not needed to break the fall or to suggest life, such a fly might best be dressed without a hackle. A hen's hackle, or a small bird's hackle, would respond to every moment of the current, and would thus suggest an appearance of life in action, which is very fascinating. The Yorkshire hackles and Stewart's famous trio of " spiders," so called, are based on this theory. What these flies really represent cannot always be certainly predicated. Doubtless the hackles in some cases suggest the wings and legs of hatched-out insects, drowning or drowned and tumbled by the current, and in others they suggest some nondescript, struggling subaqueous creature. In either case the mobility suggests life.

Nevertheless, an upstream wet-fly man, however keen on that method, does not always cast directly upstream, but more often up and across, and occasionally across. When he casts across or up and across, and holds his rod-top so as to bring his team of flies as nearly as possible perpendicularly across the current, a new set of considerations arises. The droppers, catching the stream more than does the gut cast, are drawn down with head upstream and tail downstream in advance of the gut cast. Here soft hackles are apt to be drawn back so as completely to enfold the body of the fly, with the points of the fibres flickering softly beyond the bend of the hook, thus suggesting a nymph vainly attempting to swim against the current. The top dropper may be dibbing on the surface, thus suggesting an ovipositing fly. Here the hackle represents the wings of the natural fly in active motion. In these conditions cock's hackles, whether dressed at shoulder only or palmerwise, are apt to impart motion to the wings and body, and to suggest life in this way rather than by their own motion, as do soft hackles. The resilience of a first-rate cock's hackle is great, and every exertion of it must react upon the fly's body, which it surrounds, and impart a motion which, whether lifelike in the sense of resembling the motions of some particular insect, or not, at least is sufficient to attract the attention and excite the rapacity or tyranny of the trout if it does not appeal to his appetite. This was the Devonshire theory that produced that priceless, but, alas! vanishing, strain of Old English blue game fowls.

We now come to the down-stream methods. Here we find the considerations which apply to across-stream methods present in even greater force, because the resistance of the rod-top, which holds the line as it swings the flies across the current, brings the current to bear upon the flies far more strongly than is the case when the angler is fishing across and up. For this reason, flies for this type of fishing should be dressed with a specially " good entry," so as not to skirt. Winged flies should have the wings low and fitting close over the back, and hackled flies should have good sharp cock's hackles, or, if hackled with hen's hackles or soft hackles, should have them supported by a wad of dubbing behind the hackle at the shoulder, so as to get the maximum of work out of them. By the across and down-stream method the top dropper may be made to dib more readily than by any other, thus imitating either spinner or sedge ovipositing.

To sum up, the fly dresser must think how and where his fly is to be used when he dresses it, and hackle it accordingly.

THE SPADE FEATHER.

It has often been a matter of surprise to me to notice what trashy feathers so many professional dressers use for the whisks of their trout flies, and that one practically never sees the best feathers for the purpose used.

It is not suggested that stiff and bright hackles are always necessary for whisks. A soft feather has advantages for a sunk fly intended to represent a nymph. But a bright, sharp, stiff feather undoubtedly assists flotation, and far better for the purpose than the saddle hackle so often used is the spade-shaped shoulder hackle of a cock of suitable colour in its finest fettle, especially for spinners.

There is no difficulty about getting such feathers of excellent quality in all the common colours. The fowl has to be obtained before it has been plucked. That is all. A very few feathers will go a long way. They stand out straight, and should not be tied in so as to cock up. Being sharp and bright they throw the water well, and give as much help in floating a fly as a number of turns of hackle at the shoulder.

BUZZ.

A good deal of cheap scorn has been wasted upon the excessive number of legs given by fly dressers to the artificial fly to ensure flotation, particularly to the Sedges. I would ask, how often is it that the hackles of flies are taken for legs ? Many of the sedges flutter upon the surface; and may not the saying that they are dressed " buzz " be wiser than it looks ? The effect of fluttering and the effect of a bush of hackles may not look so dissimilar to the trout. Palmers, I have no doubt, are as often taken for struggling sedge flies as for the woolly bears and other caterpillars they are fancifully supposed to represent.

Then from certain points of view a good sharp cock's hackle with the light through it is nothing but sheer sparkle. It has no appearance of solidity at all, and it may be doubted whether the fish sees much of it as leg at all. It may merely give an effect of translucency to the wings. This is, no doubt, one reason why high quality in hackles is so desirable.

A GOOD ENTRY.

This is frankly a fly-dresser's, and, what is more, a wet-fly dresser's section. The subject is a very practical one. A natural insect, whether in nymph or other stage, does not, when maintaining itself against the stream or being carried down by it, resisting or unresisting, skirt or carry bubbles with it, and it may be inferred that an artificial fly which does either of these things is apt to offend so sensitive a fish as the trout and to put him off his feed. It is held, therefore, that a trout fly which is intended to swim against the stream in however slight a degree while being carried down by it ought to have what is called "a good entry"; that is, it ought to be so constructed as to swim with the smoothness of a nymph or small fish, and not to skirt, or to cause or carry bubbles. The commonest cause of such a defect in an artificial fly is too big and clumsy a head. This is the reason why an artificial wet fly usually has a head much smaller in proportion than that of the natural fly. It is also a reason why eyed hooks are not so suitable as blind hooks for small trout flies, the eye and knot combining to make a disproportionately bulky head. But a small head alone will not ensure a good entry for a winged fly or for a fly with stiff hackles. A soft-hackled fly adjusts itself easily to the action of the water, but a fly with stiff, staring, upright wings or hackles may easily cause such a disturbance in the water as to give proof of a bad entry. The lines, therefore, on which an artificial wet fly that is to be fished against the stream in any way is built ought to be fine, like the lines of a yacht or swift boat, or high-class motor, sloping backwards, so as to offer the least possible resistance to the current, and such resistance as there is should be elastic. The fly ought to be equal on both sides, so as to balance accurately and to swim smoothly, and any excess of bulk is to be deprecated.

It is not only the fly fished down-stream, or across and down, which hangs against the stream. A dropper on an upstream cast does so too if the angler be handling his rod as he should. By keeping the rod point forward and drawing it to right or left, so as to ensure the cast of flies swinging as soon as possible perpendicularly athwart the stream, the angler ensures that each of his droppers is drawn by the current so as to come over the water he is fishing in advance of the cast to which it is attached. The more smoothly the fly comes, the more perfectly it suggests a natural insect. Hence the importance of a good entry. It may be suggested that Greenwell's Glory, constructed with split wings, set upright and rather forward, and yet a very successful fly, cannot be said to be consistent with this principle. The answer is that Greenwell's Glory so tied is a point fly for upstream fishing, and should never be fished with a drag against the stream.

QUALITY IN FLY-DRESSING MATERIALS.

About the work of even the poorest and shoddiest professional fly dresser there is a certain snap and certainty of execution to which the best amateur but seldom attains. Yet in two respects even the best professional work falls short of that of the competent amateur—knowledge of the effect that he is groping after and command of the materials to produce it. It occasionally happens (as in the case of the late Mr. R. S. Austin) that the professional is also an amateur, with first-hand knowledge of the river and its flies, and then the supremely good work may be attained if, as in his case, his conscience will not let him put up with and issue to his customers inadequate materials.

It may be that it is not possible for the houses that dress flies in bulk to obtain the requisite materials in

adequate quantity—at any rate with their present re-
sources—and that they are thus driven to fall back upon
dyed and faked substitutes; but even so there is little
excuse for the wretchedly poor material which many houses
are content to foist upon their customers. The only way
to account for it is the excuse offered by Dr. Johnson for
a gross blunder in his dictionary: "Sheer ignorance,
madam, sheer ignorance." Anyone who, knowing anything about hackles, goes over the stock picked on the
markets for the wholesale houses, may well be astonished
to see the trash that they are content to buy at a penny a
neck or less—badly selected and badly picked, wretched
in quality, shape, colour, and condition, and actually
omitting the bulk of the best and most valuable small
hackles in the neck. Honestly, it would pay them better
to exercise a liberal right of rejection, and to pay four or
six times as much for carefully, competently chosen, and
adequately picked stuff. Again and again, when I have
lit upon a packet containing the pickings of a beautiful
blue dun cock I have found that there is scarcely a feather
fit to tie a fly as small as No. 1, and that what there are
are twisted in plucking and often foul with blood. Reds
are picked in bulk in the same way, and with a reckless
disregard of size, under-colour, texture, brightness, quality.
And so with gingers and the rest. Occasionally I have
dropped on to an excellent honey-dun hen unplucked
because the poulterer's man did not know enough to see
it was worth while.

The same ignorance which pervades the ranks of the
poulterer's men is to be found putting in its deadly work
among the professional fly dressers. The mechanical part
of their art may be, and often is, excellently done, but if
the dresser does not know what effects he is aiming at,
how is he to know how to get them, or how important it
is to have the material right and high in quality? There

are many books which profess to teach fly dressing, but none that I am aware of (except Cutcliffe's—this only to a limited extent) that tells the dresser what effects he is to aim at, and how, and why; and it may be doubted if more than one here and there has any idea of what he or she is purporting to express. Even if given the natural insect to dress to, it may be doubted if the dresser realizes that it is a semi-translucent being that he is reproducing or seeking to reproduce, and he must, therefore, either reproduce by means of his materials the effects of transmitted light, or, if his materials be necessarily dense, like quill, he must get or suggest by reflection from the surface of his material the effect of transmitted light. If the body of a real spinner be held to the light, it looks very different from the same insect looked down upon and seen only by reflected light, but it is rare to see an attempt made to reproduce the effect of transmitted light by translucency of material or by reflection from an opaque surface. The tendency is, almost necessarily, to reproduce unintelligently stereotyped patterns which go on diverging further and further from type. And when this is done with poor materials which are dull in colour, and poor in translucency, texture, and quality, and when, to crown all, hackles are cut, it is little to be wondered at that the trout so often exercises the prerogative of rejection. In the days when anglers habitually dressed their own flies there were to be had hackles and dubbings, but especially poultry hackles, such as neither love nor money can buy nowadays. And it is because I want to see things go back to the conditions of the palmy days that I would like anglers to learn, at any rate, to dress their own flies not merely as a mechanical art, but as a means of rendering in colours the effects which, so far as man can judge, the natural insect produces upon the eye of the trout.

IV

SUNDRY OBSERVATIONS

WHAT MADE THE DRY FLY POSSIBLE.

IN the pleasant pages of " Chalk Stream and Moorland,"
Mr. Harold Russell, in tracing the early history of the
dry fly, comments on it as somewhat strange that fishing
with a floating fly did not become general in Southern
England many years earlier than it did, but he does not
advance what I conceive to be the true reason. The use
of the dry fly connotes the ability of the angler to fish
upstream whatever the state of the wind. The clearness
of the chalk stream required the casting of a longer line
than was necessary on rough streams. The silk and hair
lines which, prior to the coming of the American braided
oiled silk lines, were the best that could be produced could
not be cast into an adverse wind. They could be cast
upstream with the wind, across-stream with the wind, and
down-stream with the wind, but, as a general proposition,
casting against the wind was beyond them. A fly cast
upstream or across with the wind might very well float
or sink—in either case it might be taken by the trout—
but a fly cast down-stream was *bound* to sink. So as
anglers had to make their account with fishing down-stream,
'heir flies were dressed to sink. And as any violence in
'king when the fly is down-stream is apt to be visited
a smash, rods, though built long to fish far off, had
'loppy in the top to ensure gentle striking. The

result was also the keeping light of the reel line, and thus was produced a combination which, exquisite in its way, was the very worst that could be conceived for dry-fly fishing. Stewart preached the stiff rod and the upstream cast, but his was necessarily a short cast. The things which made the dry fly generally possible were the coming of the heavy American braided oiled silk line and the split-cane rod. I remember buying my first length of oiled silk line in 1877, but I knew so little of its purpose that I used it for sea fishing, and it was, I think, in the eighties that, stimulated by American progress in the building of split-canes, our makers began to build split-canes suitable for carrying these heavy lines. The heavy line was needed to deliver the fly dry and to put it into the wind, the split-cane, or a wood rod on the same lines, was necessary to deliver the heavy line. With the hour came the men, Mr. H. S. Hall, Mr. G. S. Marryat, and Mr. F. M. Halford, who evolved from the poor feeble types of dry fly of the seventies the efficient dry fly of the eighties and the present day.

THE EXCOMMUNICATION OF THE WET FLY.

I have been trying for some time past—but hitherto in vain—to discover the precise moment of time when the theory that it was not sportsmanlike, and therefore not permissible, to fish with the wet fly upon chalk streams was given to a reverently awaiting world, and who was the prophet from whose lips the words of wisdom fell. I recall some years ago seeing it propounded in the Press—I believe in the *Fishing Gazette*—that it was a rule upon chalk streams that the dry fly only must be employed, and I remember being not a little amused, for up to that time, though fishing quite a noted length of a crack chalk stream, and meeting upon it many excellent fishers with the fly, I had never heard the theory propounded by any one of them. True that almost without exception, as I myself at the time, they fished dry, but that was because they believed that thus they were more likely to be successful. Frequently, and perhaps more often than not, that would be so; but they made the error of mistaking the particular—the frequent particular, the pretty general, if you will—for the universal, and I believe that, if once they had been convinced that it was not always the dry fly that paid best, but that on parts of most days the wet fly, properly applied, was the more attractive, they were open-minded enough to be ready to reconsider their practice on its merits, and would still be so but for the edict that the wet fly was anathema on chalk streams. Yet, though I laughed, the writer was right and I was wrong. So perhaps I may be forgiven if I take up a little space in examining the question historically, to see just what it all means, and to discover, if possible, how it came about.

Whatever may be the present state of chalk-stream opinion on the subject, there can be little doubt that, in its inception, the dry fly was not adopted for any other reason than that it was found to pay—that is, to kill trout which would not yield to the seductions of the wet fly as then practised. Francis Francis was a broad-minded angler, with ample experience of wet-fly fishing, whose period comprised the early days of the dry fly, and, writing with a knowledge of both, he used, in his " Book of Angling," these wise words: " The judicious and perfect application of dry, wet, and mid-water fishing stamps the finished fly fisher with the hall-mark of efficiency." What was it that led chalk-stream angling opinion so far from these ideals ? The words quoted by me are quoted with approval by Mr. F. M. Halford in chapter xi. of " Dry-Fly Fishing in Theory and Practice," headed, " Floating

Flies and Sunk Flies." That chapter is written with the fair-mindedness and intellectual honesty which characterizes everything that came from his pen. And yet I think I detect in that chapter, and in that volume, much that has lent support to the tendency of thought which we are inquiring into. It was there argued at considerable length and with much acuteness that *on chalk streams the wet fly does not pay*, that the dry fly is successful on these streams when the sunk fly is utterly hopeless. It is not suggested that it is wicked to use the wet fly, only that it is ineffectual. But, in order to test this argument, it is necessary to see what Mr. F. M. Halford meant by the wet fly. Let me quote his exact words:

" The sunk fly is an imitation of the larva, or nymph, moving in the water, or of a winged insect when waterlogged or drowned. . . .

" With the sunk or wet fly he (the angler) casts to a likely place, whether he has or has not seen a rise there (more frequently he has not), and, in fact, his judgment should tend to tell him where, from his knowledge of the habits of the fish, they are most likely to be found in position or likely to feed. Thus wet-fly fishing is often termed ' fishing the water,' in contradistinction to the expression ' fishing the rise,' which is applied to the method of the dry-fly fisherman."

Mr. Halford, therefore, understood wet-fly fishing as fishing at large all over the water as against fishing the rise. Would he at that time have objected (had it occurred to him to do so) to a wet-fly fisherman confining himself to fishing the rise, or the located fish, with the wet fly? I can hardly think so. He was more open-minded than that. He said, in the same chapter which I have quoted:

" Some dry-fly fishermen are such purists that they will not, under any circumstances whatever, make a single cast except over rising fish, and prefer to remain idle the entire day rather than attempt to persuade the wary inhabitants of the stream to rise at an artificial fly, unless they have previously seen a natural one taken in the same position. Although respecting their scruples, this is, in my humble opinion, riding the hobby to death, and I for one am a strong advocate for floating a cocked fly over a likely place, even if no movement of a feeding fish has been seen there. . . . There is no doubt that an angler catching sight of a trout or grayling lying near the surface, or in position for feeding, can often tempt him with a good imitation of the fly on the water floated accurately over him at the first cast."

Would he have denied to the wet-fly man—had he believed that the wet fly paid—the same privilege as he would accord to the dry-fly man? I see no reason to suppose so. But it will have been seen from these quotations that at that time at any rate the idea of the wet fly being used much as the dry fly, and cast only to rising fish, to fish seen " hovering " in position to feed, and to likely places carefully chosen, had apparently not occurred to him. In fact, the comparison which he has made is between the dry-fly practice of chalk streams and the unintelligent wet-fly practice of rough rivers, applied, if you like, to chalk streams, and not between dry-fly practice and wet-fly practice deliberately thought out and adapted to use on chalk streams.

He says of the wet fly, it is true, " It is said that there are days when, even in the clearest of them, the sunk fly is found more killing than the floating one. This may possibly be true, but in many years' experience such days have not fallen to my lot, and I should be inclined to consider them as *happening ones*, or, in other words, as the rare exceptions which go to prove the rule."

I propose to give later on my reasons for doubting

whether, with his special dry-fly equipment, Mr. F. M. Halford often made the whole-hearted experiments essential to bring this comparison to a real test.

He never believed the wet fly on a chalk stream would pay, and in his autobiography, published in 1903, he gives an account of a week's fishing of the Test by a very skilled Yorkshire angler of my acquaintance, which leads him to the same conclusion. Here it is:

" I was much interested, some years since, watching a first-rate wet-fly man, a Yorkshire fisherman, on a portion of the Upper Test. His flies were Olive Quills of various shades, Iron blues, Red Quills, and such patterns, all of which he used on his native streams, and were dressed with peacock quill bodies, very meagre upright wings, and a single turn of hen hackle for legs. He did not in any way practise the ' chuck-and-chance-it plan,' but moved slowly upstream, carefully studying the set of the current, and quickly deciding where a *feeding fish should be* in each run. Sometimes it would be close under the bank, sometimes on the edge of a slack place, and sometimes on the margin of an eddy.

" Whenever he had made up his mind as to the most likely place, there he would make one, or at most two, light casts, placing his fly with great accuracy and letting it drift down without drag. Now this, I take it, was the best possible imitation of the work of a dry-fly fisherman, except that he had not spotted the fish and his fly was not floating in the dry-fly sense. His patterns were very similar in size, colour, and form to those of the ordinary chalk-stream fisherman. He used very fine drawn gut, and worked hard from morning to evening, never passing over a likely place without putting a fly into it, and very seldom losing a hooked fish.

" It was in the early part of April, during strong westerly

and south-westerly winds, when the hatch of duns was sparse, and when, in fact, all conditions were favourable to the sunk and unfavourable to the floating fly. He fished six days on a well-stocked reach of the river, and killed in the aggregate seven trout weighing nine pounds. Candidly, I was somewhat surprised at the good result, and have often wondered whether he could repeat the performance. Of course, the average weight of the fish, one and a quarter pounds, was very small for the Test, and two or three of them would have been returned by many dry-fly fishermen.

" Let it be clearly understood, however, that this fisherman was most skilful and painstaking, and was a past-master in the art of selecting the right spot, and in placing his fly accurately and delicately there at the first attempt. Had he merely fished the river up or down, or had he bungled his cast or moved about rapidly, or, in fact, made any mistakes, I do not believe he would have killed a single trout; so that his bag represents the best possible result under existing conditions for a wet-fly fisherman on a stream like the Upper Test."

The points which strike me about this account are these: (1) That the Yorkshire angler fished "from morning to evening " at a time of year when two hours, and often less, will cover the time of the take; (2) that we are not told that the Yorkshire angler ever cast to a rising fish or a bulging fish, but only to likely places; (3) what would have been the score assuming the Yorkshire angler had had, in addition to his own special skill and equipment, Mr. Halford's knowledge of the water and the position of its fish ? (4) a week at a time of year when the time of the take is so limited is a short time for even the most accomplished angler to get on terms with a strange and notoriously difficult river.

But we have it here again, not that the wet fly is wicked, but that it does not pay.

Now, where in the writings of any angling authority do we get it laid down that the wet fly is wicked, and that the high-and-dry school are entitled to look down from a height of ethical superiority upon those who can, and do, alternate wet with dry? I have looked in vain.

Viscount Grey, at p. 123 of "Fly Fishing," says: "Some dry-fly anglers may have spoken of wet-fly fishing as a 'chuck-and-chance-it' style, by which small fish are caught easily in coloured water on coarse tackle. Some wet-fly anglers, on the other hand, may have expressed a belief that all the talk about dry flies is superfluous, and that large, well-fed trout, in clear, smooth water, can be caught by the methods skilfully applied which are successful in North-Country rivers. If there be any angler on either side who still holds such opinions, he can but be advised to put them to the test in practice, and so bring himself to a more just frame of mind."

Not a word, be it observed, of deprecation of the wet fly because it is wicked, but merely that it does not pay. He goes on: "I have known and tried enough of the wet fly to be sure that the use of it has very narrow limits in a pure chalk stream, well-fished, where the season does not begin till May." If Viscount Grey does not mean that he has tried it in chalk streams, his evidence does not go very far. If he does mean it, he clearly does not deprecate it on any ground except that it is not effective.

Mr. H. S. Hall, in the Badminton Library, is silent on the subject, beyond suggesting that there is no hope for the chalk-stream angler in anything but the dry fly.

Mr. G. A. B. Dewar, again, in the "Book of the Dry Fly," compares the dry fly on streams to which it is peculiar with the wet fly on rough streams, and fails, for some reason unexplained, to compare or contrast it with the wet fly on what, for brevity, we may call dry-fly streams; but he has not a word of deprecation for the wet fly, except on the ground that it does not pay.

I have searched a number of more recent writers for light and leading on the subject, but in vain. It may be that there are papers in the *Field* and other journals which may throw more light on the subject, but I do not recall them, and I have not the means at hand of making a search.

The fact, however, remains that there *is* or *was* a body of opinion hostile to any use of the wet fly upon chalk streams, and apt to claim a higher ethical standard than is enough for those who do not object to fish these rivers on suitable occasions with a wet fly; and it would be interesting to see how it came into being. I suspect the evolution was much as follows:

The necessity of casting upstream in all weathers evolved the heavy tapered line, and that again seemed to necessitate, and did in fact evolve, the heavy rod and the double-dressed floater. This equipment was quite unsuited to wet-fly fishing, and so employed was quite as likely to result in scaring the fish as in catching them. Then wet-fly fishing, in the sense of casting across or across and down stream a dragging fly, was apt to attract small fish, and to result in their being hooked, or pricked, and scared. This was undoubtedly bad for the water. *Ergo*, wet-fly fishing is bad for the water, and ought to be barred.

This opinion became firmly rooted in many minds, and no doubt it was easier to make a rule of no wet fly, especially as the wet fly was not believed to pay, than to make a distinction between wet fly according to knowledge and mere wet fly. It was, no doubt, suggested and believed that even a wet fly cast upstream to bulging fish was apt to line them and scare them. (I believe this is quite incorrect, for the trout must constantly be having weeds and other matter brought down-stream quite as likely to touch and scare it as the line, and would think nothing of a touch from a line merely carried by the current.) So the wet fly became anathema with some folk. In brief, it did not pay, and it did harm.

But when it has come to be shown that, rightly fished in the right conditions, it does pay, and does no harm, unless adding to the angler's sport and the weight of his basket be harm, the ground of objection is changed. It is too deadly. It is as bad as worm-fishing or the use of an Alexandra. It is not fly-fishing at all.

These violences defeat themselves. I am quite willing to admit that whatever is unfair to the brother angler or damaging to the water is rightly to be barred, but to say that it is fair to cast a dry fly persistently over a bulging trout with no genuine hope of getting him, and is unfair to cast a sunk fly to him with a good chance of getting him, seems to me absurd. The water is far more hammered in the former case, and the education of the fish far more likely to be advanced. Everyone who has fished hard-fished waters knows how hardened trout become to being cast to, how they will go on feeding gaily and never making a mistake however often the dry fly is put over them. Viscount Grey gives an excellent description of these conditions in writing of his Winchester days. Yet such fish will often succumb readily to a judicious wet fly, and it is my contention that such fish are better out of the water, to make room for others less over-educated. The Germans know a great deal more about trout management than we do, and their system is to keep the stock moving, and to kill off the older stock quickly, to allow room for growth of the younger fish. A fishery is like partridge or grouse lands. The stock of game, when not shot down, quickly deteriorates in numbers and quality. So I put it forward that if the wet fly used to supplement the dry fly involves the more rapid killing off of the older stock, it does good to the fishery and not harm. The only thing to be guarded against is injury to the young stock, and that may be done by prohibiting down-stream fishing with a dragging wet fly. If the stock be found to be diminishing too rapidly, the basket may be limited, but the angler who only comes down for a day, which he would not have chosen had he foreseen what it would be, has at least a chance of putting some fish in his creel which the conditions might otherwise have barred.

If I am right, the opponents of the wet fly fairly used seem to be driven upon the argument that it is not fly fishing. This is a mere verbal distinction culled *ad hoc*, and as an argument it leaves me cold. For generations wet-fly fishing was the only fly fishing—on waters, too, where the dry fly now reigns supreme—and in those days, if records do not lie, baskets were not inferior to the best of the present day. And if a method of wet-fly fishing, which, in the sense only of its giving one an added chance of trout, and no other, is detrimental to the water, is a sin, then I am quite content to remain in my iniquity with Kingsley and Francis Francis, and a host of other good anglers, and I deny the right of users of Wickham's Fancy, Gold-ribbed Hare's ears, Pope's Nondescripts, Red Tags, Macaw Tags, and Bumbles, and fancy flies generally, to cast the first stone at me. The light rod, casting a medium line, available for either dry fly or wet, and a supply of a few patterns, specially dressed for sinking, in addition to one's floater, render it possible for the angler to cast up-stream to his trout dry fly or wet, as he may judge best, with no more fear of injuring the young stock in the one case than the other, and with an added chance of sport by a method no whit less difficult or fascinating than the dry fly.

THE CULTIVATION OF SHYNESS.

There are two kinds of shyness in trout—man-shyness, which is the prerogative and part of the charm of the wild fish, and gut-shyness, which is sheer sophistication. Man-shyness is instinctive, but cases must be within the observation of every angler in which trout whose haunt is near some stream of traffic of mankind, and whose food must be taken under man's observation or not at all, get over it to a surprising extent, and feed as readily under the eye of the passer-by as if he were not present. The shyness of the fish that is hammered by anglers is another kind of shyness. It has two stages. The first is where he stops feeding when cast to, the last is when he does not; and the last stage is worse than the first, for it combines the wariness of the first stage with the elimination of man-shyness, and the contempt for his lures that is born of knowledge.

This is the stage in which the trout of the Old Barge at Winchester, so feelingly described by Viscount Grey in his chapters on his schooldays at Winchester, must undoubtedly have been when the most successful tactics were to cover the rising fish time after time with the greatest possible rapidity in the hope that, sooner or later, he would make a mistake. It is perhaps impossible to hope that there will not continue to be hard-fished public or club waters in which these conditions prevail, but of the undesirableness of such conditions there can be no question. Nor can there be doubt of the cause. It is over-fishing or hammering, and it is a condition only conspicuous, I think, on waters known as dry-fly waters. That dry-fly fishing should make trout more gut-shy than wet-fly fishing seems probable enough, inasmuch as the phenomenon of surface drag is peculiar to the dry fly, and the under-water movement of a wet fly may be attributed by the fish to the volition of a live insect, whereas the draw of the gut on the surface is an open betrayal of the guile. It is true that the opinion used to be expressed by dry-fly anglers of immense experience and authority that the use of the wet fly on chalk streams tends to make the trout shy more rapidly than does the use of the dry fly; but I confess I have seen no facts put forward to base such an opinion, and, indeed, the use of the wet fly upon chalk streams was for years, until comparatively recently, so much of a dead letter that it is hard to see whence these anglers have obtained the data to justify such a pronouncement. Certainly neither the rods nor flies used on the first-class dry-fly streams were until recently in the least suitable to wet-fly practice, and they are by no means universally so yet. On the other hand, the experience of the hard-fished Scottish border streams, such as the Tweed, tends to show that the persistent use of the wet fly is nothing like so pernicious in its effect upon trout as an even less constant and persistent application of the dry fly. My own experience of chalk streams—much less extensive, it is true, than that of the authorities referred to, but directed with some persistence to this investigation—points the same way. The dry-fly authority rightly insists that in his angling the true sportsman should abstain from adding needlessly to the already too advanced education of our chalk-stream trout, and thus prejudicing the chances of sport for the brother anglers who will follow him on the water. But when he goes on to insist that this proposition involves a restriction to the use of dry fly only, I venture to think that the logic of this deduction is faulty. The deduction should be that the chalk-stream angler should not cast his fly without some reasonable hope of attracting the trout to which he casts it. To lay down that he should never cast without the certainty of killing would ensure the extinction of chalk-stream trouting in a month. Now, to throw a dry fly to a bulging trout is to cast without any reasonable hope of attracting the trout. I have done it many times, and I ought to know. But to throw an appropriate wet fly to a bulging trout is not to cast without any reasonable hope of attracting the trout. I have done it many times, and I ought to know. The former method undoubtedly adds needlessly to the already too advanced education of the trout. The other method involves giving the subaqueous-feeding trout an opportunity of taking the fly where he is engaged in taking his food, just as the dry-fly method involves the giving to the surface-feeding trout an opportunity of taking the fly where *he* is engaged in taking *his* food. The exclusive dry-fly man is therefore driven—and rightly driven—to deprecate casting the dry fly to bulging trout, but he is not driven by any logic that I have yet seen put forward to deprecate casting the wet fly to subaqueous-feeding or even to surface-feeding trout.

Not only are there hours and occasions when the wet fly make a sounder appeal to the trout than does the dry fly, but also places; and more incidents than one strongly confirmatory of this proposition have occurred within my own experience. The first I quote was in this wise: On a mid-July day I sat down by the Itchen to wait for the beginning of the time of the take. I occupied my time of waiting by putting a fine muslin net over the ring of my landing-net, and making a few forages in the celery bed at my feet. The net came up wriggling with nymphs of various colours and sizes. I selected from my stock an imitation dressed with bear's hair and olive seal's fur, which, when wet, looked likest to one type of nymph, and put it in my cap. There was no bulging in the morning, and the few fish which rose fed on the surface.

In the afternoon I saw two fish feeding cautiously under the edge of a long bank of cut weed which had effected a lodgment along the opposite side of the river. Now I saw at once that, if I cast a dry fly to either of these fish the odds were long that there would be a drag ere the fly reached him, and a needless addition to his already too advanced education. I might, of course, have left those two fish severely alone. But that nymph was in my cap, and presently it was attached to the end of my line and dropped, thoroughly wetted, an inch from the edge of the weed-bank, and a foot or so above the lower trout. He was not a bit scared until he had become attached to my line, which took about one second, and then it did not matter so much. Precisely the same thing occurred with the trout at the other end of the weed-patch five or six yards farther up, and I repeated the successful experiment at a second bank of weeds a few yards higher. Now my alternatives were these: (1) To cast a dry fly with no reasonable hope of catching these trout, and every prospect of adding to their education; (2) to leave them alone; (3) to do what I did. And I leave it to the reader to say which was the reasonable course to take.

The next incident, or, rather, pair of incidents, occurred on one fast shallow, where the trout have the reputation of being almost uncatchable. So they are with the dry fly, for no skill—at any rate, none at my command—can avail to prevent a drag being set up within a moment of the delivery of a cast from the only position from which it can be made with any hope of concealment. Yet one morning, when there was a rise of tiny little pale duns, and the fish on the shallow were bulging gaily, I killed there in less than ten minutes a brace of handsome trout on a tiny dotterel hackle dressed Stewart-wise on a No. oo hook to gut. Each took the fly eagerly. I detected no shyness of the sunken fly, but a dry fly always put them down with great suddenness. Then a moment later, on a smooth length just above, there was a big trout rising under the opposite bank, protected by the stump of a giant rush in such a way that every fly put to him dry was bound to swing across current with a drag at the moment of reaching him. The Dotterel dun was still attached, and he took it at the third offer, was hooked, and was played fifty or sixty yards down from his holt, and finally lost just as he seemed to be coming to net.

On another reach a day or two earlier I saw a fish of good size lying out close to the surface, impudently visible, with his nose almost against the edge of a tiny bed of weeds which came to the surface. The result was that directly a fly was floated down to the fish it either stopped on the weed, or, if cast beyond it, swung round to his nose or his back with an aggravated and vicious drag. What that trout did not know about surface drag was not worth knowing. He knew so much that it did not disturb him a bit (the dry-fly man had hammered him into this condition, mind you!), and he placidly went on with his feeding, dropping a yard or so to take the natural flies which went by him without drag on the far side of the weed. There was a rise of blue-winged olive, and I selected a dotterel hackle with a dubbed body, giving, when wet, much the colour of the body of the natural insect. The fly, thoroughly wet, was dropped a yard the other side of the weed-bed, and it swung round under water towards our trout, who immediately turned and took it in the most confiding manner. He, unfortunately, kicked off, but that is irrelevant for present purposes. The point is, he took the fly.

I never saw a length on which it was harder to avoid a drag, and all the trout had reached one or two stages in their education; either they knew all about drag and despised it and went on feeding, or they knew enough about the floating line to realize that it indicated the presence of the enemy, and that it were wise to suspend feeding operations. Once convinced of this—too late in the rise to be much use—I restored my Dotterel dun to its place, and found it readily accepted by the only brace of trout to which I was able to despatch it without making my presence known. Now, if I were to listen to the voice of authority, I should either abstain from casting a line to any of these fish, because I should be adding needlessly to the already too advanced education, etc., and so prejudicing, etc., or I should wait until the fish were well on, and add to their education in drag and the other mysteries of the dry fly. On the other hand, there was the alternative of recalcitrancy, which I took. I can, and do, believe that hammering fish with the dry fly does advance their education, as nothing else will, but so far I have seen no scintilla of proof that the use of the wet fly cast upstream to feeding trout has anything like so disastrous an effect. There is no question of wet versus dry fly. Each in its place and used according to knowledge is surely the way of wisdom.

SEMI-SUBMERGED, ETC.

On a Sunday afternoon at the end of May I had an exceptional opportunity of observing the hatch of the May fly on the Kennet. The light, the position in which I sat, the swing of the full current at my feet, and the clearness of the water after a long drought, all combined to help me, and again and again I saw that exquisite little water-miracle recur. The dull, inert, brownish body of the nymph, swung down by the current from the swaying tassels of the water-weed, coming slowly to the surface, till somehow its head and thorax seemed to threaten to emerge. Then the bursting of the brown skin of the thorax, the six pale greenish legs gripping the surface, while the body curled tail downwards in the water, as if to let the current get a purchase on the sheath. Then simultaneously the wings shooting up, the sheath coming away and floating far down the current, and the fairy-like creature standing with wings erect and upturned tail to drift down-stream, it may be a few yards or only a few inches, before taking flight for the meadows. These few inches or yards represent the one opportunity the trout, dace, or chub has of taking the May fly in the winged stage before, as spent imago, the fly goes drifting down the stream, with wings flat on the water, dead or in the throes of dissolution. The chances, therefore, for the fish of taking the insect in the nymphal stage are obviously much greater, and it is little to be wondered at that, in the inert semi-submerged nymph just about to hatch and in the spent, water-logged, dying or dead spinner, the trout finds a far easier prey than it does in the fidgety, fluttering, newly-hatched May-fly which is so apt to disappoint him by taking wing at the moment he puts up.

If these deductions be sound in the case of the green drake and its spinners, they are probably equally sound in the cases of all the other and far smaller upwinged flies, which, in process of hatching, oviposition, and death follow the same sequence of stages as the May fly. And this probably is one good reason for the success of nymph-like, or spinner-like, flies such as Tup's Indispensable, fished semi-submerged. Dubbed with a body material which readily takes up the water and fills with light, and busked with a hackle which is enough to enable the fly to cling to the surface film, such a pattern may well be taken, at one stage of the fly's career, for the hatching nymph getting its head above water, and in a later stage for the spent spinner floating down helpless or dead. Trout rise at spent gnats and fallen spinner in a quiet, deliberate way, differing greatly from the fierce rushing motions with which they bulge at the ascending nymphs which they fear may escape them by hatching and transfer to the air.

So far we have only dealt with the fly *in* the surface, and not the fly under it, nor the fly over it, the wholly wet and the wholly dry. On the subject of these, as well as on the subject of the semi-submerged, the experiments conducted by means of Dr. Francis Ward's under-water observation chambers (of which experiments an account appeared in the *Field* of May 4, 1912, and are recorded at pp. 38 to 43 of this book) may shed a little needed light. They show that the under-side of the surface film outside a certain angle to the perpendicular above the observer's eye acts as a mirror, and is impenetrable to vision. That angle is $48\frac{1}{2}$ degrees for the human observer, but may, for all I know, be different for trout, and, again, for other fish. But whatever that angle may be, outside it the trout can only see those parts of the fly which penetrate the surface film. Thus a sunk fly is visible to a trout at any distance, a semi-submerged fly at quite a considerable distance; a line floating and not breaking or denting the surface, and a perfectly dry and floating fly are not visible at all, except within the circle of which the place where the perpendicular above the trout's head meets the surface is the centre, and the angle of reflection indicates the circumference. Within that circle a floating fly looks remarkably clear, bright, and attractive, but if the hook comes through the film it looks particularly gross and obnoxious.

The deductions which may be drawn from these facts are as follows:

1. An angler fishing with an entirely floating cast has an advantage, in that the cast can only be seen within the circle above described; and this applies equally whether the fly itself be floating, semi-submerged or sunk, but—

2. The entirely floating fly itself can only be seen by the trout if it passes over the fish within the charmed circle. Within that circle it is extremely attractive, but the cast must be extremely accurate.

3. A semi-submerged or sunk fly, being visible at a greater distance, need not be so precisely accurately cast. To counter-balance that, it is duller in general effect, and the under-water part of the gut is visible.

4. Therefore, stouter gut may be used for dry-fly fishing, or, to put it the other way on, finer gut is desirable for fishing the wet fly, but not for fishing the semi-submerged.

5. To counteract the dulling effect of the water on the sunk or semi-submerged fly something brightening is needed, such as a gold tag or gold or silver ribbing, or, better still, dubbing brightened with seal's fur or pig's wool.

6. A not very perfectly-dried winged fly, which has hackle and body as well as hook breaking through the surface film, may very well be taken for a hatching nymph.

There are probably other conclusions, but these are a few to go on with.

WIND AND THE EVENING RISE.

When I think of all the wise things which for years and years I have accepted from authorities and acted upon in sheer innocence, I could swear—swear vehemently. The number of times I have gone in of an evening because of the thoroughly well-established fact that there can be no evening rise unless the wind drops ! !

For many years, as many as I can remember during my angling life, I have heard it laid down as the one certain thing in the uncertain sport of fly fishing that with a wind there could be no evening rise. Like a fool, I believed it without testing it, and many an afternoon have I waited in anxiety for the drop of the breeze at sunset, and when the drop has not arrived I have unshipped my rod and turned my steps in disappointment home-along.

It was only in 1916 that, accident having kept me on the river awaiting the return of a friend long after sundown on a gusty June evening, I found that the true proposition probably is that there is no rise to a mere spinner-fall on open water on a gusty evening. But if there be a hatch of fly on a windy evening—and there is no obvious reason why a night-hatching fly should not come out on a rough evening, if a day-hatching fly can come out on a rough morning or afternoon—it should be just as possible to get sport as on a gusty morning.

It enrages me to think of all the good evenings' fishing I have missed through believing the pundits. The moral is, " Never believe a thing you are told about fishing until you have proved it, not only once, but over and over again."

The evening I refer to gave me three and a half brace above the average weight for the water, and is recorded at p. 205. The blue-winged olive was coming up well; I could tell it by the big splurgy rises of the trout. Saturday, June 23, 1917, was just such another evening. I had been down to look at the water between my arrival at four o'clock (summer time) and an early dinner, and I had spotted the blue-winged olive—the first of the season, the keeper said —and had caught a brace with an imitation of the nymph, but they were smallish fish, and I returned them.

The wind was then blowing briskly from the south, with a faint shade of east in it, and in gusts. Fortunately its general trend was upstream, and it served the length I meant to fish fairly well, and I needed nothing more powerful than my five-ounce nine-footer. My friend, who accompanied me, was very depressed at the strength of the wind and its obvious disinclination to drop spent at sunset. But I recalled my experience of the preceding year (repeated two or three times since) with a view to comforting him, and he decided to stay on, though a very doubting Thomas.

We waited on our separate beats, with such patience as we could muster, from seven to half-past eight. The wind certainly moderated a little, but it still blew briskly and gustily, shifting a shade more to the east. About half-past eight a small hatch of small pale watery olive, with an admixture of July dun and of spinners, including some jenny spinners, came down, and a quiet protected corner enabled me to identify them.

A fish or two began to take quietly, some clearly taking spinners, others nymphs of the pale watery olive, and occasionally the hatched fly. Soon a big splurging rise said plainly " blue-winged olive," and, knotting on a nymph pattern with which I had been successful last year, I cast to the fish. He came up at length and missed. In the meantime another fish, two or three yards ahead, had risen somewhat in the same way; but I suspected grayling, and sure enough a few moments later an unmistakable forked tail appeared and sent me on to the next fish. This was rising in a corner, and was, I judged, taking small spinner of some kind. He would not have my Blue-winged Olive nymph, so I tried him in succession with Tup's Indispensable and Jenny spinner. He came at both and missed. Then he took a blue-winged olive with the

unmistakable swirl, and a few minutes later an Orange
Quill was offered him, and had hardly lit on the water before
he had it.   He put up a gorgeous fight, and proved to be
a sixteen-inch fish in excellent condition, and to weigh
one pound twelve ounces.

Two big fish were rising in the bend just above—distant a
longish cast from cover—and I wanted to try a pattern
of Blue-winged Olive which I had picked up the previous
year, and had had some success with.   So I shifted back to
that pattern, and had both the fish up to it.   But there must
have been something wrong about it, for both rose to it
without fastening.   The same result occurring with each
of the next two fish I tackled, I put up a fresh Orange Quill
on a No. 1 hook, and put it to a fish feeding under the far
back above the bend.   He was an exasperating fish, never
still a moment, and when I dropped my fly just in front
of a ring, he would rise above or below, or beyond or nearer
me, but always safely.   At length the fly pitched right to
an inch, and next moment the battle was joined.   He was
a lustier fish than the last, one inch shorter but two ounces
heavier, and I had to run him down one hundred and fifty
yards before I netted him out.

I did not take long to find another fish rising similarly,
but I must have made some mistake, for he went down.
The next fish, however, accepted the first offer and joined
his companions in the creel; he was only one pound six
ounces.   It was then 9.35 p.m.

Then, though the fish went on rising for nearly another
half-hour, some change came over them; for though the
next fish took the fly quite resolutely, it did not fasten,
nor did the next.   A very big fish, if I am any judge of a
rise, was working away, absorbing blue-winged olive,
with a smooth head-and-tail action, as regular as the ticking
of a clock; but though I offered him every opportunity of

including my Orange Quill, he ignored it persistently for a while, and then suddenly stopped. I ought to have changed to a Spinner, but I had always supposed that the Orange Quill was taken for a spinner, as it is in colour so unlike the Blue-winged Olive, so I stuck to the Quill. The next fish took the Quill, but he did not hold it, and the line coming away with a jerk, went into a snarl, which occupied ten minutes of the fast dying rise to unravel. I had time to try two more risers, but neither had any use for the Orange Quill, and at 10.5 p.m. it was all over, and I was left with a leash of fish, a sense of failure and bafflement.

ON THE ACCURACY OF AUTHORITIES.

Then I never suspected the dogma that an evening mist puts the fish down for good, and for years and years I have reeled up and gone home when the surface began to smoke at night. Shall I do so again ?

On June 16 on the Itchen the blue-winged olive began to come up in some quantity about eight o'clock, and I expected to find the fish taking them freely. But the moon was behind my hand, and I found every fish stopping at once when I began to cast, and when nine o'clock came the evening rise had yielded me nothing. Then, creeping round the next bend, I saw the ominous mist approaching, and I began to despair, as in duty bound. I was, however, the wrong side of the river for leaving it to go in, and I had to walk up the bank a mile or so to reach a bridge. So I moved on to meet the mist. I had not dismantled my rod, and presently I became aware of a good trout rising in the middle, and apparently rising quite well, despite the mist. The size and shape of the ring showed that he was taking the blue-winged olive. So I gave him my invariable prescription, the large Orange Quill.

In vain. But he went on rising. He did not appear to be
taking flies on the surface. So I took off the Quill, tied on
a Pheasant tail on No. 1 hook, moistened it in my mouth
to make it sink and look like a nymph, and despatched it
to my trout. He was my trout all right, and the keeper
put his weight at two pounds two ounces.

Then I remembered that a bit farther up was a place
where I had seen a good trout as I went by in the morning,
and I approached it gingerly. Yes. Just a little farther
out in the stream than I expected a trout was rising busily.
He took my nymph the first time it reached him, and
after a battle royal he joined No. 1 in my bag. The two
fish were as like in size and make as two peas, and they
weighed two pounds two ounces each. I was pleased
enough at the moment, but when I think of all the sport
I have probably missed in the past by believing the
authorities, instead of finding out for myself about the
behaviour of trout in mist, I refrain from good words.

DRIFTWEED AND BAD ADVICE.

The days when weeds have been cut and are floating down
in quantity are sufficiently distressing to the angler who
must take his water-side pleasures when he can. But even
on them, despite fouling of line and fly, one may occasionally manage to pick up some sport with the aid of a
tinselled fly, such as a Pink Wickham or a Pope's Nondescript.

But when the cutting is over and the stream is free of
weeds, except such as are caught against the banks, though
for a day or two the trout have left their usual hovers
and are nervous and uneasy, it is quite possible for one
who makes it his business to get at the reason of things to
fill a modest basket in the course of the day.

To begin with, the bottom, or much of it, has been shaved, often too bare, and the weeds in which the trout used to shelter and over which they used to hover, conscious of shelter in case of need, and all the bolder for that consciousness, are not in their places. Yet shelter the trout must have, and so the piles of weed which make little rafts hitched against the banks are pretty sure finds. The cut weeds will hold quite a supply of insect food, and in the absence of a hatch of fly the trout may still be on the alert under their shelter for such nymphs and other small peoples as leave the haven of the weed-jam. Thus a nymph pattern, well submerged and drifted close along the edge of the weed-rafts preferably under the far bank, is quite likely to be taken, and the floating part of the gut, drawn suddenly under, will give the angler his cue. For this game the long patches of cut weed should preferably be picked. Under one's own bank the game is not quite so easy, but it can be done. There is another alternative, however; and a small Sedge deftly floated along the edge of the patch is often surprisingly remunerative.

Before approaching such a patch, however, from below one should spend a little time watching the eddy just downstream of it. Then, if there is, or has been, any recent rise or fall of fly, little fleets lie becalmed or circling slowly, and the trout venture out and cruise among them, picking up one here and there. Here the drag is often difficult to negotiate, so a wet Tup's Indispensable or a small wet Alder will generally prove better policy than a floater.

Again, above the weed and close to the bank, there is another hopeful spot, especially if there be a small rise of little duns. Hidden right under the weed-pile a good trout will often lie, putting up his nose an inch or two above the weed-pile to intercept the small olive. He cannot see the angler, and is often surprisingly unsuspicious of guile if the first cast be delivered aright. One may find a string of weed-rafts under one's own bank all thus tenanted, especially if there be only a light wind and that upstream. One must expect in such circumstances a large proportion of failures, as if the fly be not taken the first time it is apt to catch in the weed-pile and put the trout down. The fly may, however, often be rescued, not by drawing, but by a forward and downward switching action, which picks up the fly upstream of the weed-pile, and carries it into the air before it is drawn backwards for the next cast.

Sometimes just after weed-cutting there are curious collectings of nymphs just under water in bays under the bank. One sees not a fly on the surface, but the trout are feeding hard all the time, and if you catch one and open him his stomach will be found to contain nymphs in quantity and no winged duns. In such conditions a tin-selled nymph is more likely to attract attention than a closer imitation of the nymph disclosed by the autopsy. The closer imitation is likely to pass unnoticed in the crowd. In these conditions the trout, though apparently well on the feed, are extremely difficult. A small black Alder will, however, sometimes do the trick after the May weed-cutting.

When evening draws on the trout venture out more freely, and are to be found rising wherever the current will bring them duns or spinners, and if one finds the right fly one is more apt to get sport than at any other time of day, though it is not so interesting, nor does it call for the exercise of so much intelligence. One recent May evening I rose and touched no less than eighteen trout under these conditions. The Tup's Indispensable brought them up, but was not quite right. There had been iron blue during the day, and it may have been taken for the jenny spinner, but it was the other sex, the claret spinner, that was being taken. For when at length a seal's-fur-bodied imitation was presented three handsome trout, one after another, accepted at the first offer, and then all was over for the evening.

Had it been July there might have been a prolongation of sport by reason of the blue-winged olive rise coming on after the fall of spinner. This fly the trout will be found to take as well and boldly in open as in weedy water.

Enough has been said to suggest that the advice frequently tendered to keep away from the river for ten days or a fortnight after weed-cutting is not particularly good advice.

V

B. W. O.

B. W. O.

I WANT to sing the praises of the blue-winged olive. As
a sport-providing fly it can give the May-fly several stone
and a beating. From mid-June to the end of the season
there is scarcely an evening when it may not put in an
appearance. When it does put in an appearance there is
always a chance of a big fish. When it puts in an appearance in quantity there is the chance of a big basket,
and all the fish in the basket big.

The hour of the hatch is usually late. A sprinkling of
blue-winged olives will go down almost unregarded while
the light lasts, but in the gloaming, after a pause, the
fly will sometimes hatch out in quantity, and at once
every big fish in the river will be busy gulping them
down.

It is at this point the angler needs to be careful about
his fly. He must be sure what the trout are doing. At
one time the trout will be nymphing, and the only way
to take them will be with a sunk, sparsely-hackled, dark
brown olive pattern. At another time, maybe later in the
same rise, the trout will be taking subimago. Then, according to my experience, a large Orange Quill, No. 1 size,
is fatal. At times, however, I have killed well with a fly
of the same size dressed thus:

Wings.—Darkest starling or medium coot.
Body.—Greenish-olive seal's fur.
Tag.—Flat gold.
Whisks.—Pale dun cock.
Hackle.—Medium olive.
Hook.—No. 1.

Another pattern which occasionally kills well is dressed in the same way except that the body is of heron herl dyed a greenish-yellow olive, and there is a rib of fine gold and no tag.

But at times the trout will concentrate on the spinner. It may be, and generally is, the male spinner—of a dark, rich brown sherry colour. On such occasions I have found a fly dressed as follows deadly:

Hook.—No. 1, round bend or equivalent in Limerick shape.
Body.—Dark sherry-brown seal's fur.
Rib.—Fine gold wire.
Whisk.—Honey-dun cock.
Hackle.—Six or seven turns of dark, rusty dun cock.

As an illustration of the importance of a correct diagnosis, let me quote a recent experience on the Itchen.

On June 21, 1919, the small fly evening risè was over, and I judged from the large and violent kidney-shaped whorls made by the rising trout that they had come on to the blue-winged olive. I offered a big fish under my own bank an Orange Quill with some confidence. He took no notice at first, but presently stopped, and I moved on to another fish. He was taking just above a large clump of a big umbelliferous plant, and I had to throw over it and recover my fly through it or not at all. So I calculated I had just one chuck, and if that did not come off I might as well move on, for I should not have another chance. I watched the fish for a minute or two, and concluded he was not taking subimagines. I had seen no spinner going down, so I knotted on a nymph, wetted it thoroughly in my mouth, judged my distance, and dropped the fly a foot in front of the fish and outside him. The fly went under, and instantly there was a tell-tale hint on the surface which made me pull home. I netted the fish out eventually at the place where I had put down the first fish, and the scales said two and three-quarter pounds. The next stretch was barren, but when I found another riser the evening had moved on, and the trout would have nothing to say to the nymph. I tied on an Orange Quill, and the next fish had it at the first offer. He scaled two pounds five ounces, I got one other of one and a half pounds, and then all was suddenly over for the evening.

The following week-end a friend got the fish I had begun on. He scaled three pounds two ounces. If only I——!

July 6 was another blue-winged olive evening, but as there had been a sprinkle of the subimagines coming up all day, and I had seen none on the water for half an hour, I divined, when the trout began to rise madly about 9.30, that it was spinner that was doing the trick. There were two big fish rising within ten feet of one another in a favourite bend where the current ran deep and strong under my bank, the left. I therefore tied on a hackled Ruddy Spinner, and laid it across the lower fish. He had it immediately and tore off up the stream, half out of water, for some twenty yards or more. Then I turned him down, but the mischief was done; the upper fish was scared and had gone. The hooked fish made a gallant fight, but the keeper weighed him a little later—two and a half pounds good. It was some way up to the next riser, and when I had put him down with a bad cast I thought all was over for the evening, and was making for the bridge to cross the river and so home-along, when I saw a fish rise under a tussock by my bank. I gave him the fly, and he took it gaily, and presently joined the fish in my bag—a comparatively small fish, one pound nine ounces, and not a very good colour. Then, as I came to the spot from which I had cast to him, I saw, three or four yards higher up, a series of spreading rings which called for the administration of the Spinner. Again, the first chuck was all that was necessary. At the movement of the neb I pulled in, and the line was torn off the reel as the fish raced madly diagonally across the river, and ended with a wild fling in the air that revealed his solid proportions. He put up a gorgeous fight, but came to the net at last—two pounds twelve ounces exactly. That was really the end of that evening.

The following week-end I was down again. It had rained hard in the afternoon and evening, and I did not get into position till 9.15. I was clad in a mackintosh, which covered me down to the tops of my waders, to preserve me from getting soaked by the dripping herbage, in places nearly man high. I began at the choice corner above-mentioned. There were two fish busy in it, both good ones, and I made the mistake of giving them the Spinner which had been successful on the previous occasion. I had seen a good hatch of subimago on the surface, and if I had only exercised ordinary common sense I would have put an Orange Quill, and I should probably have had one and possibly both. As it was, I put both down. I then moved quietly up to get to the fish I had put down by a bad cast the previous week-end. I found him busy, but not too busy to attend to my Orange Quill. He weighed two pounds two ounces. Next I cast right across to a fish taking steadily in the shadow under the far bank. He soon stopped; probably it was drag. I felt sure he was a good fish, and I got to the bridge

and down to him as quickly as I could. I was afraid the
rise might be over, but he was still taking at intervals
sufficiently close to enable me to cover him precisely
enough, and he had the Orange Quill at the first offer.
At first I thought I had misjudged his weight, his movements were so slow, but presently he became scared and
showed his mettle, and during the latter stages of the
battle he was half out of the water, and lashing the surface
and churning it into foam.   But the little nine-footer guided
him to the net, and he lay on the bank in the moonlight,
a perfect picture of what a chalk-stream trout should be—
deep, solid, short, and thick, in the pink of condition,
three pounds two ounces.

I have given these three evening experiences just as
illustrations of the varying ways in which trout must be
approached under differing conditions, even when rising
at the same fly. It is often very difficult to judge which
is the right or best course to adopt, and much valuable
time may be lost by an error in judgment.

It may be asked why the Orange Quill is taken at night
for the blue-winged olive. I answer frankly, I don't know.
I only know that it is. I discovered it by accident in the
early nineties, and it was a lucky accident, for it has been
worth many a good fish to me. In one season I remember
five successive Saturday evenings in June and July, each
of which yielded three and a half brace to the Orange Quill.
That experience led me astray at first, and I had some
disappointments before I worked back to the full appreciation of the fact that blue-winged olive fishing has three
phases—nymph, subimago, and spinner.

To fish the nymph at night is even more fascinating than
to do so by day. In order to divine the rise and the right
moment to strike it is essential to choose a stretch where
you look up into the light under your own bank. Then,

when the fly is taken under water, there is the faintest little heave of the silver of the surface, but as the hook goes home the resistance is apt to be magnificent.

Curiously enough, the blue-winged olive is seldom taken on the surface during the daytime, and when it is its artificial imitation is still less frequently accepted, but I have had excellent sport with a well-sunken nymph. On rare occasions I have found the female spinner on the water early in the morning, and the big fish busy. When she shows up of an evening it is with her blue bag of eggs attached.

The May fly has gone from my stretch of Itchen; but if I had to choose whether I would exchange for its return the blue-winged olive, my answer would, without hesitation, be " Not at any price."

VI

TACTICAL

GLIMPSES OF THE MOON.

MANY anglers have no doubt been driven to consider the effect of the moon on rising trout and grayling, but the moon being a lady of habits which, though regular, bear a different relation to each successive evening, and the evening rise being itself a thing of infinite variety, the study of the effects of moonlight on angling results has perhaps received rather less than its due. I thought myself lucky, therefore, in that during a holiday on the Itchen of the last week in August, 1914, I had a little moonlight on this interesting subject. The general trend of the stretch of the river which it was my privilege to fish is from north to south, with some lengths almost directly so, and in the main with few exaggerated zigzags. It thus happened that a moon showing a little east of south, even after sunset, was generally behind my hand on most of the lengths which it was open to me to select, and on only one short hundred yards was it open to me to cast across from north-east to south-west more or less into the shadow of the opposite bank. Each successive evening the wind fell in such sort as to give hopes of a good evening rise, and the time of year was not too late for a good hatch of the blue-winged olive.

As a rule the dipping of the sun's upper rim marks the beginning of the evening rise, and where a thick coppice, or spinney, or a high bank cuts off the sunlight sooner, one may hope to find a trout or two beginning earlier than where the banks are open. This suggests that where the fly is on the water the time of the take is dictated by conditions of light. Generally, no doubt, the fall of spinner on the water closely coincides with the change in temperature which comes where the sun gets off the water; but the hatch of duns, which often comes about sooner, may be expedited or retarded by little-understood conditions.

On the occasion under consideration the sunset hour, according to Whitaker, was 7.4 p.m., Greenwich time, and the moon was in her first quarter, and timed to set at 7.58 p.m. By the time, therefore, that the sun was off the water on the first evening the three-day-old moon was getting down in the sky towards a setting almost straight down-stream. It was, however, quite bright. The bend of the river which I selected was sheltered by a high bank and a spinney, and soon after sunset a fish or two began to move, but they were invariably oncers, and it was not till the moon was right down and off the water that the trout began to rise freely and to be held, and there was only time for a brace. That was on the Monday. On the Tuesday the sun set at 7.2 and the moon 8.8. On getting to the river I went farther down-stream for my after-dinner start, and got the keeper to put me across to the eastern bank at the bottom of a stretch where the stream ran deep on that side, a beat which experience told me held the best fish within the limits of my leave. The moon was low, but again bright, and right behind my rod. The fish were rising before the sun was quite off the water, and though at a distance they seemed to be feeding heartily, no sooner did one deliver the first cast than they stopped, and I had to go home content with my bag of the day. On the

Wednesday the sun set at 7 and the growing moon at 8.28. On that evening I set out to negotiate a noble two-pounder which inhabited a deep hole in a little bay in the shadow of a spinney and thoroughly protected from the moonlight by a combination of tree shelter and tussock. My plan was to take my stand in the shadow of the spinney and to switch a small Rusty Spinner across to the bay. The fish thereabouts had already begun to move when I got down to the spinney after dinner, and I thought my big friend had moved up a yard or so and was feeding carefully at the top of his hole.

I was wrong, for as my spinner was taken, and my fish went off down-stream with a slam, there was a huge boil as the two-pounder flounced off the exact spot where I had expected to find him. When the other fish—one pound nine ounces—was ashore, I decided not to wait for the return of the fugitive, so I got the keeper to put me across at the bottom of the stretch above described. It was then seven o'clock, and the sun just down. I found a few fish feeding cautiously, yet fairly freely. Yet every time I reached a fish and put my spinner over him he stopped at the second, if not at the first, cast. The moon, grown since overnight, was behind me, and if it was not the moonlight that made the trout conscious that all was not right, I cannot guess what it was. By 7.15 the rise was all over, and it set me speculating whether the moonlight had any effect in expediting the evening rise. I did not get another fish, and I turned in before the moon went down.

The following evening the sun went down at 6.59 and the moon at 8.55. Again I tried the same bank, again I found the evening rise beginning even before the sun went down. Taking the cue from the spinners I had found in the maw of the overnight trout, I had dressed some bright Orange Red spinners, and with one of these in a somewhat sheltered bay I got a trout of just two pounds with a first cast that pitched almost on his nose, and gave him no time to think. But apart from that my experience was a replica of that of the previous evening. I would have tried fishing into rises in the black shadows under the opposite bank if I could have got to a place with a bank sheltering the water from the moon, but the only bend that answered that description was a haunt of grayling, and I was out for trout.

The following evening the sunset was at 6.56, and the moon was timed to go down at 9.24. This was perhaps the most hopeless evening of the lot. The trout were as nervous as on a day of milk-and-watery glare, and if I had not had the first-mentioned two-pounder (sixteen inches and two pounds two ounces), taken in the morning on a Whitchurch dun in the hole from which he bolted on the Wednesday night, to console me, I should have knocked off in a poor humour with myself. It had been a bright, glaring day with an easterly trend in the air, and the trout had been nymphing all day, and may have been gorged to repletion. Still the rises ere I approached showed that they had not quite done.

As it was, I was inclined to kick myself for not applying during the week a lesson got some years back on a water which ran from east to west, so that an angler fishing the evening rise upstream always had the sunset glow behind him. There I found the trout almost unapproachable from behind; but, curiously enough, they accepted most confidingly a fly floated down to them. Probably I ought to have begun at the other end of my stretch and to have drifted my spinner down to my fish, and who knows but what I might have had a hefty bag to bring in. That east and west stretch, by the way, is remarkable in that a good evening rise upon it is a notable rarity. The next night I went away before the evening rise.

Now, like Captain Cuttle's, the point of these observations " lies in the application of 'em." They seem to me to establish that moonlight or sunset glow equally with daylight behind the angler reveal him to the fish, and that the eyesight which enables the trout to make fine distinctions of colour and texture on and in the water by night as by day enables him to see, and especially behind him against a diffused light, any suspicious movements on the bank. The light may also in such a position reveal the gut as it passes over the fish or alights on the water. It may conceal the ravages of *anno Domini* from the trout, but from any other point of view it is of no advantage to the angler to be " in the dusk with the light behind him."

SIDE-STRAIN: TWICE TWO AND AN EXPLANATION.

On the far side of the water, about half-way up, there is a deep muddy cross-drain unbridged, and a big willow-bush on the upstream side to mark it. Just above it I had made a note of a fairly persistent banker rising. Others had found him aggravating, for he was within a longish cast and would not endure a suspicion of a drag. But to go round involved something of a walk, ending in a cautious wade through a midge-ridden marsh. So I was—at least, I believe I was—the first to go round to see if he were more amenable to persuasion from below than from across the river. Arrived on the spot, I could not fail to realize that if I hooked my trout he had only to go down-stream fast enough and far enough to smash me infallibly. However, such a consideration never prevented me from casting to a likely trout, and I settled down to lay siege to him. This was the third week-end in July, and

I had just elaborated a nice dressing of the small darkish olive that one gets at this time of year. It was tied with a body of pale blue heron herl, dyed a greenish olive, bound down with a rib of fine gold wire, and otherwise was unremarkable enough. For the details see p. 110. The object of my attentions was rising at intervals alongside the bank, but never twice in quite the same place, and his range brought him at times so near me that I could not have lifted my little nine-footer without scaring him, and it was only when he was at the top of his beat that I dared swing my line to him. Meanwhile I crouched low, as much hidden by a tussock as possible, and keeping the willow as a background for my willow-coloured fishing suit. Presently he was taking a fly close to another tussock not ten yards up above me (about his top limit). It happened to be my fly, and I signified the same in the usual manner by raising my hand. The little rod bowed beautifully in acknowledging the compliment to my fly dressing, and the line began to cut swiftly down-stream. Another second and the trout would have been below me, below the cross-drain, safe perhaps in a bunch of heavy weed, and it would only be a question of how much of my cast I should save. Instinctively I plunged backwards into the marsh, bending my rod almost horizontally across my body as I faced upstream, and bringing to bear on the fish's mouth every ounce of cross-stream strain I could. The effect was instantaneous. He turned and plunged desperately through the weeds upstream, and I let him go, following, however, closely, and keeping a line so short that every attempt to turn down again was met by instantaneous retreat into the marsh with rod held low and side-strain reapplied. In this way I beat him upstream until I had him almost to the place where I expected to find my next fish, and then I decided that there

was room below for the normal chalk-stream tactics, and
I combed my fish down, and I netted him out from below
the tussock from which the successful cast had been
delivered. I guessed him at close on two pounds. The
keeper's scales said two pounds exactly.

Incidentally I got that other fish—but that is another
story.

I was down again on the water on September 1, and
I met one of the rods. " By the way," he said, " that
qualified trout of yours above the willow-bush at the
Moor drain was pegging away as hard as ever as I came
down." " That is strange," said I; " I was under the
impression that my family had eaten him, and I certainly
knocked him on the head and brought him in. However,
I will investigate the phenomenon."

It was all right. Crouched low behind the same old
tussock with the same old willow as a background for the
same old suit, I watched what might have been the same
old trout making the same old circuit over the same old
beat. And as he took a natural fly near the top limit,
the same old rod delivered a little Red Sedge as if it had
dropped off the tussock hard by on to the water. The
greedy neb reached for it, and I responded in the same
old manner. Off flashed the fish down-stream. But I
plunged into the marsh with rod hooped and held low.
Step for step, incident for incident, the battle pursued the
identical course of the just recounted fight of some weeks
before, and I netted out at the same old tussock a beautiful
male fish which again scaled the exact two pounds.

Incidentally there was another occupant of the next
place of vantage from which I had got that other fish,
and I approached him hopefully, with all the omens in
favour of a repetition of the luck of the previous occasion.
Unfortunately an unexpected flaw of wind dropped my

fly upon the sedge, and my attempt to recover it put the trout definitely down.

This, however, is irrelevant, the point of this narrative being that a soundly hooked trout, howbeit big and powerful, need not be allowed his own way if it be inconvenient for the angler to let him go down; and that, by judicious application of strain in the right direction, he may be persuaded that he is fighting you more successfully by boring upstream at tremendous expense of energy. The time to knock it into his head that he is wrong is when he is in the landing-net.

One Sunday afternoon some days later at the Fly-Fishers' Club I had a conversation with a guest of another member which threw some light upon this episode. I cannot give his name, so as to give him the credit due to him, for I do not recall it, nor do I recall whose guest he was. I hope, whoever he was, he will forgive me for putting about his theory with this inadequate acknowledgment.

The conversation led up to my recounting this episode. Of course, I had realized that I was applying side-strain to bring the fish round, but it was the guest who explained why side-strain was so immediately effective when no strain in any other direction would have availed to stop the fish. " You see," he said, " the trout swims with a lateral action, moving his head from side to side, and if, as he goes down-stream, you pull his head round hard sideways, half the time he must be yielding to the strain, and that makes it so hard as to be almost impossible for him to fight against it the other half of the time. So he comes round. If you applied the same amount of strain overhead it would only tend to lift him, and would have nothing like the same effect in stopping or turning him."

Very simple and obvious when put that way. Of course,

a fish forging upstream may be turned in precisely the same way if you keep opposite him or but little below. And no doubt most of us have used the method many a time. But I for one am glad to have been made aware of the cause of its efficiency, and I thank the stranger.

There is another development. At times your trout may keep so close in with a high bank above him that it is impossible to apply the side-strain. Then if you can exhibit the landing-net so as to drive him out with a rush into mid-stream it will give you a chance for a resolute application of side-strain, and the fish will be brought round and turned upstream again. One morning in May, 1920, I was on a sedgy bank in difficulties with a big fish which, boring close under the tussock, was forcing his way down towards a hedge with barbed wire in it past which I could not hope to follow him. In despair I shortened line all I could, caught up to the fish, and proffered the net. He rushed out at once more than half-way across-stream, when the rod, held low and horizontal, forced him round not ten feet above the hedge, and I kept him going upstream till he was out of danger. Twelve hours later the keeper weighed him—three pounds good.

OF POCKET PICKING.

As summer advances and the weeds are unusually high, there is to be found in a momentarily neglected fishery a chance of chances to find the trout in most unsuspecting humour for the fly, ofttimes for the dry, but more often for the wet. The celery beds are thrusting themselves, big and bold, out of the water, and the long sword blades of the ranunculus trail along the surface in dense masses at a little distance from the bank, coming closer at intervals and dividing the smooth run under the bank into a series of little pools. The day is perhaps hot and sunny, the wind fallen, the water smooth and glassy. Happy then is the angler of whom the phrenologist can say, in the words of the Bab Balladist, " unusually large his bump of pocket-pickery," for the picking of these pockets in the weeds is his game.

In many of them there will be a trout, probably not taking surface food, but willing to be tempted if properly approached. If you make up your mind to offer him a dry fly, the probability is that your first offer will be your last. Either he takes it or the disturbance necessarily made in recovering your fly puts him down, but the wet fly is another story. You want your fly to sink on alighting, so it has to be sparsely dressed and well soaked, but it is wonderful what a heavy fall a fly may make without scaring your trout, provided the line falls lightly and does not drag. Indeed, the fall of the fly serves to advertise the fish of its presence, and he often takes it immediately, on its lighting, before there is time for much gut to have gone below the surface film. But assume he does not— you withdraw your fly under water at the bottom of the pocket without making any splash or drag as in lifting a dry fly, and you cast again and again to an undisturbed trout, and if he will have none of your Greenwell's Glory or Tup's Indispensable you may still try him with a floater, or small Sedge, a Pink Wickham, a Red Quill, or whatever you may fancy. But it is surprising how confidingly a trout lying in such a position will come to the wet fly with just enough movement of the surface of the water to give the hint that bids you fasten.

OF THE WAYS OF BRER FOX.

" Brer Fox he des' lay low and say nuffin'." Very wise of Brer Fox. It is a commonplace among fly fishermen (though better observed in precept than in practice) to lie low when casting to a trout in position, but it is less known among them that there are frequently advantages in continuing the procedure after the trout is hooked and until he is in the net. Let me illustrate the point by an example. One bright July day I got down on my face and wriggled serpentwise behind a screen of flags close to the edge of a bright, gravelly shallow just below a wooden carrier which conveyed another stream over that which I was fishing. It is pretty safe to say that a strong fish that got up under the carrier and into the deep, weeded pool on the far side would take more than a little dislodging. There were several nice fish out on the shallow, and though no duns were yet showing in air or on water the fish had clearly got going, for they were active in motion though not breaking the surface. Peering between the flags, I delivered a well-soaked Tup's Indispensable with a horizontal flick above the best of the nearer fish, and at the third or fourth offer he turned to it and was fast. He seemed utterly puzzled. The rod was a light one, and I did not hold him hard. He seemed only conscious of something unpleasant in his jaw. He shook his head several times and moved about uneasily. Still I kept low and out of sight.

Then, failing to dislodge the barb, he began to get a bit alarmed, and made a bee-line for a bit of rough, broken camp-sheathing on the far side. In doing so he was travelling at an angle of about 45 degrees with the stream, so that at the critical moment I had little difficulty in turning his head down-stream and away from the point of danger. I did not take him far, however, but eased again. He seemed unable to make out what was the matter with him, and suffered himself to be led by easy stages and the avoidance of any serious pressure into the vicinity of the screen of flags, and into a gap in them where the landing-net was in readiness to receive his one pound seven ounces. The other fish on the shallow seemed quite undisturbed, and without changing my position I realized another brace in the next half-hour, and not one of the leash made a bolt for the shelter of the carrier or attempted to weed.

PICKING IT OFF: A VERY MINOR TACTIC.

It is a *very* minor one.

If it had occurred to me as having any novelty in it, I should no doubt have given it a corner in a former volume dedicated to my friend the Dry-Fly Fisherman. But in sooth, though I had practised the device for years, it was not until the summer of 1910, after the book was on the market, that anyone ever noticed it. Since then, from time to time, men with whom I have been fishing have expressed their surprise that a plan so simple and so efficacious never occurred to them, and it therefore struck me that it might be worth while to present it for what it is worth to the community of fishers with the fly. I do so with the full expectation of being told that there is no novelty in it, and that it has been practised for years. I can only say that I evolved it myself, and I never saw anyone use the plan before I did.

I put down its evolution to Mr. Walter D. Coggeshall, known to members of the Fly-Fishers' Club as the Member for America and a magician in dressing casting lines.

In 1904 he gave me a priceless casting line, with a curse to follow me to the grave and blight future generations of my name, if any, if I dared to use vegetable or mineral oil or animal fat to make the line float. Having, therefore, pity upon future generations, I did not use vegetable or mineral oil or animal fat upon the line. Having also pity on my ten-foot six-ounce Leonard, I desired to save it as much as possible from the strain of picking up and lifting a

heavy Halford line, partially sunk, from the surface of
the water. I accordingly sought for some method of getting
the line into the air without dragging it, fly and all (especially May fly and all) through the water, and the obvious
thing was to adapt a part of the switch or roll cast. I
accordingly developed almost automatically the following
method: Assume that you are standing beside a stream
running from your left to your right, that you have laid your
cast across, and that you desire to pick it up for a new cast.
You move your rod-point briskly out to the right and up
and round in a rapid curve to the left. This picks up the
weightiest part of the line and lifts it, bellying in a cork-
screw shape, into the air, leaving little but the light taper
end on the water, and before it has time to reach the water
again the entire line is lifted into the air with an absolute
minimum of strain on the rod. If the stream be running
in the other direction, the loop at the beginning of the
cast may be simply reversed, but this is really hardly
necessary if the pace of the stream be moderate. The
method is difficult to describe clearly, but it is as easy as
possible to pick up, even for an inexperienced caster.

ARGILLACEOUS.

It is said of a certain length of the Gloucestershire Coln,
by one who knows it well and has a title to his opinion,
that no man can hope to catch trout upon it with his gut
floating on the surface. He who was responsible for that
opinion is essentially a dry-fly man, and that makes his
utterance the more remarkable.

Simultaneously with a general recognition of the fatal
effect of one's gut looping clear of the water there seems
to have arisen of late years a certain amount of speculation on the desirability of sinking the gut in immediate
proximity to the fly, and on the means available for bringing

about that sinking without drowning the fly. In fact, anglers have been seeking something the converse of the wet-fly oil tip—invented by Mr. C. A. M. Skues, till 1917 the Secretary of the Fly-Fishers' Club. There the gut was paraffined down to the last link, or two links, to make it float, while the fly, constructed to sink, and the last link or two, drawn down by the fly, sank. Now, with a fly constructed to float, something is wanted to make the portion of the cast nearest to the fly sink. Some have even suggested that the whole of the gut should sink, on the ground that floating guts cast a considerable and unnatural shadow on sand or gravel bottoms, whereas the shadow cast by sunken gut is so small as to be almost negligible. It is probable that on weeds the shadow from floating gut is much less noticeable. If, however, the fly is to float, it is conceived that the current operating on a sunken line would set up drag much sooner than it would if the line were floating, at any rate, in the case of a cross-stream cast. One ingenious theorist challenges that proposition, suggesting that the deeper the cast sinks the slower moving is the stratum of water in which it is suspended; *ergo*, in a cross-stream cast the deeper the middle of the line is sunk the more easily will the fly on the other side keep pace with it.

It is unnecessary, however, for the present purposes to reach a positive conclusion in this question. The first thing is to discover what agents will cause the gut to sink without drowning the fly. Several alternative suggestions have been made. The first was no doubt due to the attempt to preserve gut in glycerine. This undoubtedly will sink gut immediately after application, but it soon washes off. Raw potato was another suggestion, but the writer was not greatly impressed with the result of the experiment. Doubtless there are many vegetable juices which might have the same effect in a stronger degree, but they have yet to be found. The most effective agent so far suggested is the discovery of Major H. J. Pack-Beresford, of the Fly-Fishers' Club. It is within the reach of the poorest, being nothing more than clay. It undoubtedly takes the part of the line to which it is applied under water at once, and it does not seem to require repeated applications. Most anglers must have noticed the extraordinary drying effect on gut of the jar which ensues on one's hitching into a tree on the back cast. It seems to have the effect of drying even the clay-dressed gut in such a way as to dry and jar all the clay off it in one action. But if the angler be a believer in the virtues of clay it is not difficult to carry a little moist lump with him, and to apply it " when so dispoged."

OF GLYCERINE.

Obviously, however, clay, with or without glycerine, is quite unsuitable for causing a fly to sink, for it would foul the material of the fly and perhaps destroy the colour. Glycerine by itself is free from this objection, and the following account of a recent afternoon and evening on the Itchen may serve as evidence of its value as an agent for taking the fly under.

I reached the river-side with a friend about half-past three on a dull afternoon in mid-July, 1920, and looking up a favourite bend I saw a series of soft rings spreading under my own, the right bank. My friend, as guest, took first shot; I looked on. Presently I became aware of blue-winged olive coming down upon the surface, and I knotted on my cast a fly which I had dressed coming down in the train from town. The hook was a No. 15 Limerick, tying silk yellow; hackle a soft, floppy, dark blue, which matches the wing of a blue-winged olive very well; body of a soft blue fur, dyed to match the body shade; and whisks of soft rusty honey dun. My friend's floater covered the trout a number of times without disturbing him and without attracting his attention, though several times the trout rose at something invisible an inch or two from my friend's fly. I made up my mind that he was not taking on the surface, and in preparation for the next fish I dipped my fly in a small glycerine bottle and ran the glycerine up the length of the first strand of gut.

Presently my friend made up his mind to change his fly, and begged me to take a cast while he was doing so. Thus it came that the glycerine-logged fly pitched beyond and just to the right of the trout and went under immediately. The trout had it at once. I did not kill the trout, for, after ploughing through several heavy beds of weed, he wore down the cast enough to break it without my ever seeing him. He was, however, a heavy fish, in the neighbourhood of, if not over, three pounds.

There was nothing else doing during the afternoon, and presently we went in for an early dinner.

Soon after nine the same evening the blue-winged olive rise began, and though there were not many fish rising those that were rising seemed to be rising very well. In vain, however, we plied them with Orange Quill and Rusty Red spinner, for not a vestige of a rise did either of us secure. At last, at ten minutes to ten, I made up my mind to try an alternative I had not tried that evening, and I knotted on a dark nymph pattern, soaked it in glycerine, and despatched it to a trout over which I had spent ten minutes with the dry fly in vain. The fly lit nearly a yard from the trout, but it was hardly under before he had it, and the keeper weighed him later at two pounds fourteen ounces.

I hurried over to my friend, gave him a nymph, knotted

it on, and dipped it in the glycerine. A few moments afterwards I heard him battling with a trout which later turned
the scale at two pounds one ounce.

Meanwhile I offered my own nymph to another fish
which was feeding steadily. Presently he took it; but
though I struck firmly, the hook did not take a good hold,
and it came away.

Then the entire rise ceased suddenly, and all was over
for the evening.

If only we had had the sense to tie on nymph, and
glycerine it, at the beginning of the rise we might have
done great things, as all the fish out seemed big. As it
was we had but one fish apiece—but each took under water
the moment the nymph was offered him.

THE SWITCH.

Years before the war I sat one morning late in May at
breakfast under the limes in the garden of a Bavarian
Gasthaus by the side of a delightful limestone river
that teemed with trout. On the far bank the river ran
alongside a public road from which it was so divided
by a tall hawthorn hedge as to be inaccessible to the
angler. On my own side the limes, coming thick down
to the river bank, made ordinary casting impossible.
But under the hawthorns lay a string of trout that
by nine of the clock in the morning were already busy.
We were to be off down-stream, my friend and I, as
soon as breakfast was disposed of; and, to save time,
our rods were already assembled, our lines threaded,
and our casts trailing to soak in the stream, and our
bags were laid out on a table ready for a start. That
string of trout was an aggravation all through the meal,
and I was tempted, in an interval of delay that followed,
to make an effort to reach one. The stream ran from my

left to my right and straightened my line nicely. A wet
Alder on a No. 2 hook had been attached before breakfast,
and I made my first effort at switching. Drawing up my
line till my rod made an angle of about 70 degrees with
the horizontal, I dipped the point sharply and brought
it round and up, and again down with a circular downward
and outward cut which brought a belly into the line carrying sufficient impetus to lift the rest of the line, the cast,
and the fly, off the water, and, without letting it go behind
me at all, carried it across river towards and eventually,
after several unsuccessful efforts, over to the trout. Owing
to their position they had never been fished for, and were
accordingly extremely unsophisticated fish, and it was not
long before I was leading one by the nose towards my
bank.

During the rest of my stay I practised my switching
under those limes at intervals before and after breakfast,
lunch, and dinner, and I collected most of the trout which
lay under that thorn hedge.

On many an occasion since I have had reason to be
grateful for the experience, and on the Itchen and elsewhere I have found it serve me well. The trout which are
protected from ordinary open casting are apt to be singularly unsuspicious of a wet-fly cast, delivered across-
stream by an angler who has tree or bush or copse behind
him, and who is careful not to shake the bank in his
approach or casting. It does not matter how smooth the
water or how bright the weather provided the wind be
not adverse. An adverse wind I find generally fatal to
the clean and delicate delivery of the fly. But if all goes
well the draw of the floating gut, or the smooth hump in
the water, indicates that the fly has been accepted.

Those who know the Duck's Nest Spinney will recall
how it comes so close up to the Itchen side as to leave no

room whatever for casting across by reason of the trees and bushes behind the angler, or for casting upstream by reason of the frequency of overhanging boughs. It follows as a natural corollary that the trout rise rather unusually freely under the big overgrown tussocks which fringe the opposite bank. From their own side these fish are almost unapproachable; and, though I have occasionally caught one from that side, it has been the exception rather than the rule, and I have far oftener been irritated by their promptitude in stopping directly my rod-tip appeared over the screen of tussocks, and by being hung up in those tussocks every third or fourth cast. Until my German visit, I had often looked longingly at those trout from the spinney side, but I had either gone back to attempt them, without much hope and with less success, from their own side, or had reluctantly moved on and given them a miss.

But one evening in the July following my German experience I was going down-stream through the spinney, to wait lower down for the evening rise to begin, when I heard a sound under the opposite bank, and saw a small, soft ring begin to spread. I looked again longingly, and twice the same thing happened. I tied on a Jenny spinner, oiled it carefully, and, drawing line off the reel, switched it out towards the rise. Each cast came nearer, and about the fourth or fifth cast the fly lit beautifully softly, just above where the fish had risen, and floated two inches or three inches under the opposite bank. Then it became submerged, and simultaneously I was playing my trout. Twice again in the same season I visited the spinney. On the first occasion I found six fish rising, and switched over to them. I pricked and turned over one and landed all the other five, one being not quite sizable. On the second occasion I killed a brace in the afternoon—the only brace rising—and in the evening I could not find the fly they were taking.

The advantage of the switch cast is the extreme delicacy with which the fly is delivered. It may be a disadvantage that the fly is not readily delivered dry, though the difficulty is not so formidable as it looks. There is, however, the counter-balancing advantage that when you want to deliver your fly wet it is quite easy.

But switching is not only a fine-weather practice. In a rough wind which drives all the duns close under the far bank a fly cast in the ordinary way across eighteen or twenty yards of water would inevitably be dried by being forced backward through the wind in the backward cast, and as a dry fly would inevitably drag in the far eddy almost directly it lit, it is practically essential to deliver a wet fly. This the switch will do with delightful delicacy and with accuracy quite as great as can be attained with the ordinary overhead cast.

VII

PSYCHOLOGICAL

HANDS.

ONE of the most enviable of the qualities which go to make up the first-rate fly fisherman is that which, in connection with horsemanship, whether in riding or driving, is known as " hands," the combined certainty and delicacy of correspondence between wrist and eye which mean so much, whether in the despatch of the tiny feathered iron to its coveted quarry, or in the skilful restraint of that quarry when hooked, and its ultimate steering to the net. After all, certainty and delicacy are correlatives—dual manifestations of the same confident power. It is, I believe, the truth that the finest handloom weavers are invariably big, powerful men, with their nerves in fine order, and that for fineness and delicacy their work far excels that of women. Anyone turning over *Who's Who*, and picking out those whose recreation is angling, will probably be surprised to see what a large proportion of these classes comes within the fraternity of fly fisherman— sailors, surgeons, and artists—all of them men of their hands, though those hands may differ in type, and there seems little in common between the long taper fingers of the artist and the skilled mechanic type of hand common among great surgeons and dentists. Probably it would be impossible to classify the hands of the sailor·man in this way, but the tendency of quality which drove them seaward made them instinctively handy men. And since the greatest satisfactions of life are to be found in the perfect performance of function, the faculty of handiness, whether in sailor, surgeon, or artist, turns the possessor instinctively to the sport in which the quality finds its finest opportunities of exposition—the sport of fishing with the fly. Watch a company of anglers at the billiard table, and it will be long odds that those with the most sensitive hands, with that quality of touch which makes for scoring, will also be the best fly fishermen.

It is the quality of hands which enables a man with the shabbiest and most hopeless equipment to make a show of the man whose hopes are built merely on perfection of rods and gear. Wise indeed was George Selwyn Marryat when he said: "It's not the fly; it's the driver." It would seem as if there could be no difference between the way a fly presented by A. and an exact replica presented by B. floats down dry over a fish when once it has lit upon the water. Yet there is some quality in some men which seems to make the fly at the end of their line exercise a provocative fascination over trout which the average performer fails to achieve. The most conspicuous example of this which I ever came across was a Frenchman, with whom I spent a couple of days on a Norman chalk stream during the May-fly season. There was a very hard-fished hundred yards of right bank in part of the water, with a good trout in every little bay. My French friend courteously gave me the *pas*, and I tried fish after fish, seven or eight in all, I think. I was not conscious of fishing badly, and I put none of these fish down, but I got no rise from any one of them; but no sooner—when I stood aside to let him cast to them—did his fly (the same pattern as mine) drift down over a fish than it rose to it almost as a matter of course. I could see no practical difference in the delivery of our flies; but, like the eliminated fee in the Edinburgh lawyer's corrected bill, it was a case of " Man, wè mayna' see him, but he's there." Hands !

ACCURACY AND DELICACY.

In a fly-fishing career over which I can look back some forty-three years I recall only two instances of anglers who voluntarily abandoned fly fishing in favour of some other amusement. One of these cases I cannot account for. The other was due to the fact that, in the course of the development of astonishing accuracy and power of casting a long straight line, the man became with every advance less and less able to catch trout, and his angling days became a long series of bewildered disappointments. It would appear that it is possible to have too much of a good thing, and that accuracy in excess may be as disastrous as any other vice or virtue. For that reason, when tempted to take lessons from Mr. Tilton, Mr. F. G. Shaw, Mr. R. D. Hughes, or any other exponent of the high art of casting, I have always said to myself: " No, no, my son. Let well alone. You catch a trout now and then with your amateur, anyhow, hugger-mugger style. If you took lessons and acquired perfection you might be even as N. and catch none, and eventually retire from the sport in despair." That is a catastrophe I am not prepared to face.

The accuracy which was N.'s bane was probably due to the nature of his gear. Gifted with a wrist of exceptional strength, he could handle a rod of corresponding power, which again needed a very heavy line to develop its capacity. The result was the propulsion of the fly with mathematical accuracy to what it is, I believe, fashionable to call its objective. A straight line, Euclid tells us, is that which lies evenly between two points. But no line remains straight for two seconds on running water. Result, immediate drag, and probably precipitate retreat of the enemy trout.

If that is a true conclusion, it would follow that it is undesirable to use gear of such exceptional power. It is probable, moreover, that a line driven with such exceptional force must be so propelled at the expense of a certain degree of delicacy. I am sure that the sacrifice of delicacy to extreme accuracy is unwise. I lately made the acquaintance of an angler who with the wind could cast with excellent accuracy and extreme delicacy. With the wind against us, or in any way adverse, I found I could beat it or cheat it far more successfully than he, but the extra cut I put in the propulsion of the fly had its effect in a sacrifice of delicacy, and on each occasion we fished together he, by reason of his greater delicacy, was the more successful by the end of the day.

Again, I remember watching a young lady, quite a novice, who was fishing one of the Aunt Sallies of the Itchen with a light rod and light line, and an upstream air rather than wind to help her. I had twice put down that trout during the day, but in the quarter of an hour that the young lady kept casting to the fish she rose him to her fly no less than four times. Unfortunately she always omitted to strike till it was too late, and the fly had been rejected. But I have no doubt whatever that her success in bringing up the fish was due to the extreme delicacy with which her light line, aided by the favouring air, enabled her to let down a fairly accurate fly over the fish.

Going back many years to my own early days on a chalk stream before ever I became possessed of a split cane, to say nothing of the miracles of Leonard, I remember that I used to get as many rises to my fly as I do to-day, but owing to nervous haste I left far too many flies in the noses of indignant trout.

In the interval I recall the successes (and they were many and great) of an angler who used to write over the signature " Red Quill," and his insistence on the virtues of a light reel line, with resulting delicacy. It is true that he lived near the water, and could practically pick his days with favouring wind or none.

For those, therefore, who are in that happy position I would say: Stick to a light line with a rod suited to it. To those who must take their weather as they find it I would say: Do not overdo your weight of line, or make too great sacrifice of delicacy to accuracy.

THE TRIUMPH OF THE INADEQUATE.

Not long since I was entertaining a comparative beginner at chalk-stream angling upon a water which it has for years been my privilege to fish. He, poor man, endowed with a superfluity of this world's goods, had, under guidance which I refrain from characterizing, expended many shekels in the purchase of an awful steel-centred column in split cane which he called a rod, of a reel of puny dimensions, and of a line so light that the rod could get no grip of it. There was another angler on the water on that occasion, and, as it is our wont, both he and I carried ridiculous little five-ounce toys, with which, nevertheless, we manage to secure our share of fish. I had offered my friend the loan of a similar little stick—with reel and line to suit it— but he politely declined, feeling more confidence in the adequacy of his own equipment.

" On the water," said the Other Rod, " we most of us use the most absurdly inadequate little rods." " Why ?" queried my friend of the steel centre. " Oh, we like it," said the Other Rod, " and we occasionally catch a trout that way."

It was not till near one o'clock that the fish began to

move, but before that I had a chance of testing the steel centre, and I soon persuaded its owner to let me lend him a reel of suitable size, carrying a line of somewhere nearer a suitable weight. But even with that I found it difficult to achieve any degree of precision. It was, however, the best I could do for my friend, and I had to leave it at that. I was not, however, surprised to know that, when the fish began to rise, one after another was put down, and not one was accurately covered. I tried the rod myself and could do nothing with it, though there was a slight favouring upstream breeze. My friend implored me to cast with my own rod, and the very first chuck put my Blue-winged Olive two inches above the fish, and next second I was turning a well-hooked pound-and-three-quarter trout downstream. Once again, later, I let myself be persuaded into casting to a rising fish just above my friend, and again my little absurdity put the fly to an inch, and I hooked a fish of one pound ten ounces.

I am not quoting this instance to vaunt any superior skill—for with my friend's rod my skill was much on a par with his own—but to afford a test example of what is real adequacy in a rod as distinguished from mere power. My friend's rod was undoubtedly far more powerful than mine. Given enough backing to one's line, one need not have been afraid to handle a salmon on it, but in point of adequacy for the purpose of chalk-stream fishing, dry and wet, it was not in the same street with what a local angler on the Tweed once called " Yon fulish wee gad." It occurred to me, therefore, to examine and, if possible, to define what constitutes adequacy in a fly rod, and it seems to me that the boast of many an angler that his rod is of special power may be a foolish one. It is not so much power as exquisite adaptation of means to end which must be aimed at. Ends vary on different waters and under different conditions, and many, indeed most men, have to make one or two rods do for all purposes. Such a rod or rods must then partake of the nature of a compromise. They may be ideal as a compromise, but are little likely to be ideal for all purposes, or, indeed, for many purposes. The ideal would be to have a different rod, with a suitable reel and line, for every new stream, or at any rate for each stream requiring a different weight of casting line.

It must, I think, be conceded that it is the casting line which conditions the make of rod required for any particular fishing. For instance, on rocky, tumbling waters, which are full of twists and kinks and drags, a heavy line that cannot be held off the water and that quickly goes under is most unsuitable. For such a stream one needs a light line and a rod long enough to hold off the water most of the short line one throws. This involves stiffness for the greater part of its length. The rod will probably be a better hooker if it is very gentle in the upper part.

On the other hand, if one is fishing a smooth-running chalk stream of crystal clearness, it is essential that one should be able to cast upstream under all conditions of wind. This involves a line of some weight. The weight can easily be overdone, but it should be adequate. Then one wants a rod of the power to carry the line, and yet of such an action that the line will develop the power of the rod. The strength of the rod may easily be excessive. The excess is worse than sheer waste. It is a positive encumbrance. It takes an exceptionally strong wrist to develop the power of such a rod. Therefore, for the majority of mankind, a rod of moderate but concentrated power is to be sought. It wants to be stripped of all unessentials, all lockfast or bayonet joints, all extra whippings, all superfluous metal, and, above all, of all superfluous timber, and to be scientifically tapered from butt to tip, and to be perfectly balanced. That is why the modern light rod has come to stay. The angler who has once handled a perfect example perfectly married to a line of appropriate weight and taper, and has had time to appreciate the gain in precision, the subtle sense of mastery, with which such a weapon endows him, is unlikely to want to return to the weaver's beam of the early days of the dry fly. The war for a time put an end to the importation of those first-rate American split canes—specially built for the English market—which were such a revelation to English anglers. But that very fact afforded an opportunity to the British manufacturer to supply the demand. Happily there seems to be a disposition on the part of some of them, at any rate, to do so. And in this they have an advantage over the American maker in their closer knowledge of British river conditions.

The product looks, it is true, a thing of frail insufficiency. But it adds enormously to the charm of angling to be able to master and defeat leviathan with a weapon apparently so inadequate. Really, the stripping of the superfluous leaves it supremely adequate by means of an exquisite adjustment of compensating inadequacies. It is strength in a triumphant combination of weaknesses.

The hook is inadequate to lift the trout. It is adequate to hold him. The cast is inadequate to hand-line out the fish, but it is fine enough not to scare him from the fly, and with the give of the rod it is adequate to bring him to the net. The rod is inadequate to lift the fish. But its pluck is unending; it is never done; it is always able to yield a bit more, and take it back again immediately. It is the conquest of the strong by the frail. The heavy rod with such a cast could put no more strain on the fish, would not bring him to the net one moment sooner, while it will take it out of the angler's wrist in the long day's fishing in the most punishing way; but the first-rate fragility, with the inexhaustible courage of the cane, works sweetly and easily from day's beginning to day's end. As an American friend of mine puts it: " You may hurt it if you run into a wall with it, or if you run a taxi over it, but short of that you cannot damage it."

There is just one thing more to be said. The choice of a rod is a matter in which temperament should be taken into account. A man of quick, impatient temperament should use a rod of slower action than would be suitable for a man of steadier nerve and phlegmatic disposition.

VIII
FRANKLY IMMORAL

MAKESHIFT.

I GOT down to the cricket-field at Winchester in time to see the players returning to the pavilion with the last wicket of the fourth innings down, and I felt stranded. I always had a rod at the keeper's, but my reels were in town. So were my fly-boxes and landing-net, and I had no creel. Still, I had a cast I had bought that morning at the Army and Navy Stores, half a dozen points in the little wallet I carry with me in my breast pocket, and in a little tin box some eight flies that I had dressed by way of passing the time on the way down in the train from Waterloo. Two little starling-winged flies with pale olive hackle and body like a Greenwell's Glory, two Spinners with crimson seal-fur's body and gold wire rib, two Iron-blue nymphs with jackdaw-throat hackle, and two Tup's Indispensables. There was nothing better to do, and if my friend " Fleur-de-Lys " had been weak enough to leave his Uniqua at the keeper's, it might be possible to rig up enough of an outfit to pass away pleasantly, if not profitably, the June afternoon and evening that were before me.

So somehow I found myself at the keeper's tucking my trousers into the top of my socks, donning my rubber knee-boots, and taking my little nine-foot Leonard from its case. For " Fleur-de-Lys " *had* imprudently left his Uniqua with the line he uses for his nine-footer. Also

there was a cap of his with a Red Sedge I had dressed for
him left carelessly in it, and a dilapidated Orange Quill.
Another rod had left a landing-net of a sort, and yet another
a knee-pad. Having taken the precaution to ascertain
that none of these rods were expected, I commandeered
reel, cap, net, and knee-pad, and proceeded, while the
keeper assembled my rod, to damp my cast in a saucer
and to put the cast, with a point or two, into my tobacco-
pouch emptied and wetted inside for the purpose. Presently the keeper came to me with a fact of grave concern.
The reel seat of my rod was too small for the saddle of my
reel. Was I done? No. I had gone too far in my
career of crime to be turned back by a little thing like that.
There was a rod on the rack, a greenheart with a splice,
held together with a sort of diachylon tape. It would
have to do without that support for a few hours.

So see me presently setting forth to the river in a cap
not my own, with a decayed-looking but capacious landing-
net, my reel affixed with a plaster, and all the apparatus of
the chalk-stream fly fisher except a creel.

It was half-past three when I reached the river, about the
dullest hour of the day, and after watching the stream for
ten minutes or so without a sign of a dimple of any sort,
I determined to take a look at a carrier hard by to see if
some more accommodating trout might not be found. I
scared the first, but presently I found a nice enough trout
lying out on a gravel patch below a culvert. The Sedge
was made for such an occasion, and presently it lit just
behind the head of the fish, who promptly turned and had
it. It was rather a nuisance carrying him in the landing-
net—but, after all, the hut was not far off. To reach it
one followed the smaller stream for a few hundred yards
—perhaps three. But now a little pale watery dun was
in the air. Should it be Tup's Indispensable or the Little
Pale Olive with the gold rib? I always rather fancied

the latter for the beginning of a small pale watery rise. So did the trout to which I offered it, and presently I was turning out No. 1 to leave the landing-net free for the reception of No. 2. They formed a pleasant-looking brace of very even weight, about one pound six ounces each. I was less fortunate with the only other riser I found before reaching the hut, for he gave a flounder on feeling the hook, and was gone. So was my fly. At the hut I deposited my brace on some flags in the corner, and turned my attention to the larger of the two streams. Curiously the fly on this is seldom the same as that on the smaller branch, and I searched an eddy to find what was on. I found an iron blue or two stationary in the surface, and I changed to an Iron-blue nymph. Very little sign of any movement. But after a while I made out a quiet rise under the far bank quite close in, and three or four times repeated. A switch took the nymph, still wet, across to the objective, but it took a number of offers to get it to the attention of the trout at the right moment. Still, at last, I diagnosed a turn under water, and, raising my rod-point, found myself fast in a strong fish. He put up a good fight, but the little stick, though bent to a hoop, was too much for him, and soon I was back at the hut to deposit him alongside the aforesaid brace. He was the best fish of the day. A careful search of the far bank revealed two more similar rises, and I left a fly in one and was entirely beaten by the other—a hardened and experienced fish that went on rising. He came up and looked at a Tup, but thought better of it in time. So I left him, and went down-stream half a mile to a bend where there are nearly always trout rising if there is anything to rise at. Difficult fish they are, for they have as much attention as a fashionable beauty, and are at least as wary. Four fish were moving in this little bay, and I tackled them with the Tup. Two I put down, but I got the third, and turned over the fourth.

Above the bend was a tussocky bank with the stream deep and rather slow beneath. So I restored the Sedge to the cast—for it is a likely length for the Sedge—and felt my way up foot by foot, getting and turning back a small trout which had no business in that place of " big yins," and retaining a fourteen-inch fish.

A little higher, where the stream ran more strongly under my bank, I put up my seal's-fur spinner, and dropping it almost to the inch upon the nose of a cruiser, I surprised him into taking it. I guessed him one pound nine ounces. He went one pound ten ounces later.

I was now not far from the hut. So I deposited my spoil and commandeered some of " Fleur-de-Lys' " whisky-and-soda, and waited for the evening rise to begin.

It was slow in coming. There was a little jenny spinner on the water, and, in default of a Jenny spinner, I put up a Tup. I had an astonishing number of rises, but the fly was not right, and it was not taken soundly, for of a dozen or more offers I only connected with one, and he kicked off after a minute's play. The seal's-fur spinner was not taken at all, and I was thankful at dusk to see the blue-winged olive beginning to show and be taken, for I had the almost infallible recipe in that water, the large Orange Quill, and in the quarter of an hour or twenty minutes of the rise I got a nice brace of hard-fighting, well-conditioned trout—one of one pound ten ounces, and one of one pound five ounces. And so to mine inn.

As a matter of precaution I unscrewed the net from the handle and carried the fish in the net, as I was not minded to break the net-ring in the neck of the screw. For the four brace of trout totted up to just over ten pounds. I have often had worse sport on that water when much better equipped, and I always look back with pleasure to that makeshift half-day.

IX

EPISODICAL

ESTABLISHED PRINCIPLES AND TROUT.

THE trout is the most extraordinary creature at bringing to nought, not only theories, but definitely established principles. I thought once that if anything in trout fishing could be called " established " (and, with every disposition towards caution in statement, I recognized that these things must be few) there were two beyond dispute: (1) That a windy evening meant no evening rise; and (2) that when the blue-winged olive was up, the chalk-stream trout will take the Orange Quill. I have before recorded experiences that disproved the former proposition, but here is an account of an earlier evening which wrecked both together.

A friend whom I asked to come and fish with me on my own little ditch failed me, and with some hesitation I took my ticket for another destination, which brought me alongside the Itchen shortly before seven o'clock (6 p.m. Greenwich Mean Time) on Saturday, June 24, 1916. A strong and slightly cold wind sprang up late in the afternoon, and showed no sign of dying down, and for some time there was not a sign of a movement of a trout on the water. I had anticipated the fitful, scattered rise of pale watery dun usual at this time of year at that time of day, but there was not even that. So, by way of occupation, I tied on a small Landrail and Hare's-ear Sedge (No. 1 hook), and began to search under the far bank. I cocked up an eye to look at a snipe, and on bringing it back to business

I was just in time to catch a gleam of a broad brown back turning downwards. For the moment I did not realize that the fish had had my Sedge. When I did so it was too late. That was all for about an hour. At eight o'clock the wind was still strong, but, to my astonishment, a fish here and there began to rise. I thought they were taking pale watery duns, and I put up a small Dotterel Hackle on No. oo hook, and presently hooked and lost a trout, hooked and landed another, and then lost two in succession. This was too large a proportion of losses, and indicated that this was not the right fly, so another had to be looked for. A few minutes' watching convinced me that, despite the wind, now abating a little but still brisk, blue-winged olives were coming up and, what is more, were being taken. Obviously the Orange Quill was indicated. I offered it to four rising fish in succession without the faintest result. I tried one more in vain. Then I tied on a fly which I consider the best imitation of the blue-winged olive to look at that I know, oiled it, and presented it to the nearest banker. The result was so prompt and surprising that he kept the fly. I tied on another and a new point, and promptly established connection with two pound-and-a-halfers in succession. They were the biggest fish I got that evening, and I had another two brace all on the same fly. At intervals, as the light went, I offered the Orange Quill, but in vain, and I had to return to the successful pattern. When I left off at 10.15 p.m. by the clock the wind was still blowing briskly, but I had witnessed one of the longest rises of blue-winged olives I had ever seen, and the fish taking them well all the time. If only I had been able to fish with the precision which is possible on a still evening I ought to have done much better. Still, three and a half brace is not a bad evening's sport.

Next day I began by exploring some ditches in search of

a feeding trout, but, finding none, I turned my thoughts to
the bank under which I had seen that broad brown back
turning down.   The same little Red Sedge was available,
and the wind served to place it nicely under the opposite
bank.   The fourth cast was a shade higher than the preceding casts, and a little dimple under the bank seemed a
disappointing result, until the quick, instinctive response
had driven on the steel, when the line was torn off with such
fury that my reel was three-quarters emptied in a moment.
Then a fine trout flung himself into the air, and again and
again.   This part of my story is irrelevant to the subject
of this paper, so I omit to describe the splendid fight this
gallant fish put up before my net received his two and a
half pounds of weight.   After this, though the trout began
to rise well, the morning was disappointing, for fly after
fly—Dotterel, Greenwell, Tup, Iron-blue dun (dry and
wet)—the fish either ignored or took so half-heartedly that
the hook did not hold, and one o'clock found me with only
one other trout in my bag.   Then I noticed a sprinkling
of blue-winged olives coming down to the river, and,
watching them, I saw one or two taken, but many neglected.
Again I tried Orange Quill in vain, then the winged pattern
of Blue-winged Olive, getting only a few false rises, until
I got one foul-hooked just above the upper lip near the
right nostril.   I obtained from him a disclosure of the
contents of his stomach, and found a long string of blue-
winged olive nymphs.   A search in my box revealed a
single attempt to reproduce the blue-winged olive nymph
in seal's fur.   It was soon knotted on, filled up with
glycerine (a foot of gut also being glycerined), and despatched
above the first feeding trout.   He recognized the resemblance right enough, as did several others between then
and three o'clock, and I wound up at the latter hour with
four brace to my credit, including my big friend.   I have

often seen blue-winged olives taken in the daytime on other rivers, British and foreign, but this is the first time I ever saw a rise to it during the daytime on the Itchen. So there is another established law broken.

It was interesting to note that the fish which were taking blue-winged olives could be clearly distinguished by the size and shape of the swirl, by day just as by night.

Saturday, July 1, was a mixed kind of day. Fine warm morning, but windy; afternoon, windy and cold, with a fine drizzle about five o'clock. Then a burst of warm sun, but no drop of the wind. I got on to the water about seven, and again, despite the wind and despite the fact that I was fishing an open reach, the fish began to rise before eight. Again there was a plentiful supply of blue-winged olive; again the trout refused the Orange Quill until the wind dropped about 9.45 p.m. (summer time), after which they took it well; and again three and a half brace succumbed to my little rod.

AN ABNORMAL DAY.

It is generally believed by chalk-stream anglers that a rise of fly—preferably duns—is necessary to bring the trout into a taking humour. But that, if a good working hypothesis, is not invariably true; and the day following the Coronation was, upon the Itchen, one of the exceptions to the general rule. The wind, which was very light, blew from the south-east, almost directly upstream, the sun was bright, and the water glassy clear. A survey from the railway bridge decided me to open my campaign from the left bank. I was on the water soon after nine, but ten struck, and eleven, without a sign of a dun in the air or on the water, and except for a ten or eleven inch grayling not a rise broke the surface of the water. There are limits to the patience of most anglers, and mine ends sooner than that of the most patient. So I began, when things got to this pass, to examine the herbage for sedges. Finding one or two about, and, in the course of doing so, bolting two or three trout from under the bank, I knotted on my favourite Landrail and Hare's-ear Sedge dressed on a No. 1 hook, and proceeded to beat slowly up my own bank. How slowly I proceeded may be judged by the fact that it took me three hours to work up six hundred yards of bank, dropping my fly into every likely corner, over the edges of cut weeds collected along the bank, in quiet bays between tussocks, in little clear spaces between weeds, and wherever there was a little fast run of water against any excrescence on the bank. It was not long before the first trout took hold, making a ring so small and delicate as to be scarcely noticeable, but it was enough, and he found his way to the net and to the basket. Then came a grayling of a pound and a half, lying a little farther out. Then a second a little smaller. Then a run of bad luck due to some bad points, trout after trout hooked and lost, sometimes breaking in the strike, sometimes later in playing, a thing which had not happened to me for many a year. But by degrees, picking up here a trout and there a trout, the bag worked its way by 3.30 to the comfortable total of four brace, including the brace of grayling. And all the while not a dun or sedge showed on the water. The strap of the bag began to cut uncomfortably hard into the shoulder, and an adjournment to the lodgings was taken for a siesta and a meal before the evening rise. On the Tuesday evening there had been quite a good evening rise in spite of a rough and cold wind—quite an abnormal experience. On this occasion there was rain as well as wind, but, in order to see if the abnormal occasion would repeat itself, in despite of rain as well as wind, my companion and I sallied

forth and stayed out till dark. By 8.30 another trout
and another grayling had been basketed, but there was
not any fly in evidence. Then, in spite of a cold wind and
continuing drizzle, there came on a strong rise to some
pale dun; but neither of us succeeded in fixing its identity
closely enough to provide the taking imitation. Had we
done so, we might with luck have been able to point the
more definite moral from what was decidedly an abnormal
day.

ONE OF LIFE'S LITTLE CAST IRONIES.

Just at the top of a club water on a tributary of the
Wey stands the keeper's cottage in a nook which Sutton
Palmer has selected to illustrate as one of the beauty
spots of Surrey, itself not the least beautiful of counties.
The stream hereabouts runs from fifteen to twenty feet
in width, with a nice pace on it and plenty of twists
and turns in it, and all sorts of little backwaters and
eddies.

At the point where the stream gathers to its narrowest
below the keeper's cottage a big ash-tree leans across from
the right bank at so violent a slant that a tall man walking
along the left bank has to stoop to avoid injury, and just
above the bole the current has carved a little bay in the
bank which forms a perfect lie-by for a fish which desires to
keep out of the strength of the stream, but to be ready
for any provender which may be brought down under his
bank. In the autumn of 1915 this bay had a constant
occupant in a dark-coloured fish, which throughout the
season had defied the allurements of the members of a club
which contained some good average fishermen, and of some
guests who were something above the average. He was a
fascinating fish, and when he was moving it was difficult
to refrain from spending much more time on him than was

for the good of the creel. And so one of the guests referred to found on an August afternoon when a sprinkling of pale watery duns was coming down, and the trout's neb was tipping up through the surface at intervals.

Crouching low a little down-stream of the tree, and negotiating with difficulty the rising bank to his right and behind him and the tree bole and branches above him, the angler switched a short line to the trout, and covered him again and again with all possible neatness for a time. Then he made a mistake, and the fish slid up a foot or so under a length of wire which had at one time fenced the edge of the wood opposite, but now had fallen nearly to the water's edge. The angler gave him a rest, and presently the fish, with a suspicious eye, turned backwards, and began to rise again, but kept close to the wire. Presently the angler cast again, but to the difficulties he had hitherto been negotiating was added the problem of getting his Tup's Indispensable under the wire. Presently the fly dropped over the wire and held. The spectator offered to go round and release it. But the angler, of a more patient temperament, declined this aid, and let the line drag in the water in the hope that the hook might come away. The finer end of the gut was almost over the fish's back. Suddenly he dropped back a few inches and tilted his head, and as he did so there was a distinct jar of the line. The fish had taken one of the knots on the gut. The angler lay low, and presently—whether by aid of the tug of the fish this deponent sayeth not—the fly came away from the wire and dropped on to the stream. The next cast lit like gossamer exactly right, and in a moment the trout was on. He proved to be just over a pound, and though above the average for the stream, not by any means of exceptional size for the water. But it was a satisfaction to see him brought to basket after his long immunity from capture, and no small part of the satisfaction lay in the fact that by one of life's little ironies he had possibly, by his tug at the gut, released the fly, and so contributed to his own undoing.

ANOTHER OF LIFE'S LITTLE CAST IRONIES.

It was where the Enz runs under a primitive log bridge at the head of a big flat, bounded by the timber-yard at Calmbach. On the right side below the bridge the bank was camp-sheathed, and about a foot above the water a fringe of extremely adhesive herbage grew out of a gap between the boards, which were laid lengthways and not perpendicularly.

One July afternoon in 1907 I crossed the bridge and was about to walk down the timber-yard, when just below me I saw a handsome trout a long way on towards two pounds. I stopped dead, but unfortunately he had seen me, and he made off. I made a mental note, however, of the particular flower-head under which he had lain, and as I came upstream again I made two or three tentative casts to the spot. Several times I covered the place perfectly, but my Tup remained unappreciated. Then I made a cast which took the gut over the herbage, and promised me a fully-fledged tangle. I thought that my chance of the fish was all up for the moment, but I crawled up, as much out of sight as possible, and, lying on my face, sought to lift the gut by hand from the clump of blossom through which it passed, and taking the line betwixt finger and thumb I raised it and drew it gently. For a moment it came easily. Then, to my astonishment, the gut was jerked from between my fingers. I leapt to my feet, rushed to my rod and raised it, to find that not only were line and fly clear of the weed, but that the fly was firmly fixed in the trout's jaw. There are no finer fighters anywhere than the Enz trout, and it was a good five minutes (and seemed like ten) before I could prove that the weight of this one was one pound fifteen ounces.

A BORROWED ROD.

In early June the Valley of the Erlaubnitz is a dream of heat. On either side of its fringing water meadows there stand, either upon the level or stretching up the lower slopes of the hills, larch poles in serried rows, evidences of the heroic German endeavour to accomplish the impossible —to assuage the unassuageable Wurstphalian thirst— while higher up the slopes, and clustering close round the picturesque oolitic limestone crags, no less serried pines— planted by the same foreseeing and provident German mind—made provision to cope with the almost equally unassuageable national demand for toothpicks. But whatever their ultimate destination, the effect, alike of pine and hop, is to protect and shelter the river valley, and to conduce to an activity and a fulness of insect life for which there is no parallel on any English river. Alders in this season hum round the alder bushes in countless myriads. Sedges of all sorts and sizes—many of them large and juicy—flutter along the river banks from morn to dewy eve, and long after into the dark, when the law has put a stop to angling. Of stone flies there is copious variety. May flies in their season are alike splendid in quantity and quality, while the rises of upwinged duns are to be envied in Hants and Herts.

Duns and May fly come on at intervals, but there is seldom a moment of the day or night when sedges of some sort or another are not offering temptation to trout and grayling, scuttering along the surface in the pursuit of happiness, or dibbing thereon in the discharge of function. So it happens that the trout of Erlaubnitz, though sus-

picious enough to drag in a tiny fly, are peculiarly amenable
to the seduction of a large fly corresponding generally to
some trichopterous type. This the native fishermen—both
numerous and keen—know well; and, as a result, every
good fish who haunts the open has every evening during
the summer one team at least of large flies, more or less
sedgy in character, drawn across his nose, and Sunday
gives him even larger opportunities. Thus it comes that
the stock of large trout feeding in the open is early weeded
out, or driven to safer quarters under umbrageous boughs
or tangles of thorn or roots, or in deep pockets among
lily pads or water-weed. It is here that the wandering
angler who has learned to drift a fly close under the opposite bank, or to float it down a narrow runnel in the grasses,
makes his account, and has such an enormous advantage
over the native sportsman. He, poor man, with a cast
that must last him one, two, or even three seasons, cannot
afford to risk flies or tackle by casting among the boughs,
and his team of three or four flies would soon be in difficulties if he attempted to extract the big trout from their
weedy fastnesses. Yet it is wonderful what he will do
with his primitive tackle. We have seen a rustic angler
with ten or eleven feet of hazel, tipped with an umbrella
rib from one of Fox's "Paragon" frames, laying his
coarse lures and heavy line with exquisite neatness and
accuracy across eighteen or twenty yards of water. In
the days when the May fly is coming on he makes much
hay of the foible of his trout for a large dragged fly, and
with a white May fly with a brown cork body and a ginger
hackle he will at times fill portentous baskets when your
dry-fly expert's creel is comparatively empty. One gets
lessons that it is not perfection of rod or tackle that makes
the fly fisherman. Once in June, 1909, it befell the
Englander to have his fly rod disabled in the course of a

promising afternoon. Returning to the inn, whose water he had been fishing, he was met by the kindly hostess with the offer "*Brauchen Sie dies*" (" Use this "). *This* was a three-piece rod of assorted parentage. The butt was from a green-heart pike rod of sorts, the middle joint came from a Castleconnell of uncertain age, and was fastened in with an extra ferrule to make it jam and so as to show the rings at the side, while the top, spliced to the middle joint by a piece of stout string, was once an integral part of an eight-foot American bait-casting rod. The top carried its rings on the upper side. Thus, though a line put through the rings pursued a spiral course around the rod from butt to top, though the rod was a flail of flails, the angler had a weapon of some sort in his hands and two hours to use it in; so he put his pride in his pocket and his reel to the reel seat, ran his line through the rings, and returned to the water-side. Just above a long weir-cauld the fishing began, and just over the edge of a broad bank of lilies—those with the pink lanceolate leaves and the exquisite wax-pink flower which come at the end of July—three trout were rising. With painful strain of a damaged wrist, a Red Sedge was got over No. 1, and a trout of one and a quarter pounds was promptly hustled ashore. No. 2 was a somewhat similar fish, and was similarly treated. No. 3 took the same fly, and after several times displaying in the air proportions proclaiming " two pounds," he allowed his chin to be got over the edge of the lilies, and he was being steered to the net when, just as he was in reach of the net, the hook came unstuck, and for a moment he lay on his side on top of the lilies. The lame German gillie made a desperate dig under him with a landing-net, but the mass of foliage and roots was too dense, and he failed. So dense was it that it took Titanic struggles on the part of the fish to worm himself into the shelter of the lilies, and for more than a minute his struggling tail stood upright out of the water, the mark for frantic efforts on the part of the gillie. A little higher up another pounder came to net, and then the angler, standing among bushes and under a railway bridge, flicked a Crosbie Alder upstream to a cruising fish, and got a bouncer of about two and a quarter pounds.

Another fish of one and a half pounds followed at the next bend, and then the angler came to a spot where he wished to put in practice one of his pet and frequently successful devices. A willow-tree had fallen into the water. The bank above it had been wattled, but was eroded by the current, and the wattling had been torn away, leaving the uprights only in the river-bed, two feet from the side, and standing three or four inches out of the water. Against one of these had accumulated a mass of thorn and bramble. Above and at the side were dense weed-beds, flushing the surface except for a narrow channel, and on the bank a big thorn-bush, whose boughs dropped to the water and trailed with bramble and other débris. Between the bank and the upright, on which the thorn and bramble had lodged, lay a big trout—three pounds was not an unfair estimate of his weight—and it was the angler's design to get him out of this impossible holt—not by force, but by guile—by hooking him and letting him run free and imagine himself lightly hooked, so that he might rush out into the open and try to kick himself free upon the surface.

Alas! it was not to be. The borrowed rod, whatever its virtues, was not delicate in the strike, and perhaps a tired wrist was not well designed to mitigate its hardness. Nothing could have been nicer than the way the fly dropped above the trout. For a moment it drifted slowly, then a huge neb came up and annexed it. Alas! the response

was too definite. There was a frantic wallow and a huge
wave as the frightened fish dashed out between the uprights into the open. If only the gut had held and the
line run free !

A sympathetic rain began to fall in a soft drizzle, and
turned the angler homewards. Just below the railway
bridge he heard a sound like a huge kiss, and where the
current swung into a large, slow back eddy he located a
nice cruising trout, which was absorbing stray morsels
with great enjoyment. It took no time to knot on a
Hare's-ear Sedge—as large as could be found in the box—
and to drop it, when the cruiser's back was turned, well
in his beat among the scum. The first time round the
fish did not see it, nor the second, nor the third. The
fly began to sink, and finally went under. The fish was
too near to let the angler pick out his fly for a fresh cast.
Was that a flash of a white belly under the scum ? If not,
what is the meaning of the screaming reel and that big
trout yonder flinging himself violently out of the water
time after time some twenty yards away ? By degrees
he was brought back, and the best of gillies netted him
out—as perfect a three-pounder as river-side ever saw.

A LOCAL FALL.

It had become a disastrous day, even for August. Four
of us in the water meadows, with an average of a mile of
water apiece in the twin streams, and only one of us had
a fish when we went in at five o'clock, and that was a
grayling. The day had been still but not hot, but there
had been no life in the air and no rise of fly, and scarcely
a fish had moved all day. Yet as, on my way in, I crossed
a corner of a meadow to reach a plank bridge which
straddled the mouth of the big tributary meadow drain
that discharges into the Eyrie length, it seemed that the

air was all gauzy and shimmery with the wings of innumerable spinners tossing in their love-dances. So that
even if there were no fresh rise of fly to bring the trout
on in the evening, there was just a chance of sufficient
fall of spinner to do the trick. The prospects, however,
were not such as to bring us out specially early after dinner,
and it was only just sundown that I found myself at the
bottom of the Eyrie beat. It did not look encouraging.
Not a fin was moving, not a fly could I see on the water,
and for the time of year the temperature was cool. So
with what patience I could muster I set myself to wait,
with my eye on the deep run under the tussocks opposite
the Eyrie. But the minutes slipped by and not a nose
put up, and after half an hour's wait I moved out of the
Eyrie and prospected slowly up my beat with my hopes
fading as the minutes sped by and the darkness gathered.
At length I reached the bend where the big drain runs in.
Here there is a big eddy in which at dusk one may often find
two or three cruising trout busy in absorbing spinners. By
this I paused for a while, for it was my last hope. But still
the darkness gathered and nothing moved. Stay ! What
was that ? It sounded like a rise, but there was no ring
anywhere. I waited a moment. It was repeated, upstream to my left. Cautiously I moved up to the corner
to see whether a trout was feeding in the mouth of the
drain. None. But there was a " gluck " again, and still
to my left up the drain, beyond two cross-drains which
entered it on either side ten or twelve yards up. Yes.
A fish was rising in the slow, almost still water of the drain,
and rising, too, in a way which, to my mind, indicated
spinners. A fish did I say ? There were one, two, three,
four, and all busy. It did not take long to knot on a
Pheasant-tail Spinner, and, creeping over the plank bridge
which crossed the side-drain, cautiously, so as to send no

warning wave into the drain, I got the fly to the lowest fish right and turned him down so as not to disturb the others. We fought it out at the corner, and I netted him out. The other three were still busy, and it did not take me long to establish a connection with No. 2. I killed him also without disturbing the others; and then No. 3. It was now pretty dark, but I wanted two brace, and I cast, therefore, for No. 4. Whether it was my fault or not I cannot say, but probably something was wrong with my timing, for though the hook seemed to hit his jaw with quite a jar, he was off with a flounder. So I had to be content with my leash —one pound six ounces, one pound ten ounces, and one pound thirteen ounces—all caught in a place where I had never before seen trout rising of an evening, and all attracted by the local fall of spinner. It must have been local, for not one of the other rods saw a trout rise during the evening.

AT THE SECOND CULVERT.

I have never quite forgiven the farmer who first, some seven years back, began to maintain an open post-and-rail fence across the carrier a few yards below the second culvert after one enters the water meadows from the Abbot's Hyde on the west side of the valley, and fortified it with barbed wire to prevent the big Herefordshire steers from wading up the gravel shallow and breaking into the lush meadow on the right bank. The object was laudable enough. The method was what I objected to. Other farmers had effected the same purpose by erecting their fortifications entirely on the eastern bank in continuation of the barbed-wire line which still runs along all the deeper part of the carrier. Great moments have I had on that carrier in days gone by, the great scenes usually on the shallow, gravelly pool just below the culvert. The carrier runs off from the main river on the east, and after a straight course of some two hundred and fifty yards or so, during which it receives the contributions of innumerable ditches, bends at right angles just above the culvert which carries the farm road that leads across the meadows from Abbot's Hyde back to the main river.

Duns are seldom seen in any quantity on this carrier, and as a consequence such few trout as it from time to time contains, though generally fat and lusty, are more amenable to the persuasions of a fair-sized fly than are the dun-fed beauties of the river proper. They have, moreover, no set feeding times, and there is always a chance with one of them, provided the approach be made with becoming reverence. The best, perhaps, of my experiences under the older conditions was one August Saturday afternoon, somewhere about 1905. The year was distinguished by exceptional flights of large dusky ants; and one day in London I caught a few that were running on the stucco of a friend's gateway, and when I got home I dressed an imitation in pig's-wool. The three or four patterns I turned out were rough, uncouth-looking objects—two blobs of rusty dun pig's-wool with a waist between—the blobs trimmed into some semblance of roundness by means of curved scissors. There was a sparse but stiff short hackle turned twice behind the upper blob.

The following Saturday I reached the keeper's somewhere about 2 p.m., and donning waders, etc., I made my way, rod in hand, across the meadows by the farm road. Approaching the second culvert I became aware of a buzz of insects hovering over it, and was delighted to find my friends, the big dusky ants, in force; still more delighted to see that within thirty yards below the culvert were no less than three good trout busy with the ants in three successive pools between weeds. Creeping cautiously across the carrier on the upstream side of the road, keeping low so as to be out of sight, and opening the gate wide so as to get through as near the upstream side as possible, I took a wide detour in the meadow and got below the lowest of the three trout. It did not take long to knot on a big Ant. Hardly had it lit above the fish before my line was taut, and my little nine-footer was making the arch of beauty. Down-stream the trout was bustled to the ready net. Now for No. 2. No less willing was he, and in a moment he was on. Down he came plunging, leaving No. 3 quite unscared, and after some anxious moments the net was put under him. The third fish was on the gravel shallow just below the culvert, and took the fly as gaily as the others. He ran for the culvert, but the little rod was equal to its job and beat him down. None of the trio reached two pounds, but none was under one and three-quarters, and all were as handsome as pictures.

That was an exceptional twenty minutes. Seldom is more than one good fish to be found within, say, a hundred yards of the culvert, and the gravel shallow (with a retreat to the culvert handy) is the usual spot to find him. The new fence run across at the bottom of the gravelly shallow has not altered that. When there is a trout thereabouts, that is where he will be out to feed. What it has altered is the chances of getting at a fish in such a position.

Still, no position is absolutely impregnable, and twice in two successive years, by good luck, perhaps, as much as by good management, I have extracted a good trout from the culvert pool above that abomination of barbed wire and wood.

The first occasion was in June, and the grass in the meadow to the west had not been cut. The keeper had told me there was a good trout at the culvert; and, risking the farmer's wrath, I had entered the meadow, waded down a drain so as to damage the grass as little as possible, crossed a table and walked up another drain till near the aforesaid abomination; then snuggled down in the grass and crawled on my stomach till I could see the mouth of the culvert and a broad tail fanning half in sunlight and half in shadow. There was a No. 1 Landrail and Hare's-ear Sedge on my cast, and as, uncomfortably, I drew off a little line to get my fly to the spot, the trout dropped a couple of feet and took something, and again moved up. He did not keep still for many moments together; he kept moving up and down and from side to side, and in ten minutes may have taken three or four flies. Several times I chucked a fly which could have covered him if he had stayed where he was when I slung. At last, whether owing to the draught up the culvert or some other stroke of luck unexplained, I switched the little Sedge right up under the culvert farther than I could have conceived it possible. Next moment there was a smacking suck and my trout was on. Where I lay I was level with the fence, and I dared put no pressure on the fish to bring him down, for it meant a certain bolt under the fence, probably on the far side of the middle stake, and then good-bye, possibly a smashed top for my delicate little split cane. So I lay still, and keeping a light touch only on my fish, I could feel him beating savagely under the arch, but too puzzled at what was troubling him to bolt. After some moments of this he made a rush into the deep pool on the upstream side of the culvert. There I began to fight him. I was bound to keep him from getting round the bend. I could not let him get to weeds on the left, nor into a rat-hole in the northern bank, nor into the lily pads in the backwater farther up on the left. So I held him firmly enough to keep him fighting, but not for quite a while hard enough to bring him down. Gradually he yielded and came back into the arch. Then I began to get my net out and down to the water's edge, and at the critical moment when I turned him down I stripped my line by hand through the rings, and rushed my fish tumbling demoralized into the net just above the middle stake of the fence. He was two pounds one ounce, and in fine order. At the moment I thought him well earned. Looking back I see how easily the result might have been reversed but for unimaginable luck.

The other instance happened in this wise. The weeds in the carrier had been cut in late July of 1914, and had not had much time to grow again. The sedges, however, overhung the carrier from one side, and I thought it possible on a still and hot August afternoon I might find a trout in their shade by means of my favourite Landrail and Hare's-ear Sedge. So again I waded down a drain, crossed a table at the bottom near a cross-dyke, and getting alongside the carrier began to search the edge under the sedges by a cast every yard or two. I hooked and lost one nice fish, and had come almost to the abomination aforesaid, when some instinct bade me not to show my head. Crouching down I drew several yards off my reel in excess of the length I meant to cast, and dropped my fly a yard or more over and across the fence. Striking at the sound I found myself fast, and, the fish darting down-stream under the fence, fortunately my side of the centre stake. Loosing my casting line, I flung all I could up over the fence towards the culvert and let off more as I ran up to the fence. By the time I reached it my reel was all but empty, but I had time to turn my rod-point under the fence and to pass the whole rod under. Then with all my line out I had to follow and hold a strong fish fighting down an almost weedless carrier, and stop him before he got to the cross-dyke, which would have stopped me, but not him. It was a breathless run, but I got below the fish in time, turned him upstream again, and killed him when half-way home. He scaled one pound fourteen ounces.

I am driven to speculate whether the excitement of these two incidents may not have been worth more than the easier conquests of the earlier conditions.

BOBBING REED.

It is curious how the incidents of a day of a bumper basket will often leave no special memory behind them apart from the total of numbers or weight, while some little incident in the taking, stalking, or losing of a single fish, perhaps of no great size, on a day otherwise undistinguished, will stay on in the memory and recur freshly again and again after the lapse of years. Such a little incident was the following:

On a day in August some fifteen years gone I had fished upstream with but modest success until about three o'clock, when I arrived at a big red-brick bridge spanning my chalk stream, standing below which on the right bank I saw the current setting strongly against the pier on the far side, carrying all flotsam swiftly along the brickwork into the tumbling hurly-burly of the eddy below—an eddy which was often the haunt of big trout; but they seldom seemed to venture up under the bridge.

For an hour or more not a dimple had marked the surface, and I recalled my forgotten sandwiches and took my seat upon a cattle fence commanding a view of the eddy and the river under the span. Often on days following rain I had heard the drip of water through the arch on to the surface; but there had been a spell of drought, and this was a dry day. So, when presently I heard a sound like the fall of a drop of water on the surface, and presently another, I looked to see where it could be falling. I did not see another falling, but presently I heard the sound again, and, after an interval, again; but still no splash. A little intrigued, I watched, and again I heard the sound, but saw nothing to suggest a cause. I seemed, however, to place it near the lower end of the arch, and there, caught against the pier on the far side, I saw a long spear of giant rush, and when the dripping sound recurred I saw the rush give a little jump, as if rebounding after the drop of water struck it. Still not satisfied, I kept my eye on the reed, and presently became aware of a tiny pale dun being swung along the current, close to the arch, hugging the brickwork, then alongside the reed, and—then the reed bobbed again and the dripping sound recurred. Just long enough I waited to see the incident recur. Then, knotting on a pale pattern of Tup's Indispensable on a No. 00 hook, I began to let out line. Presently I thought I had enough to cover the eighteen or twenty yards of water between me and the farther pier of the bridge, and I let my Indispensable down on the water. It was, of course, a sheer fluke, and I daresay I should not have done the same thing again in a hundred, perhaps not in a thousand, casts, but the fly lit within an inch of the reed about two-thirds of the way up it. The current took it swiftly down—again there was that dripping sound, again the bobbing reed—and in a moment a beautiful yellow trout leapt a yard into the air and fell back with a resounding smack. He did not, however, shake out the hook, and presently I laid him, decently wrapped in a napkin, along with his predecessors of the morning. He was only one pound five ounces, but somehow his capture gave me extraordinary satisfaction.

*   *   *   *   *

Ten years later, on a small Surrey brook, I was accompanied by a friend one August afternoon of a day that had proved aggravating and disappointing to a degree, when we saw a giant rush, which had caught against the herbage growing on the far bank, move as if struck by something small. "A rat," said my friend. "A trout for a tanner," said I. "I know that bobbing-reed trick." The hackled Red spinner on my cast was good enough to try with. It lit at the first instance within two inches of the reed and went under. As it did so the reed bobbed again in the swirl of the pounder which came up and fastened, and was presently carefully restored to the water.

SPORTING HAZARDS ON A BERKSHIRE BROOK.

The drought of 1911 must live long in the memories of fly fishermen, and it may be that in the rough streams commonly known as wet-fly waters sport was at a standstill for months; but for those whom fate or fortune confines to waters within easy access of London there was still sport to be had through the most blazing weather—and sport, at that, at times scarcely inferior to that to be had in more normal seasons. Yet it was with little hope of trout, though with a fixed determination to enjoy the lovely conditions of country and weather, that I descended the hill one mid-September day into a Berkshire valley, traversed by one of the most exquisite winding brooks in the countryside. If the banks are tangled with a wild profusion of bramble and thorn, willow-herb, and mullein; if wild cherry, hazel, and ash are interspersed with alder and willow along its course, with marshy stretches dense with sedgy tussock and flags intervening at intervals, the shallow stretches of the little river-bed are no less overgrown with flag and cress bed, giant bulrush, water crow's-foot, and other vegetation, while snaggy roots of the overhanging trees, stumps that have fallen into the water, and cut brambles piled with driftweed, hanging, perhaps, to broken lengths of barbed wire, provide the trout of this gin clear little river with such shelter as to embolden them to feed at all seasons when food is to the fore. Between these weed-beds, snags, and other obstructions the water runs briskly, scouring little stretches of gravel and shallow silver sand to a dazzling cleanness. Out upon these stretches the smaller trout lie in wait for the hatch of duns which, sooner or later, will provide them with entertainment; and it is hard to look over the edge anywhere along the course without driving upstream one or more of them, to startle and send to hiding the better fish above.

At the spot where I put my rod together the river-bed was too densely fringed on both sides to permit of my casting a line from the bank, and I was thankful for the forethought which had provided me with rubber boots reaching to the knee, and thus enabled me to enter the water and prosecute my campaign from midstream or from under banks, as seemed best from moment to moment. The first thing, however, was to stand still awhile to allow my startled friends to regain their composure. It was wonderful how quickly they did so, seeing that where I stood the water barely covered my ankles and there were few parts of the brook where it would reach to mid-calf— say eighteen inches deep. There was no harm in waiting, as there was yet no fly up, and there were all sorts of delightful country sights and sounds to occupy my attention. A pair of water-rail in particular charmed me with the grace of their movements as they ran along exposed stretches of margin which in ordinary seasons would have been under water. Presently I made out a trout, at a guess a short three-quarters of a pound, lying in the neck of a run near the left bank, a cast up stream. By his poise he was ready to feed, if not actually feeding, and I despatched a small Red Sedge—no duns being yet up—to light a foot above him.   He flashed at it—but either he missed or I did—and he went to cover.   His doing so, however, made it safe for me to move up two or three steps to within casting distance of a delightfully snaggy holt.   On the left bank the crumpled roots of an over-hanging alder turned the current outwards towards mid-stream, where it poured over a brilliant bed of water crow's-foot into a weed-pocket, and the rest of the stream was driven by a weed-piled snag at right angles to the course into the roots of a chestnut which overhung the right bank with its feet in the water.   In great good-humour I waited for the manifestations which were due from so promising a spot, and I had not long to wait.   A few minutes after eleven o'clock chimed a dimple occurred on the edge of the crow's-foot, and it was repeated in quick time.   Clearly some upwinged fly was being taken, either in the nymph or spinner stage, for no dun was on the water.   I took off my small Sedge and put up a chestnut-coloured Seal's-fur-bodied Spinner, and the first time I got it right to my friend he took it.   He was only a half-pounder, and I turned him in down-stream with care, for while I had been fishing to him I had seen a suspicious movement in the elbow of water just above the alder roots. It was not an easy feat, with the bushes behind me on my left hand and a drooping branch from the big tree over-hanging, to get my fly to the spot—twice I was hung up in the process, but each time the fly came away kindly—yet presently it dropped lightly on the spot I aimed at. There was no response till the fourth or fifth attempt. Then, just as the chance seemed past, a grey-brown neb with open pink mouth flashed at my fly, and I was not too late to pull in the point.

The line, however, was by luck almost slack, and the fish, instead of going to snag or weed, began to thrash about on the surface; and before he could bethink himself I had steered him down-stream into comparatively open water. Here it was not a long business ere the net received his sixteen ounces.

Cautiously retracing my steps I waited to see if there was anyone at home in the hole under the chestnut roots. Presently there was a rise in the eye of the run just above the midstream snag which divided the current. So I had to cast across the stump to reach my fish. On ordinary days I should have been hung up to a certainty, but this was one of the days when I could do nothing wrong. I had no intention of hooking my fish and having to pull him into the snag, so I determined he should see my fly and come back for it. I therefore cast wide of him to the other side of the gut of the stream, and slightly below the spot where he continued to break water. Sure enough he came after the fly with his head down-stream, and was hooked and steered away from the snag and out of the rooty hole before he had time to turn. He was just above the twelve-inch limit which I had set myself, but I turned him down without regret and moved on.

To pass the snaggy corner without risking a bootful I had to get ashore and re-enter the shallows above the alder roots. The trees behind made it impossible to cast to the next trout available without getting too near him, and I sent him to cover and disturbed one side of another twenty yards of brook. The other side, however, contained a run, from which I extracted another eleven-inch trout, which went back.

I had now reached a spot where the character of the stream was somewhat changed. It was somewhat deeper, and the bottom was still silver sand and gold gravel, but it was so overgrown with bunches of serried flags that, in order to cast over them to the little runs between the flag masses, it was necessary for me to regain the bank, here fortunately open enough for the purpose though packed with wild herbage and in places showing a couple of yards of black mud left by the stream between the water and sound footing. There was hazel and alder behind, near enough to keep one guessing, and it was easy to be hung up, and what with the overgrowth on the banks and the overgrowth in the water one began to wonder how it was possible either to hook a trout or to land him if one did so. For the sake of the bigger hook, I changed my Spinner for the discarded No. 1 Red Sedge with hare's-ear body, and looked about me. Presently I became aware of a trout lying under the opposite bank beneath a hazel bough and against a small pile of brambles, with three broad bands of well-grown flags between him and the black mud and dead brown flags at my feet. I do not pretend to have conceived a plan for extracting that trout if I hooked him, but he looked so nice a fish for the stream that I could not leave him untried, and, after several essays and several times pulling my hook through the leaf of a flag, I dropped my fly on his tail. He turned and took it at once, and I kept his head down-stream away from the brambles till a chance came a few yards down of steering him out of the farthest run into the next. Up this he bolted, and with a shortened line I pulled him through a weak place in the next regiment of flags, and with a little more manœuvring got him through the next, when I found myself able to lift his chin on to the edge of the black mud and to bring him slithering on to it. Then the hook came away just in reach of the rim of my long-handled landing-net, but too far away for me to get it under him. But as I touched him with it he kicked and fell upon the mesh, and presently was laid alongside his predecessor in the bag, a better fish than my first by a couple of ounces.

A fly or two could now be seen in the air, and Whirling Blue dun was clearly the order of the day. So I changed once more, oiled my fly, and looked out for another victim. I found my next fish a few yards down-stream of the last, in a run under the opposite bank, with still three thick strings of flag between me and the bed of crow's-foot from the shelter of which he seemed to come up. I say seemed, because, though I could see the tail of the crow's-foot bed through a gap in the screen of rushes, I could only hear when he rose, and see the lower end of the ring as it spread down-stream. I dropped the fly over the screen, however, struck at the sound of the rise, and got my fish down-stream and through the gap on the surprise. Once this was done the main part of the difficulty was over. I soon worked him through the rest, and to a place on the bank where there was no mud to prevent my netting him out. He was just over the twelve inches. Thoroughly drying my fly with a sheet of amadou and re-oiling it, I moved up a few yards, not ill-pleased with myself, to find another quarry. I came to an open pool with two or three fish in it, one of them, looking a safe pound, lying close against a deep bed of flags which fringed the opposite side, and then parted to let half the stream run one side and half the other. I first tried a brace of fish in the middle, which seemed in a feeding humour, but though both came and looked at my fly, neither would have it. So I made proffer to the third. He backed slowly before it till he was sheltered by the bed of flags which divided the stream. Here he seemed inaccessible, and I tried the other two again, but in vain. Then looking up a sort of foot-wide little lane which ran slantingly across the phalanx of flags I thought I saw the head and eye of the trout that had dropped down. I have cannoned off the red and pocketed all three balls at billiards, but I never made a more perfect fluke than the cast which fell exactly along the line of the lane, and dropped my Whirling Blue pat on the nose of the trout. He took it unsuspectingly, bolted straight into the open pool, and was presently added to the bag, increasing the weight upon my shoulders by a pound.

A brace of unsizable fish followed and were returned, and then I came to another open pool. I found myself standing over it under a tree, having approached unwarily, and eying a trout which hung poised in the centre, eying me in turn as if ready to bolt the moment I raised my hand. I did not raise my hand. I kept my eye steadily on the eye of the trout and dropped my Whirling Blue, which I had forgotten to dry and re-oil, with a wrist flick delivered from trouser-pocket level, so that it lit in front of him, rather on the far side from me. What possessed him to take it I cannot conceive, but take it he did, and was in due course knocked on the head.

Then there was a change in the humour of the fish, and, I think, in the level of the water—bless the millers! Though the fish lay out in position to feed, they let the fly, natural as well as artificial, go over them unheeded. Still, it might have been worse. I had had out five brace and killed two and a half brace.

One o'clock ! !

Lunch !

FOUR.

In a certain chalk stream which has not been stocked for many years, but breeds its own trout, the two-pounder was, before the war, a comparative rarity. On the length which it has been my privilege to fish for a number of years the annual tale of two-pounders could be counted on the fingers, generally on those of one hand; 1915 was an exceptionally good year in this respect, or I should be inclined to think I had monopolized more than my due proportion during August and September.

The first occasion was a Saturday early in August. The rise began tentatively about 10.15 a.m., soon after my arrival on the water. The first fish seen to rise was cruising for position, and whether he was scared or not he was soon lost; but, while he was being cast to, a bumping big trout flung himself out of the water about one hundred and fifty yards higher upstream, and fell back with a resounding splash. " I wish I had that chap on my fly," was in my mind. No other fish putting up in the interval, the one hundred and fifty yards were slowly passed by, and about eleven o'clock the place where the big fish had broken water was reached. There he stood poised in midstream about two feet down over a deep hole or pocket, at a point where a certain narrowing of the stream concentrated the current towards the middle. He was not rising, nor was it apparent that he was feeding; but he looked willing to feed. Accordingly a wet Pale Greenwell, and subsequently a wet Pale Watery dun, were successively submitted to his attention, and were allowed by him to pass without notice. Then a fair fish rose thirty or forty yards farther up, and I moved on to him, and was just netting him out when I became aware of a rise twice repeated at the point where the big fish had lain. A wide circuit into the meadow brought the nine-footer behind the trout. He was taking with a head-and-tail porpoise-roll sort of rise, and I diagnosed the fly as spent spinner. I quickly changed my wet Pale Watery for a small, floating Tup's Indispensable. The trout continued to rise, not frequently, but steadily. As the Tup lit a foot or so above him and a little to the left, he took another fly with a head-and-tail rise, and then reached for the Tup. . . . Two pounds two ounces.

Next time I visited the water was for two days at the beginning of September. Apart from their heat, there was nothing worthy of recording about these two days. On each occasion I had my couple of brace before the evening. On each occasion the evening rise was in two stages. First, there was a sudden wild outbreak of the surface into a flutter of tiny little pale duns. They were not Cœnis; the body was a pale greenish primrose, and nothing in the fly-box would imitate them. A few— a very few—fish began to rise at them, but these all fed steadily. One in particular, rising at the head of a long bank of weed which showed out of the water two-thirds of the way across, impressed me as being a real good fish; but he was plied with Quill Marryat and No. 1 Whitchurch on 000 and Pale Olive Tup in vain, and ultimately went down, and I moved on to another fish. At this time the heat was so oppressive that the perspiration constantly clouded the eyeglass, and rendered it a gymnastic feat to keep it in position. Suddenly the rise stopped, and for a moment it looked as if, with the cooling of the temperature, all was over for the evening. Presently, however, there were seen on the surface a few of the large blue-winged olives which so often lead to priceless sport. That made the big chap at the head of the weed-bed worth thinking of. There sure enough he was rising, taking the fly with the large, bold, distinctive swirl which spells blue-winged olive to the initiated. In the fly-box was a new effort at the representation of that insect.

Wing.—Coot secondary—rolled and reversed.
Body.—Greenish-yellow seal's fur, rather rough.
Tag.—Flat gold.
Hackle.—Blue dun dyed greenish-yellow olive.
Whisk.—Ditto.
Hook.—No. 1.

It lit exactly right first chuck, and in a moment the nine-footer was a hoop, and the trout racing down-stream on the far side of the big weed-bed. This suited me well enough, and I, too, ran to keep the move on the fish, and race him down below the weed-bed before he turned. The manœuvre almost succeeded, but suddenly the trout became aware that he was missing chances, and plunged into the weed-bed. Held lightly, however, with the hand high, he soon beat himself free of the weeds, and before he could bury himself again he was turned and rushed down-stream into a more open part, where presently the battle ended. . . . Two pounds four ounces.

The rest of the evening yielded further sport, but it is not worth recording.

During the afternoon of the following day, when nothing was doing, two fish were observed under the far bank, about thirty yards apart. The water was fairly open, weeds never growing very strongly in that bend. The lower fish looked a big one until the upper one was seen. The latter looked three and a half pounds, and the former was guessed at two and a half pounds. He flooped the Whitchurch dun offered him. Both fish were noted for reference, and the place from which to approach them was carefully marked.

The evening was distinguished by just such a rise of tiny pale duns as was that of the previous day. Again there was a somewhat sudden fall in temperature, and again the blue-winged olive rise began. The new pattern, however, was contemptuously rejected, so the old stand-by, a big Orange Quill, was knotted on. In quick succession a one-and-three-quarter pound trout and a grayling of one pound fifteen ounces were basketed, and then the big fish round the bend were remembered. Either of them was worth a new fly, and a new one was knotted on accordingly. There they were both of them moving to blue-winged olive, with curiously enough not another fish rising in the length. The question of tactics arose, which to tackle first ? Greed won the day. Both would be a triumph. The lower one first. Out went the fly, lighting just above him as he took a blue-winged olive. There was a moment's suspense, and then a jar as the hook went into his jaw. At once it felt as if the opposite bank had been hooked, and was steadily, slowly, and irresistibly forging upstream. Then, twenty, thirty yards it went, and then with a big torpedo wave departed the last chance of the three-and-a-half pound trout. Still, the length was not quite fruitless. . . . Two pounds seven ounces.

The next visit was on September 20. A leash of fair trout and a brace of grayling rewarded the day's toil. In the course of it a good trout was observed standing under a tussock just below a certain bend where many a big fish has met its fate. So famous is it that habitués know it as No. 1 Tussock. The trout, however, was not having anything, thank you. There was no evening rise that night, but from a couple of hundred yards below it seemed as if a sizable swirl occurred once by the No. 1 Tussock. The large Orange Quill was on in waiting for the blue-winged olive rise which never came. No. 1 Tussock was on the way home to the inn. The Orange Quill fell just above it, where the current cuddles round from the bend. Yes, there had been a swirl. . . . Two pounds two ounces.

And so farewell to the river for the season.

Curiously enough, each of these two-pounders was fished to once previously during the day, and each succumbed to the first chuck on the second occasion. Lastly, it was the first time I ever took in that water a two-pounder on each of four successive days' fishing, though I once had three two-pounders in one day, and not another fin, and once four two-pounders in one evening.

NINE TO ONE.

The mill was a powerful one, or it would not have needed a quarter of a mile of head, generally deep, and nowhere less than five-and-twenty yards across, to do its day's work. That there were big trout in the head I knew. I saw one a few days ago which was not an ounce under five pounds, and for some hours on each succeeding day I haunted the head in the hope of finding him again, not only in position, but in a taking mood. Once I saw a fish rise twice in a little bay above a big tussock, which, when one got near enough to cast to him, hid the rise entirely. Nevertheless, with a good heart I delivered a small floating March Brown to the spot where I imagined the trout to be, struck at the sound of the immediately succeeding rise, felt a horrid jar as if I had hit a snag, and then the still horrider sense of slackness that tells one that one has failed to fasten. The trout departed with a great wave, but he was not my five-pounder. That, however, was the only fish I saw move during the five days which followed my glimpse of Leviathan. There were other fish there I know, because on occasion I saw the wave which a trout departing leaves behind him (as the trouty equivalent for " footsteps on the sands of time "), though a most careful inspection both of surface and bottom had failed to reveal his presence alongside the sludgy, tussock-ridden bank. The opposite bank, besides being fringed with trees, often close together, and being elsewhere clad with brambles and exaggerated specimens of nettle, dock, willow-herb, and what had once been meadowsweet, was anything from five feet to eight feet above the water. It did not therefore offer an ideal vantage ground for attacking the pool. Yet it was right under this far bank that on the sixth day I saw my only riser besides the one aforementioned. He was close in under the bank, almost beneath a large and bushy elm—the kind that wears a sort of hangmen's fringe—and under a horrid canopy of frog-bit, deceased meadowsweet, nettle, and other herbage devised for the confusion of anglers, the profit of tackle-dealers, and the despair of over-worked recording angels.

The only redeeming features of the situation were the direction of the wind (which was not unfavourable), and the fact that the trout lay just where the mill-head was at its narrowest. I calculated that with luck I might cover the fish once in thirty or forty casts, and I stuck to him for the best part of an hour, during which he rose perhaps twenty times. If I covered him during that time it was not with a fly he wanted. I must have caught up in sedges and other herbage behind fully as many times as he rose, and my damaged wrist waxed tired. I waded in at the top of the pool, and sought the high strip in the middle, to see if I could get down to and opposite the fish, but half-way down I began to ship water over the tops of my wading stockings, and retreated to *terra firma*. But I was not done yet. It was half a mile round by the mill to the opposite side, and then the fish was quite inaccessible, but still I went. It was just on noon when I arrived at the spot and began to prospect. The fish was still there and still rising—if anything, a trifle more freely than before. What he was taking I could not see, but, going down to the water behind the next tree below him, I saw some black gnat, two little pale watery duns, a blue-winged olive, and a spent red spinner go down, and a sedge go scuttering along the water. The tree was about twenty feet from the elm below which my trout lay, and against it, waist high, swayed a very friendly and prehensile bramble-bush, covered with succulent black-berries. It sufficed to hold me back some six or seven feet from the edge, so that when my rod was held out at right angles, some two or three feet only would project over the stream. Then the line would have to be delivered over (1) bramble-bush, (2) a thick clump of willow-herb, (3) a thick clump of meadowsweet, (4) a long and particularly offensive nettle-head; and it would have to avoid a long, trailing bramble-sucker. But before I could begin to think of casting there was the tree to consider. Its branches hung low, and some clearance was indicated. Five minutes' faithful work with a pocket-knife made just a possible room for me to swing my Leonard horizontally, and I calculated that I could get my line into the air under the tree at my back without inevitably hanging up every time in the tree in front, and could then draw it back by switching my rod horizontally across the bushes, so that once in a while, with luck, my line might all fall clear of the objectionable herbage, and my fly even cover the trout.

Then I put on my mackintosh, hardened my heart, and cuddled as deep as I could into the bramble-bush which banked against my tree, and saw to my joy that I could spot the rise of my fish just beneath the solitary nettle-head. I had quite made up my mind that if a cast failed it would be ten chances to one against my recovering my fly. I began with a Pale Watery dun, and to my delight managed to get my line on to the water just as I had calculated. The fly, however, fell a foot short of the fish, and though I let it drift down so as to clear most of the herbage, and pulled it very gently through the rings, the meadow-sweet got it, and kept it and the point of my cast. I put on another, and this time I covered my fish nicely. But he took no notice, and the fly, after being recovered once successfully and represented in vain, followed its predecessor's example in yielding to the clinging affections of the meadowsweet. Then I tried a Red Quill, and after he had been rejected, I left him and more of my gut in one of the trailing brambles. Followed a home-made hackled Red spinner, tied with a priceless honey-dun cock's hackle, a Whirling Blue dun, and two Orange Quills on No. 1 hooks. There were two of these, because the first was hung up before I got him over my trout. There were fully two yards of gut left when the first Orange Quill left me, there was but one yard when I was orphaned of the second. Then I bethought me of the scuttering sedge, and I put on a good big wholesome Red Sedge, with an orange silk body on a No. 4 hook. All the time the trout had continued at intervals to take some fly or other, whose nature was not revealed to me, with a sullen, consequential " ploop," occasionally displaying his back fin and the extreme tip of his tail as he went down. All this time he had never been scared. The Sedge went over him beautifully (I had no nerves about my casting, having not the least hope or expectation of getting my fish), there was a little hump under the surface, and then the Sedge floated on undisturbed. So was the Recording Angel. Once I recovered the fly, and again put it before my fish. No notice taken, but when I tried to recover the Sedge again there was passive resistance, and I lost not only the remaining yard of gut, but the loop of my casting line.

I put a new cast into my damper to soak, emerged from my bramble-bush, sat down, frayed out the end of my casting line, waxed it, waxed a doubled length of silk, and whipped a new loop in the end. Then I put on my freshly damped cast, and as I glanced over the fly-box, looking up by chance, I saw a willow fly on the elbow of my mackintosh. Now I pride myself on my Willow Flies. I tie a spent Willow Fly which has a most life-like way of lying dead with wings outspread on the water, and I had one left. I grudged it to the bushes, but it was almost the end of the season. So on it went. Four or five switches through the air to get distance, and then the Willow Fly dropped just a foot in front and to the outside of the spot where I imagined my fish to be. Once again there was that solemn consequential suck, once again the back fin and the tail tip successively appeared and disappeared, and then, scarcely believing in what had happened, I pulled line and raised rod together (so as not to hit the tree above), drawing the hook gently but firmly home. In a moment my rod and line were drawn into the straight as the fish tore madly up under his own bank, emptying the reel of almost all its thirty-five yards of line in one streak. Then he seemed to be seeking cover in a weed, and, forcing my way through the bramble and other tangle, I crept up to and close under the upper elm, and tried to pass round it to get nearer my fish. Holding him lightly with the rod just arched, I could feel him beating savagely in the weeds, and presently, as he came away, I began winding him down quickly with my rod well hooped, and butting him out of reach of several likely-looking snags on the way down, I got him at length opposite to me in deepish water, and more than a little tired by his exertions. Keeping low, and as much out of sight as possible, I dipped the net through the herbage, and a moment later I was hoisting my fish ashore. In landing him I nearly broke my rod-point through the line catching in a bramble, but I saw what was happening just in time. Though perfect in colour, shape, and condition, deep and thick, he was not a big fish—only two pounds four ounces. But I do not recall many other trout the catching of which has been a greater satisfaction to me than his.

One o'clock.

A TRAVELLING COMPANION.

I had secured a window seat, back to engine, on the sunny side of the two o'clock train for Winchester, had extracted from my kit-bag my little travelling wallet of fly-dressing materials, and had settled into my corner, when I became aware that I was not to travel alone. A passenger who had already come up from somewhere down the line—Winchfield or Old Basing, or farther south— was to go down again with me. It was a mid-July day, and my companion was no less a personage than a dark sherry spinner. He had placed himself obligingly on the lower ledge of my window-pane, and had disabled himself from flight by the loss of his setæ. He therefore offered himself most conveniently as a model for imitation, and as soon as the other companions of my journey were seated, and the train was moving out of the station, I fixed a Limerick hook of the correct length in my little hand-vice, selected a little batch of ruddy-brown seal's fur dubbing, matched it against the model in the sunlight, waxed a length of hot orange tying silk, selected a rusty blue-dun cock's hackle of appropriate size, and whipped it on to the hook, broke off the waste end, whipped to the tail, tied in three bright honey-dun whisks and a length of fine gold wire, spun on a tapered length of the dubbing, wound it to the shoulder, wound on the wire at nice intervals, secured it at the shoulder, broke off the waste end, nipped my hackle-point in the pliers, wound the hackle some six turns, wound the tying silk through it, pushed back the hackle fibres, and finished with a whip finish on the neck of the hook. Twice the process was repeated before the train ran through Farnborough, when the wallet was tucked away.

Seven o'clock saw me on the water; but it was nearly two hours later before the evening rise began. There were a few—a very few—blue-winged olives, and the trout were obviously not taking them, and were equally obviously sipping spinners. In the bend up to which by the time the rise began I had sauntered there were three fish rising, perhaps once a minute. The first was a very *rusé* and experienced fish, in a strategic position of great advantage for observation (his observation), and he went down at the second offer of the Indispensable. The second stood better, and rose several times within an inch or two of the fly without touching it; but while I was changing to the pattern of the afternoon's manufacture he took fright at something, and bolted before I began to get out line again. Thus it came about that the next fish I covered was No. 3. He was moving a bit from side to side on the margin of a slow eddy, but presently the fly almost dropped on his nose, and he had it as it lit. At the tightening of my line he was off with a swift violence rectangularly across-stream, tearing through bunches and masses of weed, the line taut as a bowstring, then up and back and across to my own bank again, hooping the little rod and keeping me moving to prevent a smash. For a long time nothing I could do would turn him down, but at last I took a lucky chance and got his head down-stream, and from that point I kept beating him down, turning and checking every attempt to get up again to his corner until I had got him down a hundred and fifty yards or so below the point where I hooked him. Then he made a violent effort to turn upstream, and, that defeated, rushed across to the far side. All this time I had never seen a glimpse of him, and I was fated never to do so, for at the effort to start him down again he gave a plunge of startling violence, and the hook came away. Judging only by the force of his play, he was easily the biggest fish I ever hooked on that water, and I had had trout there up to and a little over three pounds.

On the way back to the corner where I hooked him I observed a rise of a big grayling, and, more in wantonness than from any desire to catch him, I put the fly over him. He came up at once, and I had him plunging and twisting at the end of my line, and led him down-stream plainly visible—a heavy grayling, for that water, of fully two pounds—and then, just as I began to get ready the net, the hook came away again.

I should have looked at my hook when I lost the big trout. When I did so now my two losses were explained. The hook was of soft metal and had pulled out, not straight, but enough to render my hold most insecure.

Meanwhile the dusk had deepened apace. The evening rise wore out rapidly, and the only two fish I found rising had to be chucked to from a bank where I had the red glow of expiring sunset behind me, and neither materialized. Bitterly disappointed, I made my way slowly up to the hut where I was to meet my friend, and I did not find a riser till just below the point of meeting. The trout placed himself nicely enough as I came up, and I offered him the new fly three or four times. He took it presently, and was gone with a slash. This time I looked at the hook and found it all right.

My friend was not at the hut, and so I strolled a yard or two above it to see if a certain persistent riser, even more *rusé* and experienced than the first I had attacked, would give me a final chance. Yes, he was still up, and the first cast landed the fly absolutely right. I tightened, felt his rush, and then again the sickening slackness. Sadly I began to wind in, when, to my astonishment and delight, I found he was on and had merely run down. Directly the line tightened he was off upstream, and led me battling for a hundred yards along the bank before I could turn him. To say sooth I was not anxious to do so too soon, for below me was a low boat-shed, over which it was just possible, with luck, to pass rod and line, but it involved risks which rendered it most undesirable to do so. So I wanted to kill him above the shed. Gradually I beat him down, and several times I brought him to the side. He did not seem a very big fish, but he felt far too strong for any liberties to be taken; so strong, indeed, that I wondered if he were not foul-hooked. So I made up my mind I must bring him below the boathouse. Therefore, offering him the net when just above the shed, I sent him off at a tangent across the stream, and throwing my body forward on to the roof, and stretching out my arm to its fullest capacity and giving line freely, I brought the rod and line over the dangerous corner; then, recovering my footing and holding the rod high, I ran down below, winding in line rapidly, and was once more on terms with my fish. He was, however, a long way from being beaten. My friend came up and relieved me of the long-handled landing-net, and made several vain efforts to fetch him out. The fish, however, was full of fight, and had he not attempted a rush into a raft of floating weed by the margin he might have got away. But as I made my effort to get his chin on to the weed the net went under him, and he was out on the bank choking and gasping and still full of fight and fury. The hold of the hook, however, was of the frailest, and another minute might have seen his escape. He was hooked all right, in the roof of the mouth. My friend guessed him at one pound ten ounces, and he had a brace of one pound twelve ounces and one pound fifteen ounces to go by. The keeper's balance, however, said two pounds four ounces; and I am sure he wasn't a patch on the first fish I lost on the simulacrum of my travelling companion.

THE FOLLOWING DAY.

The hour at which the fast afternoon train lands one in the Cathedral City is not a satisfactory one, for one reaches the water to find the two slackest hours of the chalk-stream angler's day in progress. In the days before the Summer Time Act I should have had tea and gone out for the evening, relying on a good supper when I came in. Now I go out for an hour's look round, in which I do not count on doing much—and am seldom disappointed—and come back for a solid meal before starting out for the evening rise. July 28 proved no exception. I found some four trout moving, raised two of them, and failed to hook either, and put down all four. One of them, however, had an effect on the evening's movements, for he was that aggravating fish which rises—rose, rather—a short cast above the dead hedge on the left bank. I was specially annoyed at missing him, for I had often fished to him and had never got a rise out of him, and I never knew anyone who claimed to have done so. The other fish was near the surface on a bank of weed, just above a point where a spike of celery emerging from the surface divided the current. He was only accessible from the right bank, so when I came out for the evening I strolled up to the appropriate distance below him and knotted on a wet Greenwell double on No. oo hooks tied on gut, and waited to make sure of my fish before casting. As I did so I became aware of a movement of a fishy character—it was not a rise, nor was it tailing—under my own bank, in some shallow water, at a point where the stream bent rather sharply from south-east to south. The light prevented me from seeing if a fish were there, but I sent my Greenwell double to explore. The first cast was short, but the second was there or thereabouts. There was a little hump under water, which only

broke the surface when I tightened. The kicking pounder
was soon ashore, but incidentally he put down the fish I
had come for, and so, having performed the obsequies and
wiped my hands, I turned down-stream again, crossed at
the mill, and walked up the other side, wading through a
stretch of marshy meadow, alive with floating water-snail,
to the dead hedge, determined there to await the meal-
time of the aggravator aforesaid before beginning operations. It was striking eight as I arrived, and I fully
expected to have to wait an hour before the serious business
of the evening began. But I had scarcely arrived, and had
noted a stream of miscellaneous fare coming down on the
surface—a small, dark sedge, some spinners of two or
three varieties, black gnats, a winged black ant, a gnat
with a green body, a couple of July duns, a pale watery
dun or two, and one blue-winged olive—when a soft suck
a yard above the projecting frond of vegetation where
that fish was usually to be found roused me to consciousness that I need not sit down. A moment's consideration
led me to decide that I would not cast from the bank.
If I went far enough from the dead hedge to avoid being
hung up in it, I should be so near the fish as certainly
to be seen by him. No, the bottom was sound where the
village boys had waded, and I had on waders which came
well up the leg. So I stepped cautiously into the water,
let out line down-stream, incidentally soaking my
Greenwell Glory, and delivered my first and only cast to
that fish. It was not a good cast, but it was probably
better than a more perfect one for its purpose. The fly
lit nearly a yard to the left of the fish, and very little above
him; but immediately that slight surface indication which
betrays the turn of a trout under water occurred, and softly
but firmly I pulled home the wires. Away went the
trout with a burst, and I let him run while I got out on to

the bank. I could feel the gut sawing through beds of weeds, then up into the air sprang a fish, which, if not so big as I thought him, was still satisfactorily solid. Coming down, he was off down-stream, and nearly emptied my reel before I caught him up and got below him—trespassing, by the way, in so doing, for the field below the dead hedge was not in my leave. Then, after a couple more excursions into the air, the trout was off upstream again, and this time he absolutely emptied my reel, and would infallibly have smashed me had he not brought up against a heavy bed of driftweed on the far side. Baffled in trying to bury himself in this, he turned after the third attempt, and swimming deep and fast came towards me under several heavy masses of weed. I ran down-stream to straighten and disentangle the line, and got it out and wound in rapidly. But by this time the trout was plunging through vegetation under my own bank, and got my line under a pile of driftweed which had caught on that vegetation. I began to fear he was lost, but, putting down my rod so that the line would run easily, I reached the drift weed with my long-handled net and shovelled it off in six or seven instalments. Resuming my rod, I was pleased to find the trout was still on. Upstream he went, ploughing through more water growth, but I was over him with a tight line and beginning at length to lift him. Presently I had a shot at him with the net. That was more than he could stand, and he was off into open water again, and for a long time resisted my persuasions. But at length he rolled over, and I guided him into the net at the very spot at which I had stood to cast to him. He was not a long fish, but quite a shapely one, and he turned the scale at exactly two pounds.

The fight had been an exciting one, but I rather grudged the time expended when I saw two more fish rising close together some forty or fifty yards up, and a third about the same distance beyond. I selected the banker, on a comparison of the rises, as the better of the two fish which rose alongside of each other, and I sent my little Greenwell on its errand to him. The cast was a trifle short, but the fish turned and came for it with a boil which indicated a very big fish indeed. But either he missed or I did—for I did not feel him. And as neither he nor the other fish showed any symptom of rising again, I moved on in search of the third, whose ring I had noted. He too, however, had stopped, and I had not placed him accurately enough to make a cast or two on speculation worth while.

At the bend immediately above there are two or three perennial feeders—very good fish, but extremely wary and gut shy. A friend coming up on the right bank endeavoured to lure me to spend my time on them; but, with my mind's eye on an upper stretch, I was not for wasting time on them, and I moved on.

The next stretch, however, proved very disappointing. Not one of these big fish which I had counted on to give me a chance was at home; and in the next three or four hundred yards the only rises I saw were made by two grayling. I felt sure from the size and nature of the rings they made that they were taking sherry spinner, and I took off the Greenwell's Glory and knotted on a home-made Sherry Spinner with a rusty dun hackle too priceless to be wasted on grayling. Each of the two, however, took it at the first offer, and after an obstinate resistance was netted out—one pound ten ounces and one pound eight ounces respectively. It was not nine o'clock, and I had reached a bend where, on a gravelly shallow, the fish, both trout and grayling, seem to be rising if they are rising anywhere. But not a dimple broke the surface. The blue-winged olives which were coming down were too few to bring on the fish. Moreover, the moon was up and bright and behind my hand. I looked up the next reach, and waited, for it is usually a productive one. Presently a fish made a ring and then another near the bottom of the stretch, but he would not stand to be cast to with the moon behind me, and he stopped at the first cast. Then a little later a second trout behaved in the same way, and I made up my mind to get round the next bend, where the moon would throw the shadow on my rod across-stream instead of up, and to finish out my evening there. But as I made my way up I saw a fish out in the stream dropping foot by foot and feeding freely. I dropped as low as I could and cast to him. It had to be a very short line, as he was almost on me; but he took the Spinner at the very first offer, and after violent splashing play on the surface was netted out some forty or fifty yards down-stream—one pound thirteen ounces.

It may seem strange to change one's fly immediately after killing a fish with it, but it was growing dusk, and my sight is not very good, and I wanted to tie on my Orange Quill for the end of the rise before it grew too dark. So I did so, and made my way round the bend to the very best holding stretch in the fishery.

At the lower end of that stretch the current sets under the far bank, so I did not waste much time on that part, but settled myself to wait at the point where the set of the current was under my own bank and the light right upstream, so that I could see every movement on my own side. I was bitterly disappointed, however, to see no sign of a rise. It was 9.30, and it might be that all was over. Presently a big rise under the right bank showed the distinctive features of a fish taking blue-winged olive. But I was not casting to him, for another rod was on that bank. Then there was another rise a little farther up—again under the far bank—and still none under mine. I looked right upstream, and near the top of my cherished stretch I saw a ring of the proper kind, and then another. But still I hesitated. I did not want to walk down good holding water. But still there was nothing rising near me. So very slowly and unwillingly I moved on—almost to within casting distance of the trout—when, close tucked up against the bank, a little below him, I saw three rings in quick succession, and then two more. I dropped my line across the herbage, guessing the distance to a fraction, for the next ring, almost simultaneous with the fall of my cast, absorbed my Orange Quill. There was no end of a rumpus, and a stubborn battle ended over a hundred yards downstream with the transfer to my bag of a beautiful thick-set, small-headed trout.

Feeling decidedly better, I went on to see if the fish above was still feeding. He was. Again the fly lit exactly right at the first cast, again the little nine-footer humped as I pulled home into something that felt like a live snag, and again some way down-stream the net performed its office.

It was still short of ten o'clock, and I had not covered the entire stretch. So, having washed the slime from my fly, I sped back, drying it the while in amadou. Sure enough, close under the bank another fish was rising at short intervals at inches only from the bank. It was, in that owl's light, a chance whether a second cast would be possible if the first failed, for a hang up seemed a certainty. But again the beautiful little rod did its work perfectly. The fly lit three inches above the last ring but one, and in a moment was gone in the last.

The fish was quite soundly hooked (in the tongue as it proved), and he came in, compared with the others, somewhat speedily; but then each of them had put up a very specially big battle. He made the third of a glorious leash from that stretch—two pounds four ounces, two pounds one ounce, and two pounds three ounces.

He was also the last fish of the evening; for though I waited till after the stroke of ten, not another dimple, not a sound of a suck rewarded my patience.

So I went back to the bottom of the bend, where Keeper Humfry waited in the boat to ferry me over to the other side, to the fishing-hut, to a much-needed drink, and the short road home.

  *   *   *   *   *

I wanted the short road, for the strap was quite uncomfortably tight across my chest, with within an ounce of fourteen and a half pounds of fish to tighten it.

  *   *   *   *   *

It was a good evening—four brace, and every fish on the first cast. I have not been able to make out why I had a bad night after it.

  *   *   *   *   *

Oh, ah, yes! about the following day! On further consideration I draw a veil over the following day. I leave it—appropriately—blank.

MY STICKING-PLASTER TROUT.

What great events from little causes spring! If the reel-seat of a May-fly rod of mine had fitted the reel which was bought to go with it this story would have had a different ending, and I should not have had that in my pocket at the critical moment which was destined to convert disaster into—but I am beginning the story at the wrong end!

I had killed quite a nice trout—something better than two pounds—that July evening. I had spotted another, and, I thought, a better, feeding under the far bank, and

put him down. I had come to a place where the sedges
and flowering reeds grew so high and dense that it was
useless to attempt further fishing there. So, though 9.30
had struck, and the blue-winged olive rise had begun to
slacken ominously, I pushed through a coppice, across a
clearing, and on through a wire fence to the road leading
to the bridge which spanned the river, and was hastening
down the other side when I noticed that the top of my rod
had an ominous kink in it. I did not think it could be due to
the two-pounder, and I put it down to some strain incurred
in the coppice or in getting through the wire fence; but
I was not prepared to feel the top snap in my fingers as
I sought to straighten it. I climbed disconsolately down
the embankment, and was about to make my way home,
when a tinkle from something in my pocket gave me an
idea. It was a tin box of Seabury's adhesive tape—a
form of diachylon plaster—which I had bought to strap
down that ill-fitting reel to the handle of that May-fly rod.
That was quite an idea. I laid the two broken ends alongside for a distance of two and a half or three inches, and
laid on spirally a strip of the tape, and, to my delight,
found it made a firm, if rather ungainly, job of it. Instead,
therefore, of striking across the meadows I followed the
river down to the point where I had put down the fish
from the other side—incidentally putting down on the way
a fish of two pounds five ounces, which I got on the following day—and made a little detour into the meadows,
got well below the place, and presently had the satisfaction of finding my fish up again and feeding with quiet
resolution. The Orange Quill was still on my cast, the
line ran clear despite the sticking-plaster, and the little
nine-foot rod really worked wonderfully well, considering
its handicap. Anyhow, the fly lit in front of the fish
without any splash, and was accepted without a trace of

suspicion. The hook went home, and still the splice held. The fish tore off finely; it bent the rod into a hoop, but still the splice held, and presently it struck me that it was not the top, but the middle joint that was doing the work. The battle became more and more strenuous as its climax approached. Again and again the trout sheered off desperately into deep water as it neared the net. It lashed the surface in a series of frantic struggles, it made long rushes with its back fin out of the water, but at last the net received it, and I laid its lovely length (and depth and width) on the turf. In a season in which the fish had been from May 1 on in exceptionally fine condition, this was the stoutest, cleanest, best-built trout I had ever had out of Itchen, and the heaviest—three pounds two ounces—and I got him out with a nine-foot rod with the fine end of the top mended, in the dusk, with sticking-plaster.

X

WHAT WE HAVE TO PUT UP WITH AT THE CLUB

DOGGEREL FROM THE CLUB JOURNAL.

THIS is mine:

LITTLE BROWN WINK

I.

Oh, thrilling the rise at the lure that is dry,
When the slow trout comes up to the slaughter,
    Yet rather would I
    Have the turn at my fly,
The cunning brown wink under water.

    The cute little wink under water !
    Mysterious wink under water !
        Delightful to ply
        The subaqueous fly,
    And watch for the wink under water.

II.

Let the Purist rejoice in the fly that he dries,
And look down on my practice with hauteur,
    But for me the surprise
    Of the flash of the rise,
The rosy-brown wink under water.

    The dear little wink under water,
    The yellow-brown wink under water,
        The subtle delight
        Of the line that goes tight,
    At the shy little wink under water.

III.

Oh, give me the day when the fresh from the wold
Comes down with rich colour of porter,
    And tinges with gold
    That is flashing and bold
That yellow-green wink under water.

That orange-brown wink under water,
That ruddy gold wink under water,
    Oh, the glorious thrill
    That the bosom will fill,
At that rollicking wink under water.

IV.

Or a day on some smooth-flowing stream from the chalk,
When Æolus no ruffle hath wrought her,
    The keen subtle stalk
    And the reel's sudden talk,
At the rusty-brown wink under water.

The heavy brown wink under water,
The fatuous wink under water,
    When the bumping big trout
    That has got to come out
Gives his solemn brown wink under water.

V.

I care for no trout that comes up with a splash
To capture the fly that I've brought her;
    Let the trout that will dash
    At my fly with a flash,
But tip me the wink under water.

The gleaming brown wink under water,
The golden-brown wink under water,
    When I think I descry
    The quick turn at my fly,
The fleeting brown wink under water.

VI.

When trouting is over, and autumn is here,
The days growing shorter and shorter,
    The grayling will steer
    For my fly with a mere
Little hint of a wink under water.

A silvery wink under water,
A soft little wink under water,
    But she has it all right,
    For the line has gone tight,
At that wee little wink under water.

VII.

So plunging and rolling I lead her ashore
And as to the bank I escort her,
    She repenteth her sore,
    That she'll never no more
Give that silver-brown wink under water.

That pinky-dun wink under water,
That shade of a wink under water,
    That raises a doubt,
    Is it grayling or trout
Gave that misty brown wink under water?

VIII.

So here's to the fish that is crafty and shy,
With the lore that Dame Nature has taught **her,**
Yet we'll lure her to die,
As she captures our fly
With that giddy brown wink under water.

And here's to the wink under water,
The wicked brown wink under water,
And here's to the wise
That decline to despise
Any kind of a wink under water.

This is what I have to put up with:

DINGY BROWN WINK

A SEQUEL

Puristes loquitur:

But suppose I am out on a day that is rough,
When the wind blows a regular snorter,
It's the (tommi)est rot
To suppose I can spot
That I'm getting a wink under water.

Your dingy brown wink under water—
Ineffable wink under water;
I'd like you to tell
How the (qualified) hell
I'm to know I've a wink under water.

Respondit Subaquaticus :

It would seem that the practice of fishing the **rise**
Makes the temper grow shorter and shorter;
I can only advise
You make use of your eyes
And watch for the wink under water.

The glimpse of a wink under water,
The hint of a wink under water;
Any hint is enough
On a day that is rough
To strike at a wink under water.

I cannot explain just what method is mine,
But Experience, when you have bought her,
Will tighten your line
At a hint of a sign
Of a ghost of a wink under water.

The pallidest wink under water,
The wraith of a wink under water,
And pull in your fly
Ere you've time to descry
If you've really a wink under water.

But if, after all, your experiments fail,
Then get some ecstatic supporter,
    Get from under the gale
    To your fireside and rail
At the mythical wink under water.

    The spurious wink under water,
    Hypothetical wink under water,
        And toast with full glasses
        Confusion to asses
    That prate of the wink under water.

Refert puristes:

Get along with your rabid and insolent guff,
You silly and giddy cavorter,
    I've had more than enough
    Of your drivelling stuff
And your idiot wink under water.

    For there isn't a wink under water,
    There was never a wink under water,
        And I firmly believe
        With intent to deceive
    You invented the wink under water.

Cantant omnes:

It is rude, though your feelings it seems to relieve,
To dub any member " distorter,"
    You can hardly conceive
    All the tales we believe
With the aid of a wink *over* water—

    An innocent wink over water,
    A wink over qualified water,
        Ironical wink
        Over comforting drink,
    A wink over whisky-and-water.

So why not a wink *under* water,
An adjective wink under water,
    A merry brown, very brown,
    Sherry brown, cherry brown,
    Honey dun, sunny dun,
    Frisky brown, whisky brown
    Might have been olive green,
    Yellow gold, mellow gold,
    Very gold, marigold,
    Numerous, humorous,
    Glimmering, shimmering,
    Nickering, flickering,
    Rollicking, frolicking,
    Kaleidoscopical, topical, tropical.

Finical, cynical, blithering, dithering,
Anything else that is equally withering,
Spurious, curious, furious, impurious,
Scarcely impeccable, wholly uncheckable,
Not indisputable, shockingly mutable,
Quite irrefutable, frankly inscrutable
Pure hypothetical, sheerly heretical,
Hyperæsthetical, strongly emetical,
Quite unendurable, simply incurable,
Still without rival in things adjectival,
Adjectives, more of 'em, many a score of 'em
(Subject quite deathless, but we're getting breathless),
All of 'em latent in S(omebody)'s patent,
Invisible wink under water.

AND SO FAREWELL AND HOME-ALONG.

ADVERTISEMENT

AMADOU

THE price of Amadou is going up. It is going up mainly on account of this advertisement. Buy a bull of Amadou. It will be steadier than Victory Bonds. Much steadier than War Stock.

What is Amadou ?

Amadou is a fungoid growth which is about to settle upon the dry-fly angler. Once it settles upon him it will stick. He will be unable to free himself. Indeed, he will not want to. Ask your chemist for it. Ask your dentist.

Dentists use it for drying the hollows in teeth. Dry-fly men who know what is good for them use it for drying flies. Salmon-fly anglers are going to find it first-rate for the purpose of drying and preserving their salmon flies. Wet and mangled May flies washed and then dried with it resume their pristine youth and beauty. Amadou quadruples the life of an ordinary May fly.

Has Amadou *any* drawback ?

Yes—one !

Amadou absorbs petroleum as readily as water. Therefore, when a fly is dried with Amadou it needs to be re-paraffined.

Thus the price of petroleum is going up too.

What great events from little causes spring !

The little cause that put me on to Amadou was a six-foot Berkshire parson—broad in proportion.

Bless the little cause.

A CATALOG OF SELECTED DOVER
BOOKS IN ALL FIELDS OF INTEREST

100 BEST-LOVED POEMS, Edited by Philip Smith. "The Passionate Shepherd to His Love," "Shall I compare thee to a summer's day?" "Death, be not proud," "The Raven," "The Road Not Taken," plus works by Blake, Wordsworth, Byron, Shelley, Keats, many others. 96pp. 5³⁄₁₆ x 8¼.　　　　　　　　　　0-486-28553-7

100 SMALL HOUSES OF THE THIRTIES, Brown-Blodgett Company. Exterior photographs and floor plans for 100 charming structures. Illustrations of models accompanied by descriptions of interiors, color schemes, closet space, and other amenities. 200 illustrations. 112pp. 8⅜ x 11.　　　　　　　0-486-44131-8

1000 TURN-OF-THE-CENTURY HOUSES: With Illustrations and Floor Plans, Herbert C. Chivers. Reproduced from a rare edition, this showcase of homes ranges from cottages and bungalows to sprawling mansions. Each house is meticulously illustrated and accompanied by complete floor plans. 256pp. 9⅜ x 12¼.

0-486-45596-3

101 GREAT AMERICAN POEMS, Edited by The American Poetry & Literacy Project. Rich treasury of verse from the 19th and 20th centuries includes works by Edgar Allan Poe, Robert Frost, Walt Whitman, Langston Hughes, Emily Dickinson, T. S. Eliot, other notables. 96pp. 5³⁄₁₆ x 8¼.　　　　　　0-486-40158-8

101 GREAT SAMURAI PRINTS, Utagawa Kuniyoshi. Kuniyoshi was a master of the warrior woodblock print — and these 18th-century illustrations represent the pinnacle of his craft. Full-color portraits of renowned Japanese samurais pulse with movement, passion, and remarkably fine detail. 112pp. 8⅜ x 11.　0-486-46523-3

ABC OF BALLET, Janet Grosser. Clearly worded, abundantly illustrated little guide defines basic ballet-related terms: arabesque, battement, pas de chat, relevé, sissonne, many others. Pronunciation guide included. Excellent primer. 48pp. 4³⁄₁₆ x 5¾.

0-486-40871-X

ACCESSORIES OF DRESS: An Illustrated Encyclopedia, Katherine Lester and Bess Viola Oerke. Illustrations of hats, veils, wigs, cravats, shawls, shoes, gloves, and other accessories enhance an engaging commentary that reveals the humor and charm of the many-sided story of accessorized apparel. 644 figures and 59 plates. 608pp. 6⅛ x 9¼.

0-486-43378-1

ADVENTURES OF HUCKLEBERRY FINN, Mark Twain. Join Huck and Jim as their boyhood adventures along the Mississippi River lead them into a world of excitement, danger, and self-discovery. Humorous narrative, lyrical descriptions of the Mississippi valley, and memorable characters. 224pp. 5³⁄₁₆ x 8¼.　　0-486-28061-6

ALICE STARMORE'S BOOK OF FAIR ISLE KNITTING, Alice Starmore. A noted designer from the region of Scotland's Fair Isle explores the history and techniques of this distinctive, stranded-color knitting style and provides copious illustrated instructions for 14 original knitwear designs. 208pp. 8⅜ x 10⅞.　0-486-47218-3

Browse over 9,000 books at www.doverpublications.com

ALICE'S ADVENTURES IN WONDERLAND, Lewis Carroll. Beloved classic about a little girl lost in a topsy-turvy land and her encounters with the White Rabbit, March Hare, Mad Hatter, Cheshire Cat, and other delightfully improbable characters. 42 illustrations by Sir John Tenniel. 96pp. 5³⁄₁₆ x 8¼. 0-486-27543-4

AMERICA'S LIGHTHOUSES: An Illustrated History, Francis Ross Holland. Profusely illustrated fact-filled survey of American lighthouses since 1716. Over 200 stations — East, Gulf, and West coasts, Great Lakes, Hawaii, Alaska, Puerto Rico, the Virgin Islands, and the Mississippi and St. Lawrence Rivers. 240pp. 8 x 10¾.
0-486-25576-X

AN ENCYCLOPEDIA OF THE VIOLIN, Alberto Bachmann. Translated by Frederick H. Martens. Introduction by Eugene Ysaye. First published in 1925, this renowned reference remains unsurpassed as a source of essential information, from construction and evolution to repertoire and technique. Includes a glossary and 73 illustrations. 496pp. 6⅛ x 9¼. 0-486-46618-3

ANIMALS: 1,419 Copyright-Free Illustrations of Mammals, Birds, Fish, Insects, etc., Selected by Jim Harter. Selected for its visual impact and ease of use, this outstanding collection of wood engravings presents over 1,000 species of animals in extremely lifelike poses. Includes mammals, birds, reptiles, amphibians, fish, insects, and other invertebrates. 284pp. 9 x 12. 0-486-23766-4

THE ANNALS, Tacitus. Translated by Alfred John Church and William Jackson Brodribb. This vital chronicle of Imperial Rome, written by the era's great historian, spans A.D. 14-68 and paints incisive psychological portraits of major figures, from Tiberius to Nero. 416pp. 5³⁄₁₆ x 8¼. 0-486-45236-0

ANTIGONE, Sophocles. Filled with passionate speeches and sensitive probing of moral and philosophical issues, this powerful and often-performed Greek drama reveals the grim fate that befalls the children of Oedipus. Footnotes. 64pp. 5³⁄₁₆ x 8 ¼. 0-486-27804-2

ART DECO DECORATIVE PATTERNS IN FULL COLOR, Christian Stoll. Reprinted from a rare 1910 portfolio, 160 sensuous and exotic images depict a breathtaking array of florals, geometrics, and abstracts — all elegant in their stark simplicity. 64pp. 8⅜ x 11. 0-486-44862-2

THE ARTHUR RACKHAM TREASURY: 86 Full-Color Illustrations, Arthur Rackham. Selected and Edited by Jeff A. Menges. A stunning treasury of 86 full-page plates span the famed English artist's career, from *Rip Van Winkle* (1905) to masterworks such as *Undine, A Midsummer Night's Dream,* and *Wind in the Willows* (1939). 96pp. 8⅜ x 11.
0-486-44685-9

THE AUTHENTIC GILBERT & SULLIVAN SONGBOOK, W. S. Gilbert and A. S. Sullivan. The most comprehensive collection available, this songbook includes selections from every one of Gilbert and Sullivan's light operas. Ninety-two numbers are presented uncut and unedited, and in their original keys. 410pp. 9 x 12.
0-486-23482-7

THE AWAKENING, Kate Chopin. First published in 1899, this controversial novel of a New Orleans wife's search for love outside a stifling marriage shocked readers. Today, it remains a first-rate narrative with superb characterization. New introductory Note. 128pp. 5³⁄₁₆ x 8¼. 0-486-27786-0

BASIC DRAWING, Louis Priscilla. Beginning with perspective, this commonsense manual progresses to the figure in movement, light and shade, anatomy, drapery, composition, trees and landscape, and outdoor sketching. Black-and-white illustrations throughout. 128pp. 8⅜ x 11. 0-486-45815-6

Browse over 9,000 books at www.doverpublications.com

THE BATTLES THAT CHANGED HISTORY, Fletcher Pratt. Historian profiles 16 crucial conflicts, ancient to modern, that changed the course of Western civilization. Gripping accounts of battles led by Alexander the Great, Joan of Arc, Ulysses S. Grant, other commanders. 27 maps. 352pp. 5⅜ x 8½. 0-486-41129-X

BEETHOVEN'S LETTERS, Ludwig van Beethoven. Edited by Dr. A. C. Kalischer. Features 457 letters to fellow musicians, friends, greats, patrons, and literary men. Reveals musical thoughts, quirks of personality, insights, and daily events. Includes 15 plates. 410pp. 5⅜ x 8½. 0-486-22769-3

BERNICE BOBS HER HAIR AND OTHER STORIES, F. Scott Fitzgerald. This brilliant anthology includes 6 of Fitzgerald's most popular stories: "The Diamond as Big as the Ritz," the title tale, "The Offshore Pirate," "The Ice Palace," "The Jelly Bean," and "May Day." 176pp. 5⅜ x 8½. 0-486-47049-0

BESLER'S BOOK OF FLOWERS AND PLANTS: 73 Full-Color Plates from Hortus Eystettensis, 1613, Basilius Besler. Here is a selection of magnificent plates from the *Hortus Eystettensis,* which vividly illustrated and identified the plants, flowers, and trees that thrived in the legendary German garden at Eichstätt. 80pp. 8⅜ x 11. 0-486-46005-3

THE BOOK OF KELLS, Edited by Blanche Cirker. Painstakingly reproduced from a rare facsimile edition, this volume contains full-page decorations, portraits, illustrations, plus a sampling of textual leaves with exquisite calligraphy and ornamentation. 32 full-color illustrations. 32pp. 9⅜ x 12¼. 0-486-24345-1

THE BOOK OF THE CROSSBOW: With an Additional Section on Catapults and Other Siege Engines, Ralph Payne-Gallwey. Fascinating study traces history and use of crossbow as military and sporting weapon, from Middle Ages to modern times. Also covers related weapons: balistas, catapults, Turkish bows, more. Over 240 illustrations. 400pp. 7¼ x 10⅛. 0-486-28720-3

THE BUNGALOW BOOK: Floor Plans and Photos of 112 Houses, 1910, Henry L. Wilson. Here are 112 of the most popular and economic blueprints of the early 20th century — plus an illustration or photograph of each completed house. A wonderful time capsule that still offers a wealth of valuable insights. 160pp. 8⅜ x 11. 0-486-45104-6

THE CALL OF THE WILD, Jack London. A classic novel of adventure, drawn from London's own experiences as a Klondike adventurer, relating the story of a heroic dog caught in the brutal life of the Alaska Gold Rush. Note. 64pp. 5³⁄₁₆ x 8¼. 0-486-26472-6

CANDIDE, Voltaire. Edited by Francois-Marie Arouet. One of the world's great satires since its first publication in 1759. Witty, caustic skewering of romance, science, philosophy, religion, government — nearly all human ideals and institutions. 112pp. 5³⁄₁₆ x 8¼. 0-486-26689-3

CELEBRATED IN THEIR TIME: Photographic Portraits from the George Grantham Bain Collection, Edited by Amy Pastan. With an Introduction by Michael Carlebach. Remarkable portrait gallery features 112 rare images of Albert Einstein, Charlie Chaplin, the Wright Brothers, Henry Ford, and other luminaries from the worlds of politics, art, entertainment, and industry. 128pp. 8⅜ x 11. 0-486-46754-6

CHARIOTS FOR APOLLO: The NASA History of Manned Lunar Spacecraft to 1969, Courtney G. Brooks, James M. Grimwood, and Loyd S. Swenson, Jr. This illustrated history by a trio of experts is the definitive reference on the Apollo spacecraft and lunar modules. It traces the vehicles' design, development, and operation in space. More than 100 photographs and illustrations. 576pp. 6¾ x 9¼. 0-486-46756-2

Browse over 9,000 books at www.doverpublications.com

A CHRISTMAS CAROL, Charles Dickens. This engrossing tale relates Ebenezer Scrooge's ghostly journeys through Christmases past, present, and future and his ultimate transformation from a harsh and grasping old miser to a charitable and compassionate human being. 80pp. 5¾₆ x 8¼.   0-486-26865-9

COMMON SENSE, Thomas Paine. First published in January of 1776, this highly influential landmark document clearly and persuasively argued for American separation from Great Britain and paved the way for the Declaration of Independence. 64pp. 5¾₆ x 8¼.   0-486-29602-4

THE COMPLETE SHORT STORIES OF OSCAR WILDE, Oscar Wilde. Complete texts of "The Happy Prince and Other Tales," "A House of Pomegranates," "Lord Arthur Savile's Crime and Other Stories," "Poems in Prose," and "The Portrait of Mr. W. H." 208pp. 5¾₆ x 8¼.   0-486-45216-6

COMPLETE SONNETS, William Shakespeare. Over 150 exquisite poems deal with love, friendship, the tyranny of time, beauty's evanescence, death, and other themes in language of remarkable power, precision, and beauty. Glossary of archaic terms. 80pp. 5¾₆ x 8¼.   0-486-26686-9

THE COUNT OF MONTE CRISTO: Abridged Edition, Alexandre Dumas. Falsely accused of treason, Edmond Dantès is imprisoned in the bleak Chateau d'If. After a hair-raising escape, he launches an elaborate plot to extract a bitter revenge against those who betrayed him. 448pp. 5¾₆ x 8¼.   0-486-45643-9

CRAFTSMAN BUNGALOWS: Designs from the Pacific Northwest, Yoho & Merritt. This reprint of a rare catalog, showcasing the charming simplicity and cozy style of Craftsman bungalows, is filled with photos of completed homes, plus floor plans and estimated costs. An indispensable resource for architects, historians, and illustrators. 112pp. 10 x 7.   0-486-46875-5

CRAFTSMAN BUNGALOWS: 59 Homes from "The Craftsman," Edited by Gustav Stickley. Best and most attractive designs from Arts and Crafts Movement publication — 1903–1916 — includes sketches, photographs of homes, floor plans, descriptive text. 128pp. 8¼ x 11.   0-486-25829-7

CRIME AND PUNISHMENT, Fyodor Dostoyevsky. Translated by Constance Garnett. Supreme masterpiece tells the story of Raskolnikov, a student tormented by his own thoughts after he murders an old woman. Overwhelmed by guilt and terror, he confesses and goes to prison. 480pp. 5¾₆ x 8¼.   0-486-41587-2

THE DECLARATION OF INDEPENDENCE AND OTHER GREAT DOCUMENTS OF AMERICAN HISTORY: 1775-1865, Edited by John Grafton. Thirteen compelling and influential documents: Henry's "Give Me Liberty or Give Me Death," Declaration of Independence, The Constitution, Washington's First Inaugural Address, The Monroe Doctrine, The Emancipation Proclamation, Gettysburg Address, more. 64pp. 5¾₆ x 8¼.   0-486-41124-9

THE DESERT AND THE SOWN: Travels in Palestine and Syria, Gertrude Bell. "The female Lawrence of Arabia," Gertrude Bell wrote captivating, perceptive accounts of her travels in the Middle East. This intriguing narrative, accompanied by 160 photos, traces her 1905 sojourn in Lebanon, Syria, and Palestine. 368pp. 5⅜ x 8½.
                    0-486-46876-3

A DOLL'S HOUSE, Henrik Ibsen. Ibsen's best-known play displays his genius for realistic prose drama. An expression of women's rights, the play climaxes when the central character, Nora, rejects a smothering marriage and life in "a doll's house." 80pp. 5¾₆ x 8¼.   0-486-27062-9

DOOMED SHIPS: Great Ocean Liner Disasters, William H. Miller, Jr. Nearly 200 photographs, many from private collections, highlight tales of some of the vessels whose pleasure cruises ended in catastrophe: the *Morro Castle, Normandie, Andrea Doria, Europa,* and many others. 128pp. 8⅞ x 11¾. 0-486-45366-9

THE DORÉ BIBLE ILLUSTRATIONS, Gustave Doré. Detailed plates from the Bible: the Creation scenes, Adam and Eve, horrifying visions of the Flood, the battle sequences with their monumental crowds, depictions of the life of Jesus, 241 plates in all. 241pp. 9 x 12. 0-486-23004-X

DRAWING DRAPERY FROM HEAD TO TOE, Cliff Young. Expert guidance on how to draw shirts, pants, skirts, gloves, hats, and coats on the human figure, including folds in relation to the body, pull and crush, action folds, creases, more. Over 200 drawings. 48pp. 8¼ x 11. 0-486-45591-2

DUBLINERS, James Joyce. A fine and accessible introduction to the work of one of the 20th century's most influential writers, this collection features 15 tales, including a masterpiece of the short-story genre, "The Dead." 160pp. 5³⁄₁₆ x 8¼. 0-486-26870-5

EASY-TO-MAKE POP-UPS, Joan Irvine. Illustrated by Barbara Reid. Dozens of wonderful ideas for three-dimensional paper fun — from holiday greeting cards with moving parts to a pop-up menagerie. Easy-to-follow, illustrated instructions for more than 30 projects. 299 black-and-white illustrations. 96pp. 8⅜ x 11.
0-486-44622-0

EASY-TO-MAKE STORYBOOK DOLLS: A "Novel" Approach to Cloth Dollmaking, Sherralyn St. Clair. Favorite fictional characters come alive in this unique beginner's dollmaking guide. Includes patterns for Pollyanna, Dorothy from *The Wonderful Wizard of Oz,* Mary of *The Secret Garden,* plus easy-to-follow instructions, 263 black-and-white illustrations, and an 8-page color insert. 112pp. 8¼ x 11. 0-486-47360-0

EINSTEIN'S ESSAYS IN SCIENCE, Albert Einstein. Speeches and essays in accessible, everyday language profile influential physicists such as Niels Bohr and Isaac Newton. They also explore areas of physics to which the author made major contributions. 128pp. 5 x 8. 0-486-47011-3

EL DORADO: Further Adventures of the Scarlet Pimpernel, Baroness Orczy. A popular sequel to *The Scarlet Pimpernel,* this suspenseful story recounts the Pimpernel's attempts to rescue the Dauphin from imprisonment during the French Revolution. An irresistible blend of intrigue, period detail, and vibrant characterizations. 352pp. 5³⁄₁₆ x 8¼. 0-486-44026-5

ELEGANT SMALL HOMES OF THE TWENTIES: 99 Designs from a Competition, Chicago Tribune. Nearly 100 designs for five- and six-room houses feature New England and Southern colonials, Normandy cottages, stately Italianate dwellings, and other fascinating snapshots of American domestic architecture of the 1920s. 112pp. 9 x 12. 0-486-46910-7

THE ELEMENTS OF STYLE: The Original Edition, William Strunk, Jr. This is the book that generations of writers have relied upon for timeless advice on grammar, diction, syntax, and other essentials. In concise terms, it identifies the principal requirements of proper style and common errors. 64pp. 5⅜ x 8½. 0-486-44798-7

THE ELUSIVE PIMPERNEL, Baroness Orczy. Robespierre's revolutionaries find their wicked schemes thwarted by the heroic Pimpernel — Sir Percival Blakeney. In this thrilling sequel, Chauvelin devises a plot to eliminate the Pimpernel and his wife. 272pp. 5³⁄₁₆ x 8¼. 0-486-45464-9